# WEST AFRICAN SUFI

Baba Thimbely at the grave of Cerno Bokar, Bandiagara, 1978.

# WEST AFRICAN SUFI

*The Religious Heritage and Spiritual Search of Cerno Bokar Saalif Taal*

LOUIS BRENNER

UNIVERSITY OF CALIFORNIA PRESS
BERKELEY AND LOS ANGELES

Published in the United States of America by
University of California Press,
Berkeley and Los Angeles

Printed in Great Britain

**Library of Congress Cataloging in Publication Data**

Brenner, Louis.
West African Sufi.

1. Cerno Bokar Saalif Taal. 2. Tijānīyah--Biography.
I. Title.
BP80.C46B73 1984 297'.4'0924 [B] 83-4803
ISBN 0-520-05008-8
ISBN 0-520-05009-6 (pbk.)

The author wishes to thank M. Amadou Hampaté Bâ for his kind permission to quote passages from *Vie et Enseignement de Tierno Bokar*. Literary rights to all such quotations as well as to other materials cited from his personal archives remain with M. Bâ.

*To the memory of A.H.J.*

# CONTENTS

## ILLUSTRATIONS

# ACKNOWLEDGEMENTS

Of the numerous people who assisted and supported me in my research for this book, I should first like to thank Amadou Hamaté Bâ without whose cooperation and encouragement it could not have been written; I have discussed the extent of my debt to him in the introduction. Hardly any less important to me was the assistance of Almamy Malik Yattara of the Institut des Sciences Humaines, Bamako, who worked with me in Mali as research assistant, guide and interpreter (of both language and custom). During our first meeting together he counselled me that in order to pursue research in Mali one had above all to be patient. Almamy Malik followed his own advice; he never flinched from any task or situation, be it the difficult conditions of travel or the long, enervating hours huddled together over a tape recorder transcribing Fulfulde interviews. He has become to me not only an invaluable colleague but also a cherished friend. Of the many other Malians who aided my research I should also like to mention Alpha Oumar Konaré, now Minister of Culture but, at the time of my initial arrival in Mali, Director of the Institut des Sciences Humaines; he did everything possible to facilitate my research. I should also like to thank all those who made themselves available for interview; Baba Thimbely (now deceased) and Dauda Maiga deserve special mention because of their extraordinary hospitality as well as their willing cooperation.

Field work in Mali was made possible by grants from two American foundations, for which I am grateful. The American Philosophical Society, Philadelphia, funded my transportation to Mali for an exploratory field trip in early 1977; and the Social Science Research Council, New York, provided funds for six months' field research which was conducted in three separate trips during 1977 and 1978.

I should also like to thank Annette Courtenay-Mayers who helped me to transcribe interviews recorded in French, and Georgina Courtenay-Mayers who assisted in typing part of the manuscript. David Robinson, Humphrey Fisher and John Hunwick all read the draft manuscript and offered valuable comments and suggestions for its improvement. Indeed, these three colleagues have assisted me more than they might realize throughout my research and writing.

Finally, I would like to express my gratitude to my wife Nancy and to my sons Andrew and Jonathan for their support, and especially their tolerance, over the years that this book has been in preparation.

*London,*
*January 1983*

L.B.

# ABBREVIATIONS

ANM. Archives Nationales du Mali, Bamako.
ANS. Archives Nationales du Sénégal, Dakar.
BN. Bibliothèque Nationale, Paris. Arabic manuscipts cited are from the department of Manuscrits Orientaux.
CEDRAB. Centre de Documentation et de Recherche Historique, Aḥmad Baba, Timbuktu, Mali.
CHEAM. Centre de Hautes Études sur l'Afrique et l'Asie Modernes, formerly the Centre de Hautes Études d'Administration Musulmane.
IFAN. Institut Fondamental d'Afrique Noire.
JM. *Jawāhir al-Ma'ānī* by 'Alī, Ḥarāzim.
MAMMP. Malian Arabic Manuscript Microfilming Project, Yale University.
*Rimāḥ. Rimāḥ ḥizb al-raḥīm 'alā nuḥūr ḥizb al-rajīm* by al-Ḥājj 'Umar b. Sa'īd al-Fūtī.
TB. *Tierno Bokar, le Sage de Bandiagara* by Amadou Hampaté Bâ and Marcel Cardaire.
VE. *Vie et Enseignement de Tierno Bokar, le Sage de Bandiagara* by Amadou Hampaté Bâ.

# NOTE ON ORTHOGRAPHY

The conventions of orthography employed in this book are necessarily something of a compromise between the demands of precise scholarship and simplification of presentation.

Proper names have been written according to their spoken versions using the system of transcription now common in West Africa. This results in Amadu rather than the French Amadou or the Arabic Ahmad, and in Umar rather than Oumar or 'Umar, etc. Precise Arabic transcriptions of names have been given when these will aid in identifying a personality in the Arabic literature.

The transcription of Fulfulde words also been simplified. This has resulted in the suppression of the symbols for the implosives: *ɓ, ɗ*, and *ƴ*. Therefore *kaɓɓe* has been written as *kabbe*, and Fulɓe as Fulbe. Pullo, the singular form of Fulbe, has been retained. The *c* in Cerno and Cam is pronounced like *ch* in "church."

# A PERSONAL INTRODUCTION

> "Cerno Bokar decided that he would work for what would bring him close to God. He became one who searched for Truth; he became a friend of religion."
> Baba Thimbely, 1977

> "The light of Truth . . . is a darkness more brilliant than all lights combined."
> Cerno Bokar, 1933

Cerno Bokar Saalif Taal was the great-nephew of al-Hajj Umar Taal, the renowned nineteenth century jihadist and proselytizer of the Tijaniyya Sufi order in West Africa. Born in about 1883 in Segu when this city was still under African suzerainty, Cerno Bokar grew to maturity in the context of the imposition of French colonial power and the concurrent erosion of Tijani political and religious authority. Despite the hardships of his youth, his own religious education was not ignored; he received a sound scholarly training and eventually became a teacher in Bandiagara. Although considered a good scholar by his contemporaries, he was not particularly interested in producing bookish scholars. Rather he addressed himself to the problem of teaching the tenets of Islam to illiterate adults, especially to recent converts. But even more important, he devoted constant efforts toward encouraging those around him to activate the principles of their religion within themselves in the context of their everyday lives. This striving to move "beyond the letter" of the written word, as he stated it, was the real essence of his own spiritual search.

This book is an attempt to explore Cerno Bokar's spiritual quest as the interaction between, on the one hand, the influences of his social and religious environment and, on the other, his own personal yearning to find the "Truth." Cerno Bokar spoke often about the "Truth," although he never seems to have given specific definition to the word. One of the Muslim names for God is *al-Ḥaqq*, the Truth. Another Arabic word, *ḥaqīqa*, can also be translated as "truth;" in Sufi terminology it refers to ultimate, divine reality as well as to the highest degree of mystical attainment. Cerno Bokar employed all these meanings in his teachings, but he also spoke of Truth as a kind of essential, universal religion and as a kind of mystical intuition. This vagueness of definition reflects an inherent characteristic of the man, because the emphasis in Cerno Bokar's life was much less in proclaiming any particular "Truth" than in constantly searching for it. Of course, on one level he taught the theological dogmas of Islam which explained the nature of God in terms of His various attributes, but as a Sufi he accepted that the comprehension of the *true* nature of God might well be beyond his capacity. The saints of Islam might achieve such a profound understanding, but Cerno Bokar never claimed to have done so himself. Everything we know about him suggests that he engaged throughout his adult life in a search for something which he could not clearly define, but in which his belief was sustained by his faith in its existence.

My attraction to a study of Cerno Bokar's life and thought resulted from my fascination with his humble yet persistent sense of search as well as with the directness and sincerity of his observations and commentaries. My first introduction to him was in the biography by Amadou Hampaté Bâ and Marcel Cardaire, *Tierno Bokar, le Sage de Bandiagara*, at a period when I had become interested in Sufism in West Africa; my particular concern was to determine to what extent an active spiritual discipline existed within the West African Sufi brotherhoods, about which most scholarly writings had emphasized their social and political aspects. Cerno Bokar convinced me that this spiritual discipline existed even in the twentieth century, and my first inclination was to translate into English *Le Sage de Bandiagara* in order to make this information available to a broader English-speaking audience. However, upon reflection I realized that, important contribution as it was, the Bâ and Cardaire book left unexplored many dimensions of Cerno Bokar's religious thought and his Sufi beliefs and practices. I therefore embarked upon a research project whose aim was to trace Cerno Bokar's religious heritage in as many directions as I was able. In this I relied heavily on the assistance and cooperation of Amadou Hampaté Bâ, through whose agency the vast majority of what we know of Cerno's life and teaching has been preserved and transmitted. But I also interviewed others who knew and studied under Cerno Bokar, I read the West African Tijani books, and I combed African archives for relevant material. In the process I discovered the collection of discourses, originally recorded by Hampaté Bâ, which are included in Part III of this book. Although about half of these discourses had already been published in *Le Sage de Bandiagara*, I was struck anew by their uniqueness. Here we seemed to have a body of demonstrably valid oral material, not only valuable for documenting Cerno Bokar's thought, but also illustrative of the dynamic and creative ways in which oral instruction could complement literate scholarship in Muslim West Africa. I was tempted to translate and publish them on their own, but I resisted that impulse as well, concluding that such a publication would take us no further in our understanding of the background of Cerno Bokar's thought than a translation of *Le Sage*.

Even by the time I began to write up some of the results of my research, I still intended to attempt a rather specialized analysis of Cerno Bokar's thought and teaching, a kind of religious study. But almost simultaneously with putting pen to paper, I realized that for several reasons I could not limit myself in this way. Firstly, my inclinations as a historian simply did not permit me to ignore the milieu in which Cerno Bokar lived his life. More significantly, his spiritual search as a Tijani Sufi led him at the end of his life to submit to the spiritual authority of Shaykh Hamallah of Nioro, an act which resulted in the harsh suppression of both Cerno and his followers. These events could not be understood without some knowledge of the conditions of French colonialism and the politics of the religious brotherhoods in the twentieth century. Cerno Bokar's difficulties resulted from his deep sense of personal integrity; he had concluded that Hamallah was the most elevated Tijani spiritual leader of his time, and it was therefore necessary to submit to him. He was prepared to keep secret his relationship to Hamallah, because he did not consider public proclamation of his beliefs to be a part of his spiritual quest. But when his affiliation became known, he absolutely refused to retreat from his position, as a result of which he suffered severe consequences. When his Sufi principles came into conflict with the conditions of his ordinary life, Cerno Bokar staunchly stood by his principles.

Pondering the significance of these events led me to a further appreciation of why one must study spiritual search in the context of ordinary life. Cerno Bokar was concerned that people activate their religious principles in their everyday lives. His is not a teaching of social isolation nor of asceticism. Ordinary life can provide aids to one's search, and it can also throw up obstacles; many examples of both are given in the discourses. But in no case can spiritual search be conducted without reference to life itself, as one lives it. For Cerno Bokar there was no search set apart from life, nor indeed was there any *real* life without search. But if my goal has been to explore these two themes in relation to one another, the result has fallen far short of my original hopes. Although we posses in his discourses a much more intimate knowledge about what (and how) Cerno Bokar thought than about many other better known West African Muslim scholars, not nearly enough detail is known about him to do justice to the kind of project I had envisaged. The discourses provide remarkable insight into Cerno Bokar's personal search for religious understanding, but they do not refer to specific events and are not very useful in reconstructing his biography. We have no accounts of Cerno's own feelings about major events in his life such as his submission to Shaykh Hamallah, his decision after much hesitation to become a teacher, his relationships with various members of the extended Taal family, nor about his views and attitudes toward French colonial authority. The absence of personal testimony by Cerno Bokar about his life is exacerbated first by the fact that very few of his close associates survive today to speak about him, and secondly, that one of these associates, Amadou Hampaté Bâ, has developed a very particular view of the man as his disciple and his biographer, and as the propagator of his teachings. No study of Cerno Bokar could be undertaken without considerable reliance upon Hampaté Bâ, who is not and has never claimed to be an unbiassed and objective critic of Cerno and his teachings. Hampaté Bâ has candidly warned me that a disciple's evaluation of his spiritual teacher has little objective value:

> He cannot *not* love his spiritual master because he *is* his master. For him, he has accomplished everything; otherwise he would not have chosen him as his master. He is his model. For example, I can say that for me Cerno Bokar is *insān al-kāmil*, a perfected man. But that does not mean that he is, *in fact*, *insān al-kāmil*, because he himself would not accept it. But for me he is *insān al-kāmil* because I have never seen anyone whom I would place above him.[1]

Nonetheless, the man who spoke these words has been an invaluable source of information and encouragement in all of my research on Cerno Bokar. Hampaté Bâ recorded Cerno's discourses in 1933, he co-authored a biography of him in 1957 (*Le Sage de Bandiagara*) which was extensively revised in 1980,[2] and I have spent many hours with him in fruitful and fascinating conversation. It therefore seems essential that I say something about him and my relationship with him by way of introducing this book.

*Images.* It is appropriate to begin with myself. In the early 1970s I developed a keen interest in Sufism. I was particularly disturbed that West African Sufism was very often depicted as being devoid of any real or profound spiritual dimension. Most scholarly interest centered on the brotherhoods as social, political and economic organizations. Passing reference was usually made by authors to what Sufism was allegedly about: mystical union with God, salvation through prayer and devotional exercises, a comprehension of the esoteric dimensions of existence; but after a few pages' discussion of these matters, most scholars devoted the bulk of their works to an analysis of the brotherhoods as social and political organizations. My efforts to move beyond this approach began with a wide-ranging reading programme about Sufism outside West Africa, the basic purpose of which was to discover what Sufism was "supposed" to be so that I could then look for it in West Africa. My thinking in this period was recorded in a review article written in 1972.[3] The immediately preceeding years had seen the appearance of a spate of new books on Sufism, and I reviewed several of them by Martin Lings, F. Schuon and Idries Shah. Although all these authors might not have been happy to find themselves associated with one another in a single article, they were definitely grouped together in my mind because each of them, along with others, had given me some essential guidance on how to approach the study of Sufism. But my conclusions about West Africa in this article were not very edifying. Aside from indicating certain underlying features of Sufism, I basically argued that one could not judge Sufism by external appearances. Just because al-Hajj Umar had led a bloody and ruthless military campaign across half of West Africa, or Amadu Bamba seemed to place little significance on whether or not his followers fulfilled even the most fundamental Islamic obligations, it did not follow that they were not *really* Sufis.

In certain contexts I would still be prepared to defend this seemingly facile comment. However, just after I wrote the above article I read *Le Sage de Bandiagara*; now I was convinced that I had found a "real" Sufi in West Africa. Cerno Bokar seemed to fulfill all the criteria I had established from my readings and I wrote another article in order to explain why this was so.[4] In it I described Sufism as a specifically Islamic response to man's universal confrontation with life and with the dilemmas of the human condition. I outlined Cerno Bokar's specific form of spiritual search in terms of a quest for self-knowledge and self-control leading toward an awakening of spiritual capacities. And I argued that the discourses published in *Le Sage* were in fact a form of Sufi teaching story. As I look back upon this article, I realize that I was clothing Cerno Bokar in an image constructed out of bits and pieces taken from my more general reading on Sufism. Much of what I said was valid enough, but the general weight of the article did not bring us much closer to understanding Sufism as practiced in West Africa.

The image of Cerno Bokar portrayed in the present book owes much more to his own West African heritage. I would not retract my statements about self-knowledge and self-control as elements of African Sufism, but they assume a somewhat more measured role in the context of a range of beliefs and practices which will be familiar to many Africanists — for example, the significance of repeated recitations of certain prayers believed to have special efficacy, the belief in saints, miracles, and what are called "secrets," the search for *baraka* (Arabic for spiritual grace) and salvation through one's relationship to a venerated *shaykh*, and the great significance placed upon dreams and visions. My recent research has been devoted to understanding these aspects of West African Sufism as its practitioners themselves see them; in so doing I have relied mostly upon the writings of West African Sufis and upon interviews and discussions with Muslims and Sufis in West Africa. These efforts to comprehend Sufi ideas, concepts and practices from the inside have not been made any easier by my tendency to filter what I hear through some supposed critical faculty in order allegedly to assess the validity of information received. This is not a bad thing for a historian to do, but it is not terribly useful if one is truly trying to take in what and how another person thinks. It was in this task that Hampaté Bâ's assistance to me was greatest, not only because he patiently and painstakingly answered all my questions (which he did), but because he spoke directly and honestly from his own sense of deep commitment about the Sufism in which he believes. He did not lecture to me; he confided in me and in so doing he helped me to attend to his words in the manner they deserved. These were the occasions on which Hampaté Bâ spoke as a disciple and a propagator of Cerno Bokar's teachings; his explications (as he himself pointed out) may not have been precisely those of Cerno Bokar, but I certainly had no means available to me to get any closer to the original teachings. Our conversations ranged over the entire spectrum of West African Islam and Sufism, and his remarks often led me into lines of investigation whose existence I had not even suspected when I commenced my research; the most exciting of these, and the one most extensively explored in this book, was the theological teaching known in Fulfulde as *kabbe*, which formed the basis of Cerno Bokar's own *mā 'd-dīn*, a kind of Islamic catechism which he taught in Bandiagara (see Chapter 4 and Appendix I).

But of course Hampaté Bâ is not only a disciple of Cerno Bokar; he has also chosen to be his biographer. Indeed, he is responsible, either directly or indirectly, for virtually everything the public knows about Cerno Bokar. Now the relationship of a disciple to his teacher could not be more different from that between an individual and his biographer, at least in the western, academic concept of biography. A Sufi disciple is meant to develop a very special association with his teacher; he seeks not only to absorb the substantive content of the teaching which is communicated by words, but also to be imbued with the "presence" of the teacher who is directing his internal spiritual development. This dimension of the relationship is almost never discussed openly and in any case is practically impossible to describe, although it is the essence of the entire exercise without which little else of real and lasting value can be accomplished. Only through this inner development can the disciple truly receive the totality of the teaching and make it his own, but having accomplished this degree of "understanding", he can then in turn transmit the teaching to others. In so doing he has no need, though he may wish to do so, to refer to his teacher, because what he is teaching comes from within himself and from his own understanding. The Sufi disciple therefore views his teacher from a privileged and very private perspective, and he seeks to allow the influences of his teacher to act upon him. He is not interested in a public revelation of the facts of this relationship, and any views or opinions of it by the outside world are considered largely irrelevant. A biographer works from a very different set of premises. Biography is about public revelation, or at least about the gathering of all kinds of information from all kinds of sources so as to describe in as full a fashion as possible the life of an individual. Biography is presented to the public from whom it invites response and reaction, particularly biography in the contemporary world.

Neither Hampaté Bâ's efforts at biography nor his endeavors to propagate his interpretations of Cerno Bokar's teaching have been without response and reaction. This is especially so within West Africa where each slightly variant form of Islamic practice tends to find both adherents and opponents. Cerno Bokar had his enemies and his critics and so does Hampaté Bâ, although not for the same reasons. Witness the following quotation from Lansiné Kaba's study of Islamic reformist movements in Mali:

In the 1950s there was in Bamako a small group of modernists whose spokesman was the distinguished historian Amadou Hampaté Bâ, whose work reveals strong influences of European education and important elements of Western thought. These are especially noticeable in his book *Tierno Bokar: Le Sage de Bandiagara*. The character depicted in this book resembles Socrates in many respects. To the Socratic method of systematic doubt and patient questioning and teaching, the learned old man also adds the high moral qualities inherent in Jesus Christ. The blending of the two spiritual fathers of the Western tradition into the person of an old Muslim teacher may be deliberate or accidental. Yet the implication is clear: Islam contains a philosophical enlightment and a degree of spirituality comparable to those of European culture. This remark will satisfy many contemporary Muslims. The portrayal, however, implies a strong intellectual reaction against traditional Muslim leadership and a clear support for the idea of change in the attitude of Muslims towards modern life. Wahhabi leaders will support this idea. However, Bâ's views go much further. They are in accordance with those advocates who hope to incorporate into Islamic doctrine certain Western principles and methods. This adoption eventually may lead to a complete syncretism of the two value systems.[5]

These remarks should be placed in context; Kaba's book, *The Wahhabiyya*, is a study of post-war Islamic reformist movements in Mali. In the 1950s Hampaté Bâ was influential in starting up a number of French-supported Muslim religious schools which used Bambara and Fulfulde as the languages of instruction. These vernacular schools were seen by many Muslim educational reformers, perhaps justifiably, as politically inspired experiments to undermine their own schools in which Arabic was being introduced as the language of instruction. I have no knowledge of Hampaté Bâ's precise intentions and actions in all this, but he was accused by some parties of collaborating with the French against reformist interests. For Kaba, the most damning aspect of *Le Sage de Bandiagara* is that it was co-authored by Marcel Cardaire, an official in the Bureau des Affaires Musulmanes (an agency devoted largely to the surveillance of Muslims) and a staunch opponent of the reformists. Certainly this literary collaboration could not have been devoid of political connotations, whether intended or not. But is Kaba justified in implying that the image of Cerno Bokar which is presented in *Le Sage* was conjured up in the midst of the modernist-reformist debate as a "strong intellectual reaction against traditional Muslim leadership" and a "syncretism" of European and Islamic value systems?

No one who has read *Le Sage de Bandiagara* would deny that in it Cerno Bokar is portrayed in such a way that few Westerners could fail to recognize him as a man of profound spiritual accomplishment. I personally would not describe that image as particularly Christian or Socratic, but one can appreciate Kaba's remarks on this. However, the public image of Cerno Bokar had begun to emerge in the journals of western academia a decade before the appearance of *Le Sage* in 1957, in the form of two articles by Théodore Monod. The first, "Un poème mystique soudanais,"[6] was the translation of a poem composed by a disciple of Cerno Bokar; the second article, entitled "Un Homme de Dieu: Tierno Bokar,"[7] offered the first published presentation of Cerno Bokar's own teachings in the form of some of his discourses. Cerno Bokar next appeared in the pages of Alphonse Gouilly's *L'Islam dans l'Afrique Occidentale Française* in a section of the book devoted to the Hamallist Sufi movement. Gouilly includes a passage on Hamallist doctrine to which is appended a lengthy footnote on the "esoteric aspect of Hamallism" provided to him by "a learned African, himself a follower of Hamallah."[8] The note explains the stages of Sufi spiritual development in much the same format as would later appear in *Le Sage de Bandiagara* where it is specifically attributed to Cerno Bokar. Gouilly's "learned African" informant was, of course, Hampaté Bâ, who had also provided Monod with the material which allowed him to publish his two articles. Much the same relationship existed between Cardaire and Hampaté Bâ in their co-authorship of *Le Sage*; Hampaté Bâ provided all the substantive material, and Cardaire put the text into proper French, adding some of his own interpretations and comments. At least Cardaire credited Hampaté Bâ's contribution by name, although Hampaté Bâ claims that he never saw the actual text before it was published.

To return to Kaba's accusations, two questions must be posed: in what way was Hampaté Bâ responsible for the image of Cerno Bokar which had been presented to the French-reading public between 1947 and 1957; and how did this image relate directly to the modernist-reformist debates of the early 1950s in Mali (then French Soudan)? To respond to the second question first, it should be clear from chronology alone that Cerno Bokar was being portrayed as a particular kind of mystic well before the reformist confrontations in Mali in which Hampaté Bâ was involved. Furthermore, those early articles were written in a context completely separated from reformist concerns; there can be little doubt that Hampaté Bâ had managed to impress Monod and later Gouilly with the teachings of Cerno Bokar. Surely his goal was to vindicate the tarnished name of his teacher and also to defend the reputation of the Hamalliyya. This view conforms to Hampaté Bâ's own version of how he and Cardaire came to write *Le Sage*, which is outlined in its recent revised version, *Vie et Enseignement de Tierno Bokar*.[9] According to him, he first met Cardaire when the latter came to Bamako to investigate his involvement in the discredited Hamalliyya movement. Not only did Hampaté Bâ escape implication, but he befriended Cardaire who himself suggested they co-author a biography of Cerno Bokar. I am unable to comment on the extent to which Hampaté Bâ either shared Cardaire's views on the reformists or cooperated in moves against them, but it seems clear that his contribution to publications about Cerno Bokar were designed to achieve a purpose quite different from challenging reformism.

Hampaté Bâ's role in the creation of Cerno Bokar's published image is more difficult to assess. As well as a historian and an accomplished poet in Fulfulde, he is a consummate raconteur. No one who has read his works would doubt his facility with words or his ability to formulate a convincing characterisation of a personality in any manner which pleased him. His reconstructions of historical events are often expressed in a literary idiom which seems to aim more for effect and impression than fact, *even if* they are accurate accounts. Nor is he unwilling to give free rein to his creative imagination, for example in providing allegedly verbatim reports of conversations at which he was not present. This particular approach to history might be described as a contemporary, literate expression of what has come to be known among Africanists as "oral tradition." This is not the place to enter into a discussion of the nature of oral tradition in Africa, but certainly one of the factors which distinguishes it from Western historical exposition is the degree to which effect is seen as a legitimate and even essential ingredient of it. We Western-trained historians are taught to search for demonstrable and supportable "facts" out of which should emerge supposedly objective analyses; oral tradition rarely makes any claims to objectivity. Hampaté Bâ's training as a historian was in the informal school of the oral traditionalists; it began in earliest childhood whilst listening to tales spun by the esteemed raconteurs of Masina; the process never seems to have ceased for him, nor has his personal interest in it waned. He has made occasional reference to this formation in his writings,[10] and its significance should not be understimated. It should also be recalled that his reputation as a published historian is based upon his experimentation with and defense of oral tradition as a valid and useful source of African history.

This traditionalist approach to history may give us pause in our search for the "true facts," but one must not forget that in his continued advocacy of this particular form of expression Hampaté Bâ gives witness to his uncompromising fidelity to this aspect of his African heritage.[11]

My experience suggests that he is unabashedly prepared to discuss Africa's society and history in all its aspects without offering apology for what it is or has been, and to do this with considerable pride. If the idiom of his communication encourages him to play to his audience or lends itself to a wide range of emotional, ideological or political colouring, this is the idiom which Africa has taught him. This is one reason why I find it impossible to understand Lansiné Kaba's charge that the portrayal of Cerno Bokar in *Le Sage de Bandiagara* "implies a strong intellectual reaction against traditional Muslim leadership." One might argue that certain of the anecdotes which Hampaté Bâ relates about Cerno are designed to cater to specific European sensibilities, such as his little lecture to his students on charity which was instanced by the fall of a baby sparrow from its nest (p. 100), or his extraordinary lesson based on the proverb, "The greatest knowledge is to know one does not know" (p. 144). Perhaps these are the kind of stories which led Kaba to feel that Cerno Bokar was being falsely imbued with what he sees as Christian and Socratic attributes; but of course the qualities of charity and self-doubt are not the special possessions of the western world, and I will argue in this book that Cerno Bokar's teachings about these and many other ideas emerge directly from West Africa's Islamic tradition, even if I have no way to prove that the precise content of Hampaté Bâ's stories is factually true. For me, then, the image which Hampaté Bâ created of Cerno Bokar in *Le Sage*, far from being a reaction against traditional Muslim leadership, inspired me with a new interest in studying it, and all of my personal contacts with him during my research have convinced me that he is in fact a committed advocate of that leadership.

*Sources.* What all this boils down to is that the major "primary source" for my research into the life of Cerno Bokar was a devoted disciple of the individual under investigation, the advocate of a particular form of history, and a delightful reconteur. For my part, I found myself perfectly willing to listen to Hampaté Bâ for hours, and by now it will be clear that my relationship with him has nurtured within me a considerable respect for him. I do not believe that a full understanding and appreciation of Cerno's ideas are possible without this respect, and I offer no apology for what some might consider a biassed view on my part. In any case, I have no intention of arguing that Cerno Bokar was a personification of West African Islam; he was an exceptional and in many ways extraordinary individual. But at the same time he was a product of the West African Islamic heritage upon which every aspect of his teaching was based. For the insight and sense of acceptance to which Hampaté Bâ led me, I am grateful; at the same time, of course, I have been left the task of evaluating his historical accounts from the perspective which I have adopted in my study.

The procedures which I have adopted are not so systematic that they deserve to be called a methodology, but they should be stated briefly here.

Hampaté Bâ's general explications of Islamic and Sufi doctrine and practice were accepted as factual evidence only for what he himself believes as a disciple of Cerno Bokar; as I suggested above, conversations on these matters have guided me in much of my research, but generally their content has not been employed in this book as direct evidence for Islamic belief and practice. Rather I have relied as much as possible on other primary and corroborating sources in order to describe and analyse the intellectual and religious background to Cerno Bokar's thought. Hampaté Bâ often pointed the way in this research, and occasionally he was able to explain certain subjects for which other indigenous sources were virtually impossible to obtain, for example, on the Sufi uses of numerology.

The situation is rather different and more difficult in moving from the background to the specific content of Cerno Bokar's thought and teaching. Here we find several kinds of material: Cerno's catechism known as *mā 'd-dīn* or "What is religion?" (reproduced in Appendix I); his discourses; and a wide range of anecdotes about, and quotations attributed to, Cerno Bokar which are found in various of Hampaté Bâ's writings and in my interviews with him. The *mā 'd-dīn* was definitely Cerno's invention and was taught by him in Bandiagara; this has been confirmed by numerous informants, although the only complete text available to me is that published by Hampaté Bâ. The content of the discourses has not been corroborated by any other source, but I have concluded, with minor reservations, that these are accurate accounts of Cerno Bokar's comments and observations recorded in special conditions by Hamptē Bâ in 1933. My evaluation of them as a source appears in detail in the introduction to Part III. I have employed the *mā 'd-dīn* and the discourses almost exclusively as evidence of Cerno Bokar's ideas, but I have generally avoided using any other scattered and more recent materials, not because I have any specific reason to believe that these are necessarily not accurate accounts but because Hampaté Bâ has made it clear to me that with time even he is no longer certain which ideas came from Cerno and which are his own. The *mā 'd-dīn* and the discourses were written down in the 1930s and do not seem subsequently to have been modified, except to be put into more correct French. On the few occasions when later anecdotes or attributions do appear in this book, the reader will easily recognize them for what they are: evocative illustrations of Cerno Bokar's characteristic behaviour, already evident from other sources.

Hampaté Bâ's historical accounts have been evaluated even more rigorously and subjected to severe critical examination whenever other sources allow for comparison. In virtually no instance have they been used on their own to establish specific facts about Cerno Bokar's life or about other events described in this book. But if Hampaté Bâ's accounts generate one kind of problem, other sources produce other problems. The French took almost no notice of Cerno Bokar until his submission to Shaykh Hamallah; then he became a major preoccupation in official reports. They knew virtually nothing about him but feared his possible influence and placed him under close surveillance for alleged "weakness of character." Their fear and ignorance contributed to producing the tragedy of Cerno Bokar's final years. Between the disparate views of devoted disciple and fearful authorities there is some, but not much, middle ground of evidence about the details of Cerno's life, gleaned from interviews with a few surviving persons who knew him and from other scattered references.

To reiterate, then, the aim of the present book is to study the interaction between Cerno Bokar's personal spiritual quest and his social and religious environment. An understanding of this interaction has necessitated an examination not only of Cerno Bokar's ideas and teachings, but also of the more comprehensive themes of religious structures, practices and thought as well as of general political evolution and conflict.

The book is divided into three parts: the first describes the relevant religious and political developments in the nineteenth- and early twentieth-century Soudan which form the background to a more specific discussion, in the second part, of Cerno Bokar's own life and teaching. The third part is a translation of a selection of Cerno Bokar's discourses. This progression from general to more specific themes is designed to illustrate the historical continuity and internal consistency of Cerno Bokar's own religious thought, as well as to reveal the forces which ultimately brought him into confrontation with the political world in which he lived. Indeed, considerations about conflict, continuity and change regularly intruded into my thoughts as I proceeded in my research. Nothing struck me more profoundly than my realization of the ephemeral and vulnerable nature of man's intellectual and cultural heritage. The scattered fragments of Cerno Bokar's thought which are contained in his discourses and in the *mā 'd-dīn* are but one tiny window which opens on to an extensive and expansive religious and intellectual tradition. These fragments only exist today because Amadou Hampaté Bâ acted to preserve them; the French and African authorities who crushed the small group of Hamallist Sufis which centered upon Cerno Bokar and who consequently terminated Cerno's active intellectual life harboured not the slightest suspicion that they were at the same time destroying a rich and vital growth-point in Africa's cultural heritage. This event represents more than the tragedy of one man; writ large, it is a tragedy for the whole of Africa where the forces of recent and contemporary change tend to run roughshod over the more vulnerable elements of the continent's ancient culture. If the present study does not achieve as full a description or as profound a comprehension of its subject as one would like, at least one would hope that other students might be encouraged by it to undertake similar studies which will aid in our general appreciation of the history and dynamics of the African religious and intellectual heritage.

## NOTES

1. Interview with Amadou Hampaté Bâ, 12 May 1978.
2. *Tierno Bokar, le Sage de Bandiagara* (Paris: Présence Africaine, 1957), abbreviated in all following notes as TB; revised edition published as *Vie et Enseignement de Tierno Bokar. Le Sage de Bandiagara* (Paris: Éditions du Seuil, 1980), abbreviated as VE.
3. "Separate Realities: a Review of Literature on Sufism," *International Journal of African Historical Studies*, v, 4(1972), 637–58.
4. "The Sufi Teaching of Tierno Bokar Salif Tall," *Journal of Religion in Africa*, viii, fasc. 3(1976), 208–26.
5. Lansiné Kaba, *The Wahhabiyya. Islamic Reform and Politics in French West Africa* (Evanston, 1974), 22–3.
6. *Le Monde non-chrétien*, no. 2(1947), 217–28.
7. *Présence Africaine*, 8–9(1950), 149–57.
8. A. Gouilly, *L'Islam dans l'Afrique Occidentale Française* (Paris, 1952), 147–9.
9. VE, 7–11.
10. See VE, 127 and the introduction to *L'Étrange Destin de Wangrin* (Paris, 1973).
11. In this regard, see J.-P. Gourdeau, "Une Lecture de *L'Étrange Destin de Wangrin* d'Amadou Hampaté Bâ," *Annales de l'Université d'Abidjan*, Ser. D., 8(1975), 153–84.

Mosque in the Sudanese style near Lake Debo, Mali.

## Part I

# THE HISTORICAL CONTEXT

"There is only one God. There can only be one way to lead to Him, one religion of which the others are only variable forms. This religion can only be called Truth."

Cerno Bokar, 1933

"The precepts of Muhammad, inspired by a superficial verbalism and by an intransigeance which allows for no conciliation, provides for no possibility of rapprochement with our ideals."

G. Guy, "L'Enseignement colonial en France," 1927

"The Sufi aspirant must seek out a *shaykh* in whose religious faith he has confidence, who is well known for his uprightness and his trustworthiness and is knowledgable about the Sufi way, and he must submit himself to his service."

al-Suhrawardī, quoted in the *Rimāḥ* of al-Hajj Umar, 1845

"The *politique des races* is one sure method for inhibiting the unification of Islam; . . . it permits us to initiate an administrative activity near each centre of Muslim influence, not to combat the dogma of a religion, but to prevent it from degenerating into a political force."

R. Arnaud, "L'Islam et la politique musulmane francaise en AOF," 1912

"On 17 July Bokar Saalif confirmed that he had become a convinced partisan of Shaykh Hamallah. . . . He refused to furnish any precise details to explain his conversion and would only say that he was free to choose his religion and that no threat or action could cause him to revoke his decision."

*Commandant de Cercle*, Mopti, 1937

"Sincerity is telling the truth in a situation from which there is no escape except by lying."

al-Junaid, quoted in the *Rimāḥ* of al-Hajj Umar, 1845

# 1

# THE POLITICAL BACKGROUND

The patterns which shaped Cerno Bokar's life were informed by three major interrelated themes: his intense personal religious quest as a Muslim and a Sufi; the demands placed upon him as a prominent member of the Taal family and as a leader of the Tijaniyya Sufi order; and the deepening impact of the French colonial presence in the western Soudan. Most of this book is devoted to the first of these themes, to an examination of the content of Cerno Bokar's religious thought and teaching and to the influences which informed it. Of course, one can only go so far in such an exploration. The broader religious and intellectual background is relatively easy to establish, but the causes of Cerno Bokar's precise orientation within this context are very elusive because their understanding requires an exploration into personalities and personal relationships about which one necessarily knows little. For example, a study of Tijani doctrine and practice in West Africa can reveal the possible sources for most if not all of Cerno Bokar's religious ideas and teachings, but this exercise cannot explain the reasons for his personal attraction to contemplative mysticism. Similarly, Cerno Bokar's position of leadership in the Tijaniyya Sufi order seems easy to comprehend when one considers his status in the Taal family and his training in religious studies; such a development seems natural if not inevitable. But this kind of reasoning cannot explain events in Cerno Bokar's later life when his religious convictions set him in direct confrontation with most members of his family. Finally, we know virtually nothing about how Cerno Bokar felt or what he thought about the colonial presence in West Africa, although the tightening grip of French authority and influence could not but have been of concern to him. The crisis which overshadowed the final years of his life was in large part the result of French attitudes and policies towards Islam.

This book explores at varying levels of analysis the interrelation of these thematic patterns in Cerno Bokar's life. The object is to present the relevant background in as much or as little detail as seems appropriate so that the development of Cerno's life can be viewed not only in proximity to the man himself but also from the broader perspective of the world in which he lived. That world was in change, and much of the dynamic tension in Cerno's life was the direct result of the varying pace and differing directions of this change. Cerno Bokar himself was the advocate and agent of a particular form of religious radicalism which he had inherited from his family forebears: he was a proselytizer of Islam among the "unbelievers," especially the Dogon among whom he lived; as a teacher he developed and improved the forms and texts of religious instruction, especially those designed for teaching the non-literate; and he was a propagator of Tijani Sufism as a leading *muqaddam* of that brotherhood. Indeed, it was as a Tijani that his radicalism was most pronounced, because he clung tenaciously to the fundamental precepts of that order at a time when many others had begun to drift away from them. This drift was the direct result of Tijani political successes, uneven as they were. In the aftermath of the *jihād* of al-Hajj Umar earlier in the nineteenth century, many Tijani leaders became rather more interested in conserving their political authority than in confronting the spiritual rigours of Sufism. This trend was only intensified by the onslaught of French imperial power; Tijani leadership was decimated and dispirited by the imposition of this alien authority. For many Tijanis the only response they could find to the new situation was political: some resisted, many others collaborated in one way or another. But Cerno Bokar, who was born only about a decade before the French conquest, found for himself a somewhat different response: he acted almost as if the conquest had never occurred. This strategy seemed to work well enough until the time when the pursuit of his personal religious goals came into direct conflict with French political interests.

Cerno Bokar was not a political man, but neither was he immune to the effects of the political forces around him. His disciples were drawn to him because of the qualities they saw in him as a man of religion, but many of these same persons were also being drawn into the political turmoil of the day. One flirted with the French Popular Front, another was active in forming the Dogon Union, a nascent political party, another was passionately and aggressively anti-French. None of them received any encouragement for their political activities from Cerno Bokar; sometimes quite the opposite. For Cerno the French presence was a fact of life which must be accepted, no more and no less important than any other fact of political and social life. What was of primary importance to him was how one lived one's life so as to prepare for religious salvation. For him rulers were necessary in society; but who ruled was not terribly important. Rulers should be just, of course, but he was not shocked to find that many of them were not. The French possessed both good and bad qualities; so did members of his own family, the Taal, who had come to power under his great-uncle, al-Hajj Umar. He believed in the inevitability of inequality in society, but also in the equality of all men before God. He did not proclaim any of these views with political intention, which does not mean they were not understood by those around him to have political implications. Cerno does not even seem to have been much concerned over whether young Muslim children attended French schools, a highly emotive issue for many Muslim parents early in the century. In his opinion one could be a good Muslim regardless of the nature of one's formal education, and being a good Muslim was the ultimate goal to which all others were secondary.

In short, Cerno Bokar was a non-political man living in a highly charged and turbulent political world. Proclaim as he might his lack of interest in politics, politics was interested in him. For much of his adult life he managed to remain isolated from direct political engagement, but he could never completely separate himself from the heritage of his own family nor could he escape the nervous attention of French colonial authority. We therefore begin with an examination of the complex interrelationship between two of the thematic patterns which shaped Cerno Bokar's life: the wave of religious renewal initiated by al-Hajj Umar and the expansion of French imperial domination. Indeed, these were two powerful transforming forces which deeply affected all the western Soudan in the nineteeth and early twentieth centuries.

## *Al-Hajj Umar and the forces of Islamic renewal*

Al-Hajj Umar Taal al-Fūtī al-Tūrī[1] is one of the most prominent Muslim figures in West African history. Born in the last decade of the eighteenth century in the Senegal River valley, he devoted his life to religious study from an early age. In about 1825 he undertook the pilgrimage to Mecca, and remained for about three years in the environs of the Holy Cities where he received instruction and guidance in the doctrines of the Tijaniyya Sufi order which he had joined in West Africa. His instructor in Mecca, one of the most elevated leaders of the order, appointed Umar a *khalīfa* in the Tijaniyya order, a position which gave him effective spiritual authority over all Tijani adherents in West Africa.[2]

Although the Tijaniyya order was not yet very widespread in West Africa, al-Hajj Umar began actively proselytizing on its behalf as soon as he had returned from Mecca. His enthusiasm was not welcomed in all quarters and he occasionally found himself engaged in serious disputes, especially with the Shehu of Borno and with the Qadiri Sufi leaders of Timbuktu and Masina. On the other hand, he got on well with the Qadiri Caliph Muhammad Bello of Sokoto, with whom he remained for some years and whose daughter he married. During these years Umar also wrote quite extensively, and the subject to which he increasingly warmed was the explication of Tijani doctrine, an interest which culminated in 1845 in the completion of what must be considered his major work, *Rimāḥ ḥizb al-raḥīm 'alā nuḥūr ḥizb al-rajīm* (The Spears of the Party of the Merciful against the Throats of the Party of the Damned).[3] Despite its militant title, the book is a detailed explanation and defense of Tijani ideas and teachings and is considered by members of the order to be one of their most authoritative doctrinal works. It must be one of the most widely read books ever written by any West African Muslim scholar and has been published in Cairo, Tunis, and Beirut.

Although upon his return to West Africa al-Hajj Umar put most of his effort into spreading the doctrines of the Tijaniyya order, this was not the only subject about which he wrote, nor the only issue which attracted his attention. He was also very disturbed about factional strife and disunity among West African Muslims, about the widespread distribution of what he considered prohibited or misguided practices by Muslims, and generally about the sea of unbelievers which often surrounded West African Muslim communities. He was extremely outspoken on all these matters. In Futa Jallon, where he finally settled fifteen years after setting out on his pilgrimage, he attracted a growing number of Muslims to his following and very soon he was himself the leader of a burgeoning Muslim community. As this community grew, relations worsened with local political leaders who began to fear a threat to their own authority. The increasing tension culminated in 1852 with an attack by a non-Muslim chief against al-Hajj Umar, who consequently declared *jihād*, or religious war, against the "unbelievers." Local success by the Muslims was followed by more far-reaching campaigns northward toward the Bambara[4] kingdom of Kaarta, conquered in 1857, and where a new Muslim administrative centre was established at Nioro. An unsuccessful confrontation with the French in 1858 turned Umar's energies eastward toward a second Bambara kingdom, Segu, the conquest of which in 1861 led to conflicts with the neighbouring Muslim state of Masina. Masina had aided Segu against the Umarian forces, and even though he now found himself in the midst of the kind of intra-Muslim conflict he had so often condemned in the past, Umar refused to seek a compromise with his adversary. In 1862 the Masina capital, Hamdullahi, was captured and its ruler subsequently put to death.

Umar and a large contingent of his forces settled in Hamdullahi. Geographically, the fruits of the *jihādi* conquests had been extensive. Umarian lieutenants were established over a wide territory as local rulers; nascent Muslim administrations were functioning in many formerly non-Muslim districts. But the position was far from secure. Bambara rebellions were widespread, and the defeated Fulbe of Masina were not idle. By 1863 they had formed an anti-Umarian coalition of Muslim groups in the Niger valley which counterattacked Hamdullahi. Warfare continued for months and Umar was besieged in Hamdullahi. Early in 1864 he managed to escape eastward, only to be surrounded again among the hills and rocks near a village called Degembere, and

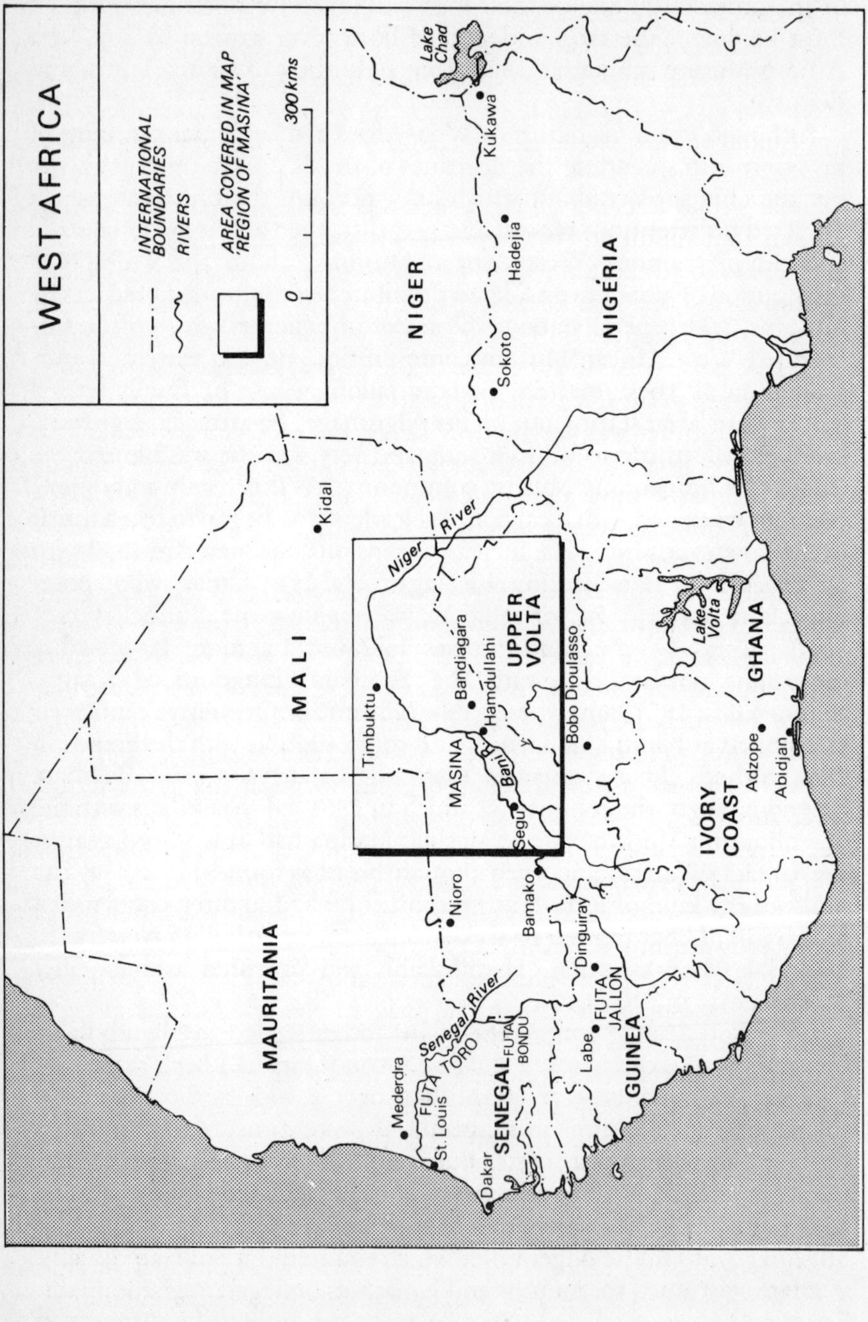
WEST AFRICA
INTERNATIONAL BOUNDARIES
RIVERS
AREA COVERED IN MAP 'REGION OF MASINA'
0
300 kms
MAURITANIA
MALI
NIGER
NIGÉRIA
UPPER VOLTA
GHANA
IVORY COAST
GUINEA
SENEGAL
Lake Chad
Kukawa
Hadejia
Sokoto
Kidal
Niger River
Timbuktu
Bandiagara
Hamdullahi
MASINA
Bani R.
Segu
Bamako
Nioro
Bobo Dioulasso
Lake Volta
Adzope
Abidjan
Dinguiray
FUTA JALLON
Labe
FUTA BONDU
FUTA TORO
Senegal River
Mederdra
St. Louis
Dakar

there, in circumstances still not fully explained, he died apparently from the effect of an explosion of gunpowder.

Following Umar's death, the coalition of his enemies began to split apart. The Umarians regrouped their forces, defeated the Fulbe, and set about the task of tightening their grip on Masina. They established a new capital on the plateau east of Hamdullahi at a Dogon village called Bandiagara.[5]

Umar's conquests not only changed the political face of the western Soudan, but modified its religious complexion as well. This was not only due to the establishment of new Muslim regimes in formerly non-Muslim areas, but also because Umar never ceased to proselytize on behalf of the Tijaniyya Sufi order. Large numbers of those who joined the *jihādi* cause became adherents of the Tijaniyya, and every administrative centre in the Umarian organisation was also a centre from which the religious order was proclaimed. In the inland Delta regions of the Niger valley, where Islam had enjoyed a lengthy and often illustrious history, Umar's movement met not only political and military resistance, but also serious doctrinal opposition to some of the basic teachings of the Tijaniyya. The spiritual leadership of the long established and eminent Qadiriyya Sufi order was centered among the Kunta in Timbuktu. Qadiri objections to Tijani doctrine were not new to al-Hajj Umar; he had encountered them soon after his return from Mecca. But during the *jihād* there was an intensification of the doctrinal debate, in which the political and military stakes which were very high. The disputes were resolved on the battlefield; the doctrinal debates themselves cooled as the antagonists came to accept the new political order, unstable as it was. The Tijaniyya spread into former Qadiri areas, and eventually adherents to the two orders adopted attitudes of mutual tolerance. The expansion of the Tijaniyya continued unabated and even gained momentum in the twentieth century; today the order exists throughout Muslim West Africa.

Upon al-Hajj Umar's death, his eldest son Amadu, whom Umar had named as his successor, sought to pick up the reins of his father's political and spiritual authority and to unify the newly conquered territories into a centralised state. For almost twenty-five years he struggled from his capital in Segu to achieve this goal, but the odds were overwhelmingly against him. Not only was there the constant problem of retaining control over conquered territory, but many of those to whom Umar had delegated administrative authority, for example in Dinguiray and Nioro, refused to accept Amadu's claims to leadership. Dissension in these areas erupted into armed conflict. In Masina Amadu's cousin, Tijani, who had founded the new capital of Bandiagara, maintained a peaceful but nonetheless carefully guarded attitude of independence. These internal divisions prevented the

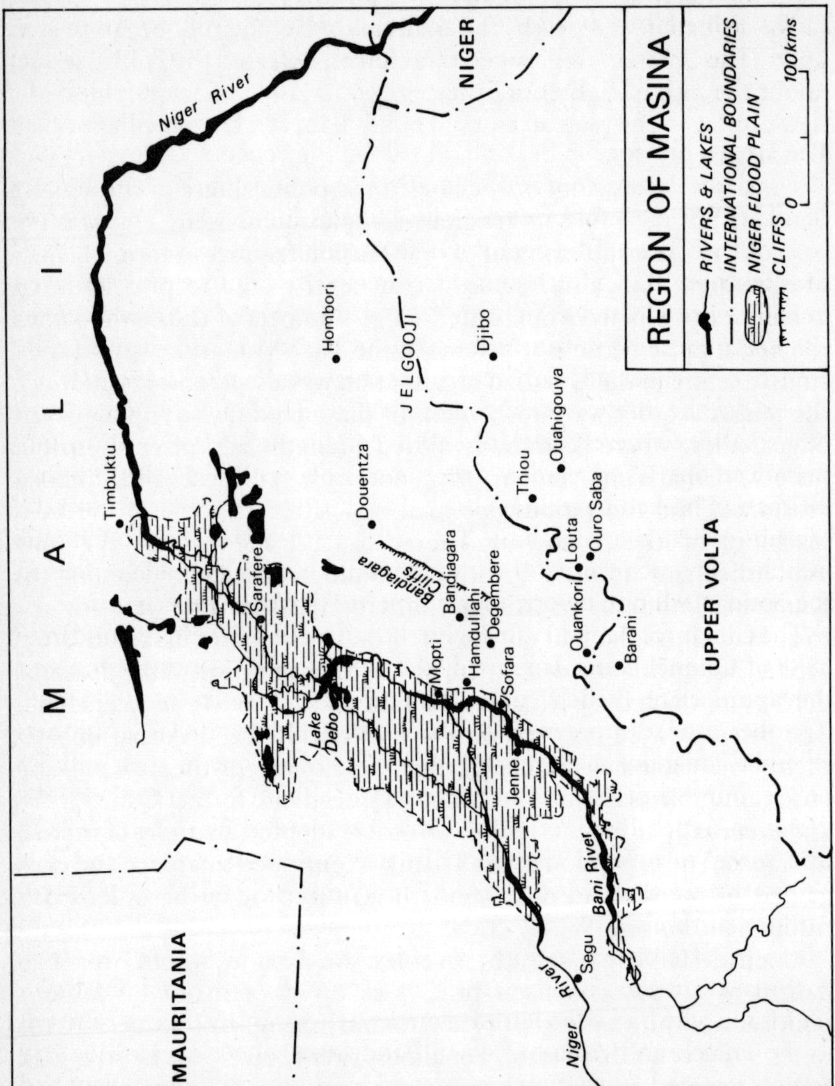
REGION OF MASINA
RIVERS & LAKES
INTERNATIONAL BOUNDARIES
NIGER FLOOD PLAIN
CLIFFS
0
100 kms
M A L I
MAURITANIA
NIGER
UPPER VOLTA
JELGOOJI
Niger River
Niger River
Bani River
Lake Debo
Bandiagara Cliffs
Timbuktu
Sarafere
Hombori
Douentza
Djibo
Ouahigouya
Thiou
Bandiagara
Louta
Ouro Saba
Mopti
Hamdullahi
Degembere
Ouankoro
Barani
Sofara
Jenne
Segu

consolidation of the Umarian conquests into a cohesive Muslim state, but the collapse of the entire political edifice was precipitated not by an internal threat but by an external one: French imperial expansion.

## *French conquest in the Western Soudan*

The French presence in St Louis and along the Senegal River valley had affected the entire course of Umar's *jihād*. Umar had undoubtedly cherished the hope of extending his Muslim community to his homeland of Futa Toro. This dream was shattered by defeat at the hands of the French in 1857, after which he redirected his efforts eastwards. Even in 1864 when Umar was fighting for his life in Masina, a French envoy was in Segu seeking to conclude a treaty of friendship with Amadu. The French were eager not only to protect their position on the coast, but also to tap the interior trade potential of the Soudan. Opinion on how best to achieve these goals differed depending upon who was making the decisions, and policy alternated between negotiation and ultimatum backed by military force. But during the final decades of the century, when the "scramble for Africa" reached a fever pitch, the militant approach gained the upper hand, and the Umarian centers in the Soudan fell one by one to the superior power of French arms.

The climax for Amadu came with the arrival in the western Soudan in 1888 of Colonel Louis Archinard who was in no way ambivalent about the appropriate French course of action. In a series of dry season (October-June) campaigns, Archinard drove Amadu and large numbers of other Umarians and Muslim leaders not only out of their seats of power, but completely out of the western Soudan. Not even under the threat of French force could the Umarians forget their differences and find a way to unified resistance. In the mid-1880s Amadu found it necessary once again to suppress the independent tendencies of Nioro. Additional threats to security forced Amadu to remain in Nioro from where he attempted to forge an anti-French alliance. But in 1890 Archinard launched a direct attack on Segu, and Amadu was unable to aid his son who had been left in command there. In 1891 Nioro also fell to the French and Amadu fled to Bandiagara where he was not very warmly received. Although his independent-minded cousin Tijani had died in 1887, another of Umar's sons, Muniru, now ruled and many of the Bandiagara notables had no desire to fall under the direct command of Amadu. In the end, however, Muniru agreed to abdicate in Amadu's favour; he died shortly thereafter and many claimed that Amadu was responsible for his death. In any case, Amadu was not long in Bandiagara; in spring 1893 Archinard captured the Masinan capital and Amadu fled eastwards toward the Sokoto Caliphate (in present-day northern Nigeria) where he died a few years later.

The Umarians who remained in the western Soudan were in almost complete disarray, stunned and leaderless. As if this widespread defeat were not enough, early French policy seemed designed to humiliate them completely. In Segu the French placed in authority a member of the former Bambara dynasty which had been defeated by al-Hajj Umar. He did not long remain in power because the French could not abide his excesses, but his presence was enough to spread considerable consternation among Umarians still in the region. To Bandiagara Archinard brought a younger son of al-Hajj Umar, Agibu, who had decided to throw in his lot with the Europeans. Agibu was made the chief of all Masina and given power to organise and administer this region.

The establishment of a protectorate in Masina was for the French but a single step in the construction of their West African empire. Masina would soon become integrated into an entirely new political entity of French invention, the colony of Soudan (or French Soudan) which in turn would become part of a French West African confederation governed from Dakar. The boundaries of the new colonies were drawn in response to French concerns about the administration and economic integration of the region into an efficient and productive unit. Politically, however, the French wished to maintain the disunity of their African subjects so as better to control them. In this the Africans managed unwittingly to aid their colonial rulers, because although most Africans might well have perceived the French presence as a profound challenge to the old social, political and economic order, they could not agree on a unified response. In the Soudan, one possibility for widespread African unity lay in Islam and in the heritage of tentative political hegemony and religious authority which al-Hajj Umar had established over that part of the region lying south and west of Timbuktu. But for all those who might have rallied to the Umarian heritage, there were many more who were its avowed enemies. In any case, Umarian political authority had been crushed by French arms; and as the new colonial structure became more firmly entrenched, the French became very sensitive to the emergence of religious movements which might bring a modicum of unity to their subjects. We can here survey only the broad interplay of these forces in West Africa, and present two specific case studies which illustrate both French-African and intra-African conflict and which relate specifically to the life of Cerno Bokar. The first is that of Agibu himself, who attempted to strike an Umarian compromise with the French from his new capital in Bandiagara; his case illustrates a political response to French conquest, and it is important because of its ramifications upon Cerno Bokar who lived almost all his life in Bandiagara. The second case is that of Shaykh Hamallah whose religious movement was perceived as a threat by both the French and by many Umarians alike.

## *Agibu, "King of Masina"*

The case of Agibu vividly illustrates both the factional strife which plagued the Umarians after the death of al-Hajj Umar in 1864 and the political pressures to which they were subjected by the French conquest. Agibu had remained with his elder brother, Amadu, in Segu after the Umarian conquest of that city in 1861. Between 1870 and 1874, when Amadu, in an effort to enforce his authority as successor to his father, was campaigning against several of his dissident brothers in the Western provinces of the fragile Umarian state, Agibu had been left in Segu as his regent. On his return, Amadu apparently became jealous of Agibu's popularity, and some evidence suggests that members of his court capitalized on these feelings to drive a wedge between the two brothers so as to isolate Agibu and limit his influence. This same faction encouraged Amadu to appoint Agibu governor of Dinguiray when the post fell vacant in 1876 (following the death of yet another brother), thus removing him completely from court politics. In spite of some interpretations to the contrary,[6] Agibu and Amadu do not seem personally to have been on such bad terms at this time; otherwise, why appoint Agibu governor of an important province? The issue is confused, however, by a letter from Agibu to a French official in which he claims that he had later sided with the French because Amadu had taken one of his wives from him, as well as some 200 slaves and "3000" in gold.[7] The letter does not state precisely when this alleged seizure took place, but had it been before Agibu went to Dinguiray it would hardly have provided assurance of loyal behaviour by the new governor.

Agibu and Amadu certainly drifted apart, but some doubt must remain as to when the rift between them became serious. Even by the late 1880s, when French pressure upon him to conclude a separate treaty with them was intensifying, Agibu refused to act independently of Amadu. What is more clear is that the closer Amadu came to ultimate defeat by the French, the more evident became Agibu's desire to succeed him, although his motives are obscure. French reports favour the interpretation that Agibu was driven by self-interest and a kind of juvenile avarice; he seemed to covet the material rewards that cooperation with the French brought to him.[8] But certain of his African partisans have argued not only that Agibu was seeking to preserve some semblance of the Umarian state, but that Amadu had instructed him in writing to do so; however, the purported letter which could prove this assertion was allegedly destroyed in a fire![9] Perhaps each of these extreme views contains some truth; no doubt Agibu, along with many other Umarians, would have wanted to retain a degree of administrative authority even under the French, all the more so in order to ensure the security of Degembere, the site where Umar had died and which had

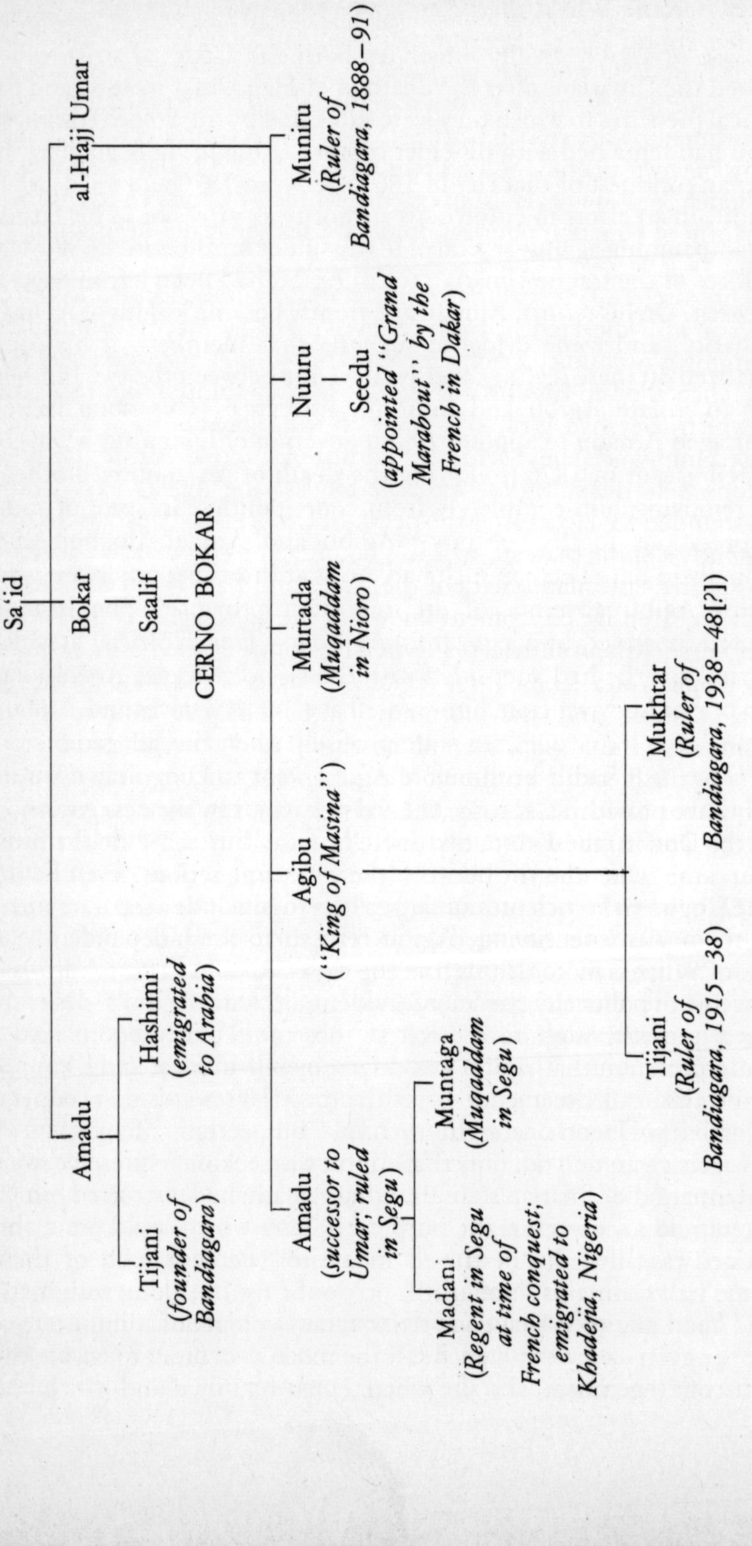


Genealogical table of the Taal family, showing only those persons mentioned in the text.

already become a holy place for Tijani pilgrims.[10] Going to Masina afforded Agibu these opportunities. But even his protagonists have quoted him as saying that he wished to go to Masina because of its "handsome horses and beautiful harnesses."[11] The fact is that Agibu's appointment by the French stirred up all kinds of contradictory feelings among his own people. Some detested him for his collaboration with the French,[12] while others supported him in his efforts to reconstruct some form of Umarian political unity and authority out of the ruins of defeat.

Events after 1893 reveal that Agibu had definitely decided to throw in his lot with the French, but whatever plans he may have nurtured for forging a new unity among the Umarians never advanced very far. The French allowed him little free rein; they appointed him to a position which they had created — that of King of Masina — and they deposed him when they saw fit. In addition, internal African political divisions were deep. Agibu was invested as king in Bandiagara, the town founded by Tijani after the death of Umar. Bandiagara is located on a gently sloping plateau, which is bounded on the west by the flood plains of the vast inland delta of the Niger and Bani rivers and on the east by an extensive escarpment known as the Bandiagara cliffs. At the foot of these cliffs an alluvial plain stretches south-eastwards into what is today Upper Volta. These three regions — parts of the flood plain, the central plateau and the northern reaches of the alluvial plain — comprised the Masina over which Agibu had been given putative control by the French.[13] Although the region was inhabited by members of a number of ethnic groups, the most important for this discussion were the Dogon, the Fulbe, and the Umarians themselves who in this region came to be known collectively as Futanke, the people of Futa.

The Dogon, who were primarily agriculturalists, inhabited the cliffs, but their settlements extended on to both the plateau and the alluvial plain, of which they constituted almost half the population. Although they were not politically unified into any sort of state organization, their political presence was strongly felt in the region. They had played a crucial role in aiding Tijani to gain ascendancy over his Fulbe enemies, and the first two decades of French rule in Masina were very much dominated by Dogon unrest. Indeed, final submission to the French by the Dogon came only after extreme repressive measures coupled with the decimation of the population through death and emigration which resulted from a severe drought between 1911 and 1914. Some estimates suggested that the Dogon population in the area was reduced by as much as half during this period.[14]

The flood plains of the inland delta contain a major concentration of Fulbe populations, although Fulbe are also found in considerable numbers in the plateau and the alluvial plain. Fulbe movement to the plateau occurred mostly in the nineteenth century, when the rulers of the newly founded Muslim theocracy in Hamdullahi encouraged their supporters to occupy recently conquered lands. It was in his attempts to gain control of this Fulbe state that al-Hajj Umar had lost his life, and it was upon the ruins of this same state that Tijani built his own Futanke-ruled state of Masina. Although the Fulbe, unlike the Dogon, could look to a heritage of centralised government, the political institutions of Hamdullahi were so recently imposed that they had not yet become firmly rooted. Their deeper political traditions were much more inclined toward the diffusion of political authority among families and lineages. The Fulbe proper were pastoralists, although Pullo society included groups of slaves, former slaves and other dependent peoples now acculturated to Fulbe ways, who farmed and engaged in various craft industries, such as weaving and leather working. After the death of al-Hajj Umar the Fulbe were unable to sustain a unified posture, even under the threat of Tijani's armies. Some shifted allegiance to the Futanke, some submitted begrudgingly, and others resisted and were defeated.

The Futanke who conquered and ruled Masina under the leadership of Tijani constituted a minority of the population of the region. Although there were numerous religious teachers and scholars among their ranks, they came as conquerors and they established themselves as rulers, and that for the most part was their role. Most of them settled in Bandiagara, although some were dispersed as administrators of newly conquered territory. They had relied heavily on the support of certain Dogon groups in their struggles against the Fulbe, an alliance which persisted, with occasional setbacks, into the twentieth century. The process of Dogon Islamization, which would gain pace with the increasing political and social changes of the colonial period, stemmed from their political relationship with the Futanke.[15]

During the years of Tijani's rule, the Futanke leaders remained fairly well unified among themselves. They were a minority among numerous enemies and were forced to defend their claim to suzerainty by force of arms. Tijani also maintained a quietly independent attitude toward Amadu in Segu, neither endorsing Amadu's position as successor to Umar nor openly challenging him. But this stance, of course, gave birth to a latent rivalry between Segu and Masina which developed into a fullblown political struggle with the arrival of Amadu in Bandiagara in 1891. Muniru, a younger half-brother of Amadu, was now ruling in Masina. Some Futanke felt he should step down in favour of Amadu; others encouraged him to defend what they considered his legitimate claim to rule in Masina. In the end Muniru abdicated, but when he died soon afterwards, rumours spread that Amadu had somehow been responsible for his death. These rumours seem to have originated among Amadu's enemies in Bandiagara, and they were taken up by certain French writers, endorsed no doubt as further justification for their campaigns against Amadu.[16]

Amadu's emigration in 1893 reduced the Futanke to less than one percent of the total population of Masina.[17] And the arrival of Agibu and his retinue in Bandiagara established a third political faction among this still divided tiny remnant of the Futanke population. Although the latent hostility among certain members of these three groups was to smoulder for many more years, Agibu went some distance toward trying to bring the Futanke together. He did this by attempting to establish himself as the successor to his father, at least in the sense that he was a legitimate figurehead for the Umarians and the protector of the now defeated and dispersed Futanke. He accepted into his care numerous Futanke refugees from the French conquests of the western Soudan,[18] and encouraged many of Amadu's comrades, who had fled eastward with him and then deserted him, to return to Bandiagara.[19] Of course, he did all this in the context of an extremely pro-French attitude, which alienated many Futanke from him. But Agibu was persistent in his collaboration; not only did he aid the French directly by acting as their front-man in the administration of Masina, but he sent his children to French schools, thus preparing them to work as functionaries in the nascent colonial administration. His actions may have been motivated by the sincere belief that the French intended, as his appointment suggested, to allow him to re-establish a limited Futanke hegemony in Masina. But even this justifiable expectation was to prove tragically incorrect.

From the beginning of his rule, certain limitations had been placed upon Agibu's activities; for example, he was not to go to war with allies of France, he was to welcome all French to Masina, and he was to send ten horses to Segu every year as a sort of tribute. He was also to provide rice for the French garrison in Bandiagara. In return, the French would aid him in various ways, primarily by providing the military support which would keep him in power. Beyond these conditions he was free to go to war, levy taxes and administer as he saw fit. But Archinard made it clear that he did not want Masina to become a new Umarian state, and he warned Agibu about the treachery and disloyalty of the Futanke, thus stirring the rivalries among them which were already deeply entrenched.[20]

In the event, Agibu enjoyed very little independence. Within a year of his installation he was writing letters of bitter complaint about the local French authorities: "Everything which the Commandant of Bandiagara does is specifically aimed at suggesting that I am incapable of governing."[21] He even went to the extreme of writing to Archinard pleading with him to intervene so that he might be allowed to administer the territories which had been ceded to him.[22] All to no avail; local French officials convinced themselves that Agibu was unable effectively to govern the unruly and rebellious populations over which he had been given authority. In 1895, a council of notables was appointed with powers of shared responsibilities of governance with Agibu. And in 1902 Masina was transferred to a civil administration and Agibu's title and authority were reduced to chief of Bandiagara; with this demotion he lost almost all his authority. What for the French was a simple administrative order was for Agibu a great personal blow. His mind seemed to crack under the strain; his behaviour became erratic, and by 1906 an official report stated that he no longer exercised any authority whatsoever, neither among the population of Masina nor within his own family. Indeed, one report alleged that for the most part he was "cordially detested."[23] So much for the King of Masina.

## NOTES

1. Al-Fūtī al-Tūrī refers to Umar's birthplace, Futa Toro in the Senegal River valley.
2. The Tijaniyya Sufi order is discussed in detail below.
3. *Rimāḥ ḥizb al-raḥīm 'alā nuḥūr ḥizb al-rajīm*, published in the margins of 'Alī Ḥarāzim, *Jawāhir al-Ma'ānī* (Beirut, no date).
4. The ethnic designations employed in this book are briefly described in Appendix IV.
5. Numerous studies of al-Hajj Umar exist; several of the more recently published are: F. Dumont, *L'Anti-Sultan ou al-Hajj Omar Tal du Fouta, Combattant de la Foi (1794–1864)* (Dakar-Abidjan, 1974); T. Oloruntimehin, *The Segu Tukolor Empire* (New York, 1972); Y. Saint-Martin, *L'Empire toucouleur et la France* (Dakar, 1967), and *L'Empire Toucouleur, 1848–1897* (Paris, 1970); J.R. Willis, "The Writings of al-Ḥājj 'Umar al-Fūtī and Shaykh Mukhtār b. Wadī'at Allāh: Literary Themes, Sources, and Influences," in J.R. Willis, ed., *Studies in West African Islam*, vol. I, *The Cultivators of Islam* (London, 1979). Unpublished theses include: Omar Jah, "Sufism and Nineteenth Century Jihād Movements in West Africa: a case study of al-Hajj 'Umar al-Fūtī's Philosophy of Jihād and its Sufi Bases," Ph.D. thesis, McGill University, 1973; and J.R. Willis, "Al-Ḥājj 'Umar b. Sa'īd al-Fūtī al-Tūrī (*c*. 1794–1864) and the Doctrinal Basis of his Islamic Reformist Movement in the Western Sudan," Ph.D. thesis, University of London, 1970. In addition, David Robinson has kindly allowed me to read his draft manuscript on the *jihād* of Umar.
6. See Y. Saint-Martin, "Un fils d'El Hadj Omar: Aguibou roi du Dinguiray et du Macina (1843–1907)," *Cahiers d'études africaines*, 29, viii.i, 1968, 144–78; for this period see also Saint-Martin, *L'Empire Toucouleur, 1848–1897*, and St Martin, *L'Empire Toucouleur et la France*.
7. ANS, 15-G-75, Correspondence avec les chefs indigènes. Aguibou 1888–1900, Deuxième chemise, pièce 23, Aguibou to Col. Humbert. Internal evidence shows the letter to have been written after the French

conquest of Segu, although Saint-Martin suggests the seizure of persons and property occurred at the time of Amadu's return to Segu in 1874, "Un Fils," 152. In this he follows the account of A. de Loppinot, "Souvenirs d'Aguibou," *Bulletin du Comité Historique et Scientifique de l'Afrique Occidentale Française*, 1919, p. 41.

8. This is the view of Saint-Martin in "Un Fils."
9. Ibrahima-Mamadou Ouane, *L'Énigme du Macina*, (Monte-Carlo, 1952), 48–9 and 45, note 1.
10. *Ibid*.
11. *Ibid*., 48.
12. See ANS 15-G-75, Première chemise, pièce 70, in which Agibu speaks of the hatred of his niece for him because of his cooperation with the French.
13. ANM, Fonds ancien, 1-D-7, Notice Générale sur le Soudan, "État d'Aguibou," 1896; and 1-D-47, Monographies sur le Macina, "Notice sur le Macina, Cercle de Bandiagara, 1896."
14. ANM, Fonds ancien, 1-E-24, Rapports Politiques et Rapports de Tournées, Bandiagara 1911–1920.
15. Baba Thimbely, interview of 21 January 1978.
16. These rumours spread throughout the French community. See Mme. Bonnetain, *Une Française au Soudan* (Paris, 1894), 185ff.
17. Fawtier, "Le Cercle de Bandiagara," *Bulletin du Comité de l'Afrique française, Renseignements coloniaux*, 1914, 71.
18. See, for example, ANS 15-G-75, deuxième chemise, pièce 9, in which a large number of Futanke noble captives are listed as having been sent to Agibu by the French.
19. See Ouane, 52–6, for the case of Ibrahim Almamy Ciré and his nephew Ahmadu Cheikh Khalil, who was a strong pro-French advocate in Bandiagara; see also P. Marty, *Études sur l'Islam et les Tribus du Soudan* (Paris, 1920), II. 211–13.
20. Ouane, *L'Énigme*, 49–52.
21. ANS 15-G-75, deuxième chemise, pièce 3, letter of 2 May 1894 to Commandant Plaintes.
22. *Ibid*., première chemise, pièce 77.
23. ANM, Fonds ancien, 1-E-23, Rapports politiques, Cercle de Bandiagara, 1893–1910; see March 1904 and Annual Report, 1906.

# 2

# FRENCH DOMINATION AND THE CHALLENGE TO ISLAM

The case of Agibu represents the transformation of political structure which the French envisaged for West Africa. Henceforward legitimate political authority would be exercised only within limits set by the French. The old-style ruling class built upon patronage and alliance in the courts of rulers was to be replaced by a new ruling class of Frenchmen and their African apprentices who would be trained, either formally or informally, to administer the new system. The common denominator in both the old and new systems was force and the coercive direction of the majority of the population. The motivating ideology for al-Hajj Umar had been reformist Islam; for the French it was their "civilising mission." It would be misleading to suggest that the clash of Islamic and French ideologies was the only, or even the major, theme of conflict during the colonial period. But for the purposes of the subject here under study, it was of primary importance. Nor should one suppose that either of these ideologies was translated effectively and without modification into practice. The reformism of al-Hajj Umar became bogged down in the demands of military conquest, and the Tijani Sufism of his associates and successors was increasingly obscured by their preoccupation with political power. Much the same can be said of the French, whose peculiar form of "civilisation" in West Africa often consisted of covering over the harsh realities of foreign military occupation with a thin veneer of fine words.

The aim of this chapter is to discuss only one aspect of this complex, evolving situation: the confrontation of Tijani Sufism with French Islamic policy between the two world wars. The major French goal with respect to Islam was the maintenance of political stability. The deposition of Agibu marked the demise of the Umarian political kingdom; the French next went to work on the religious kingdom, a much more difficult task because the objective of attack was very elusive. Muslim leaders were to be found all over the Soudan, and they acted virtually independently of one another. Unlike state systems, the decapitation of religious organizations, like Sufi orders, did not necessarily result in their demise. So the French conducted surveys and compiled dossiers on religious leaders; all those who refused openly to declare their loyalty to France were considered suspect and were carefully watched. Muslims were consequently placed on the defensive; but even so, Muslim activity during this period was not simply a series of reactions to French initiatives. Islam, and the Tijaniyya order, possessed an internal dynamic of their own which was not susceptible to alteration by actions against individual Muslims. Tijani leadership evolved through a process which was very difficult to understand from the outside, especially for non-Muslims, and impossible to control without suppressing freedom of religious practice, something the French were loath to do even if they had been capable of it. The French were therefore caught in the ambivalent position of trying to control Islamic political influence while not suppressing religion. For their part, the Muslims found themselves living under non-Muslim rule, precisely the situation against which al-Hajj Umar's *jihād* had been fought. Rather than expanding to meet the imperatives of its theocratic ideology, Islam was now apparently in retreat as a political force. The battle-lines became drawn in such a way that many extremists interpreted cooperation or collaboration with the French as disloyalty to Islam, and they asserted that the "pure" practice of Islam could be achieved only in complete isolation from French contact.

The tensions of this situation focused on the issue of leadership. The turn of the century found many Tijanis anticipating the appearance in West Africa of a saintly leader who would take up the mantle of spiritual authority which had been bequeathed by al-Hajj Umar. For a growing number of Tijanis in the 1920s and 1930s, this position was ascribed to Shaykh Hamallah of Nioro. But many Umarians, especially members of the Taal family, refused to accept the claims made on behalf of Hamallah; their protestations were supported by the French, who became increasingly fearful of Hamallah's burgeoning influence. The French tried to appoint their own Tijani leaders by giving their administrative "blessings" to certain selected individuals who were willing to act as their agents in smoothing over nascent conflicts. Their difficulty with Hamallah was that he refused to have anything whatsoever to do with them or their administration.

## *The nature and impact of the French presence*

Between the two world wars French authority became relatively well established in the western Soudan. Visible social and political changes were set in motion to which administrators pointed with pride. Nonetheless, the French did not consider their position secure, and they remained especially sensitive to any activities among Africans which might evolve into an organized opposition to their policies or their presence. In very broad terms, French policy was aimed at maintaining Africans in small social and political units to inhibit the development of any broad-based solidarity. Islam was of particular concern because it was recognised as one indigenous institution which had the potential to unite large numbers of Africans against foreign domination. The French were firmly convinced that gradually, over a long period, their own institutions would take root in Africa and, through the strength of their inherent superiority, undermine any lingering African resistance. A good example of this attitude was educational policy; rather early, a French educational system was introduced with the idea of producing future generations of Africans who would be prepared not only to operate the newly emergent westernized economy and administration, but who, more important still, would also be imbued with French culture and therefore understanding of and even sympathy towards French colonial aims. Such was the faith of some French administrators in the power of education. Today this view may seem vain and even romantic, especially since the eventual nationalist movements toward independence in Africa were generated by these same educated Africans. Nor should one believe that the French relied solely on such "soft" policies; control was everywhere maintained by a relatively harsh administration. The "soft" formulations were propagated for public consumption; but on the ground few Africans escaped the more bitter aspects of French domination.

Agibu is a case in point; when he had outlived his usefulness to them, the French had no qualms about treating him high-handedly, even if publicly he was always referred to as a "loyal subject of France." But they would never have been able to occupy the Western Soudan without people like Agibu, Africans who for one reason or another had thrown in their lot with the Europeans. In Bandiagara itself there were never more than a handful of Frenchmen — military officers and, later, colonial administrators — whose major task was to ensure that the cadres of African chiefs, clerks and soldiers enforced official policy. Relatively few Frenchmen ever learned any African language well enough to communicate directly with the peoples they governed. In any case, new postings were so frequent, and the different languages so numerous, that reliance on African interpreters was essential. French colonial authority was therefore represented in Masina, as elsewhere in the Western Soudan, by a tiny group of Frenchmen and a large number of Africans on whom the French depended not only for manpower but also for their information about and communication with the people at large. Frenchmen living in these conditions were isolated and certainly must have felt insecure. For the most part administrators could not gain direct knowledge of what was going on around them because of the language barrier, and even when they could, local quarrels and rivalries appeared to them extremely petty. After all, the French felt they were building an empire and extending the benefits of French civilisation to less fortunate peoples. Local disputes not only hindered the progress of these grand projects but, more important, they could lead to outbursts which might threaten the lives of Europeans. Consequently a vast network of informers and spies was developed to keep close watch on every person of the least prominence who might be able to exercise influence on other Africans. Files were maintained on such persons, providing biographical information and assessing their loyalty to France. Movement was carefully controlled; even Agibu was not allowed to leave Bandiagara without permission. The slightest hint of unrest was quickly crushed, and possible local troublemarkers were transferred to other colonies.

This system lent itself to intrigues of Byzantine proportions, from which not only the French but also various African parties could benefit. The source of all local authority was the French colonial administrator, the *commandant de cercle*. He appointed local African chiefs, oversaw the work of the cadres of clerks and interpreters, and employed spies and informers, all of whom acquired some degree of delegated authority with its attendant relative wealth and prestige. Chiefships, no matter how minor, were keenly sought after by the more ambitious. Influence upon the French administrator could be exercised through his African subordinates, through his interpreter, and even through his African mistress.[1] The administration was also subject to manipulation; information which passed up and down the colonial chain of command could be and was modified to suit the needs of certain interested parties. It was difficult to know whom to trust and believe, and the French often disputed among themselves as to who among them truly "understood" the Africans. This nether world of colonial administration has been given more attention in fiction than in historical literature, but it nonetheless provided the context in which many a local decision was taken.[2] Misunderstandings and misinterpretations, both accidentally and intentionally perpetrated, were not uncommon. It is not surprising in such conditions that young administrators often arrived at their first postings filled with idealism and enthusiasm, only to depart plagued by cynicism and paranoia, afflictions so common among Europeans in the Soudan that they came to be considered symptoms of a local disease which the French called "*la Soudanité*."

The pressures and strains of the colonial situation may have been more keenly felt by persons in authority like Agibu, or by certain French administrators, but they extended in one form or another to all levels of society in Bandiagara and Masina. Political institutions were not the only ones undergoing change; social, economic and religious relationships were also under considerable stress. Pressure for the emancipation of slaves increased during the first decade of the twentieth century with the ambiguous effect of obliging some people to work in ways they had never done before, while liberating others to employ their own labour for their own benefit. (Of course, having abolished slavery, the French adopted their own policy of forced labour for the execution and maintenance of public works projects.) The impact of emancipation was felt with varying force depending upon specific circumstances, but even if the immediate result was not particulary spectacular, the long-term implications were significant both socially and economically. The French also pursued an aggressive educational policy designed at the primary level to train Africans to read, write and speak French, and at more advanced levels to become interpreters or to pursue various technical trades. Whereas some families welcomed the opportunity for their children to gain an *entrée* into the new political order, a considerable proportion of Muslims strongly resisted French schooling. By the second decade of the century the fledgling school system was firmly established, especially in larger centres of population, and recruitment was stepped up; many children of resisting parents were placed in school by force. Often, to avoid subjecting their children to foreign or non-Muslim values, families substituted children of servile status for one of their own to fill a school place allotted to them.

The emancipation of slaves and the extension of rudimentary education were tangible evidence of the French "civilising mission" in West Africa, whose progress could be documented by numbers: so many slaves freed, so many youngsters in school. Colonial administrators were not insensitive to the possible ramifications of these innovations. Emancipation was carried out according to local conditions; for example, a compromise was worked out with the pastoral Fulbe of Masina so they could continue to receive a portion of the harvest from their former serfs.[3] With regard to education, some concern was expressed over creating a class of uprooted Africans who were alienated from their own society. But given these kinds of considerations, few Frenchmen seriously doubted the soundness of these policies, which they felt pointed the way to progress and to liberty. African reactions, of course, differed from those of the French and varied considerably among themselves. We have mentioned some of the obvious differences of attitude between former slaves and free men. The freedom and eventual upward mobility of former slaves resulted in some stress in the Soudan, especially among those who had owned large numbers of slaves. And if schools represented opportunity for some, they were seen by others as an attack on African values. This opinion was particularly strong among the religious leadership, who had real cause for concern.

Educational policy was but one aspect of a general attack on the established position of Muslims throughout French West Africa. As we have seen, prevailing conditions at the time of the French conquest compelled French authorities often to treat with Muslim leaders. Not only were Muslims, like Agibu, often placed in positions of authority, but the French adopted Arabic as their official language of correspondence with African rulers since Arabic scribes were more widely available than French ones. By the second decade of the twentieth century conditions had changed, and the opinion was growing among colonial authorities that the greatest potential threat to France in West Africa was Islam. Policy decisions increasingly took this factor into consideration. In 1909, in promulgating his new "native policy," Governor General William Ponty expressed concern that Muslims should not govern non-Muslims because such situations might encourage the spread of "Muslim clericalism."[4] In 1911 it was decreed that henceforth not only all administrative correspondence but also all judgements of native courts would be written in French. This decision was a serious blow to Islamic education in the Soudan because it eliminated the only official positions Arabists could acquire in the new colonial order. Earlier French policy had been to encourage Arabic education, albeit under their own close direction, in special schools of their own construction (in Dakar, Jenne, and Timbuktu); now such schools lost their practical *raison d'être*. In an official statement on educational policy, Ponty explained the kind of thinking behind these decisions:

> School is the best instrument of progress. . . . Everyone knows that the study of French is the most effective cure one can employ against [religious] fanaticism, and experience teaches us that Muslims who know our language are less imbued with prejudice than those who know only Arabic.[5]

Of course, these decrees did not stop the spread of Islam, which was beginning to gain adherents more rapidly than ever. Islam was the dominant religion in the growing commercial and administrative centers in the Soudan, such as Mopti, Segu and Bandiagara. New arrivals seeking work in these towns came under Islamic influences and often converted. Almost all long distance commerce was controlled by Muslims; as trade expanded, so did Muslim influence. On the other hand, the concern of many Muslims that their fundamental values were threatened by French policies was also justified. The number of Muslims was growing, but the quality of their leadership was in serious decline. Many of the most learned scholars had left the Soudan when Amadu b. Umar fled before the French armies. The economic structure which had supported religious education had been severely shaken with the arrival of the French, and the Muslim ruling classes were either no longer in power or no longer had the means to support religious schools. Many teachers and scholars found it necessary to abandon their studies and seek their livelihoods in other ways. In the new political order the educational path to personal success would no longer be Muslim schools but French ones, where children were given no religious instruction at all. Rather, they were taught "*morale*," which might best be described as how to be loyal and devoted subjects of France.[6]

West African Muslims were not deprived of the choice as to how they might respond to these changes. One must remember that the perceptions of individuals about the source of their difficulties, or indeed their good fortune, varied widely according to local circumstances. The French were not always and everywhere seen as a problematical factor in everyday life. On the other hand, it would be difficult to find an example of an African, no matter how "collaborationist" he might appear, whose interests could be interpreted as completely at one with those of the French. The question most before the Muslim community was not how to expel the non-Muslim usurpers, but how Islam could survive and grow within the conditions now prevalent. Isolated instances of outright opposition to French authority occurred, but the basic pattern for Muslim leaders was acceptence of French sovereignty as a political fact. Public attitudes then ranged from open collaboration to neutrality. True neutrality was possible only through an anonymity bordering on invisibility. The French took great pains to observe the activities of marabouts and other Muslim leaders; any indication that a marabout enjoyed an influence beyond a few close friends or students led to increased surveillance which might lead to formal enquiries. Faced with the possibility of administrative action against them, those marabouts who did not wish to be seen as collaborators adopted a position which might be called militant neutrality. They made no public utterance at all about the French, thus implying that secular politics was completely outside their concern, but given the particular context, this attitude might have profound political implications. Shaykh Hamallah had tried unsuccessfully to pursue such a policy, and the events which surrounded Cerno Bokar's relationship with Hamallah were laced with spies, informers and "collaborators." But the loyalties of persons involved in such affairs were never clear-cut. Seedu Nuuru Taal of Senegal, a traditionally educated grandson of al-Hajj Umar, acted on behalf of the French in the conviction that his interventions were in the best interests of Islam and, especially in the case of Cerno Bokar and the Hamalliyya, in the interests of the Tijaniyya order as he wished it to be constituted. By contrast, Amadou Hampaté Bâ received a French education and worked for most of his adult life for the French administration. He was drawn into the Hamalliyya movement through his long and intimate contact with Cerno Bokar; however he was not averse to providing information to his French superiors (and colleagues) about the Hamallists, because he felt that by so doing he was aiding that movement.

If the French presence divided Muslim leadership within itself about how to relate to their new sovereigns, the changing social and economic conditions brought new pressures to bear upon the marabouts from the people they were ostensibly leading. In the broadest terms, traditional Muslim leaders would come under increasing pressure to adapt their religious practices to respond to a shifting constituency. Of course, the basic elements of Islam, such as the five daily prayers, fasting during Ramadan, and so forth, are not seen to be subject to change. But religious practice in West Africa was deeply imbued with Sufi interpretations, as well as with popular belief in the extraordinary powers of some holy men, of the efficacy of supererogatory prayers, and of the value of talismans and charms.

The most direct challenge to this form of Islamic practice and belief was to come from the fundamentalist and anti-Sufi *Wahhabi* movement of Saudi Arabia,[7] which became firmly rooted in Soudan only after the Second World War. But the pattern of communications which ultimately brought this movement to West Africa began much earlier in the century. More people began to undertake the pilgrimage to Mecca; the subsequent increased contact with the outside world introduced more and more Muslims to alternative forms of Islamic social organization and of religious interpretations and expression. The situation was a dynamic one which required astute leaders who could direct the way through the transformations taking place. The French-educated Muslim who worked in the community of Europeans would necessarily view his religion differently than if he had never left the confines of his own village. But at the same time that French education could cause one deeply to question Islam, and even if not consciously then by sheer neglect to abandon it, European educational methods also brought a challenge to Muslim teachers. The adoption in the Qur'anic schools of Western teaching methods as well as curricula was initiated due to the catalyst of the new colonial situation.[8]

## *The Tijaniyya Sufi order in West Africa*

The reformist Muslim response to the changing situation in West Africa emerged in full force after the Second World War. Reformism was based on fundamentalist Muslim principles which had evolved in the Middle East; it was therefore in many ways an imported response to the European challenge designed to transform traditional West African forms of Islamic practice and to strengthen Islam in general. But before the Second World War, the Muslim movement which caused greatest concern within the French administration in the Soudan was that which formed around Shaykh Hamallah, a Tijani leader in Nioro. In order to understand the origins and growth of Hamallism, we must first examine the structure and history of the Tijaniyya Sufi order in West Africa, an exploration which takes us far away from the immediate political concerns of the French colonial authorities. But perhaps the jarring juxtaposition of subject-matter which the present discussion requires is illustrative of the nature of the cultural confrontation which was taking place in West Africa at the time.

The literature of Sufism describes the ultimate Sufi experience as a union with God, or an annihilation in God, a concept which can perhaps be better understood if viewed from its broader Muslim perspective. "*Islām*" means submission, and the Islamic religion demands submission to God through adherence to His law as revealed in the Qur'an to the Prophet Muhammad. Sufis can be seen as Muslims who seek to acquire a personal and subjective experience of their relationship to God and thereby understand more deeply their submission to Him. This rather inclusive view of Sufism is in no way designed to obscure the fact that Sufism in its particular forms of expression includes a vast and diverse range of religious practices. Even so, the various Sufi orders which grew up were distinguished from one another not by any differences in the ultimate goal of their mystical practices, but in the methods for reaching this goal. These methods constituted a kind of religious rule which was set out by the founder of an order and which was based upon his personal experience of spiritual search. The Arabic word for Sufi order is *ṭarīqa*, meaning "path" or "way;" the orders were usually named after their founders, so that the Tijaniyya order might also be described as the Sufi way, or the religious rule, of Shaykh Ahmad al-Tijani. The founder (as well as subsequent leaders) of a Sufi order, particularly in the western reaches of the Muslim world, was called *shaykh*, and he was usually considered to have acquired saintly attributes. The Arabic word *walī* is often translated as "saint," although the term "friend of God" perhaps better communicates the connotations which underly the Muslim concept. The *walī* is one who is considered close to God; through his own efforts he has traversed the highest stages of spiritual development. His profound spiritual understanding has been "opened" by God and his state of being has been transformed onto one of the highest spiritual planes. His perception transcends that of ordinary mortals, and he is considered to be in touch with extraordinary spiritual powers. One of the most salient features of West African Islam was the desire of Muslims to be associated with persons felt to have achieved these levels of saintliness.

Shaykh Ahmad al-Tijani lived in North Africa in the latter eighteenth century. He was considered a *walī* by his followers, and the order which he founded was based on his authority as a spiritual leader. However, al-Tijani was unusual in that he claimed that his "way" was unique and consequently superior to all others. The historical spread of the Sufi orders up to this period had been rather organic in nature; all founders traced their spiritual heritage back to the Prophet Muhammad through a chain of *shuyūkh* beginning with their own Sufi master, then to his master, and so on. A graphic representation of these collected spiritual hierarchies would resemble a triangle with the Prophet Muhammad at the apex and the historically most recent *shuyūkh* at the base. Al-Tijani broke with this pattern. Although he had been affiliated with several orders, as was then common practice, at a certain stage in his spiritual development he claimed to have had a vision of the Prophet, not in a dream but while he was awake. The Prophet told him that he should leave all the other "ways" he had pursued and that he himself would be al-Tijani's direct intermediary to God.[9] The Prophet also instructed him on all the prayers and recitations he should pursue. In this way, all the spiritual methods of the Tijaniyya way are claimed to have originated directly from the Prophet Muhammad, and all the usual chains of authority via other *shuyūkh* were eliminated. As a result of these visions and of the instructions given him by the Prophet, al-Tijani considered himself to have been selected for a special role in the history of Sufism. He came to view his position in relation to Sufism as analogous to that of Muhammad with respect to monotheism. Just as Muhammad was considered the seal of the Prophets, or the last Prophet whom God would send to mankind, and his religion, Islam, was considered superior to all other religions, so al-Tijani claimed to be the seal of the saints, and his way superior to all others. Adherence to the Tijaniyya way, it was claimed, virtually guaranteed attainment of paradise, and withdrawal from the order ensured damnation. Adherents were also prohibited from belonging to any other orders, nor could they visit the *shuyūkh* of other orders, thus stamping the Tijaniyya with a further air of exclusivity.[10]

These claims brought a hail of criticism down upon the Tijaniyya from both Sufis and non-Sufis alike. The Sufis have been more or less continually under attack throughout their long history from more legalistically minded Muslims who have questioned their interpretations of the Qur'an and *ḥadīth*, and occasionally declared their practices to be unlawful or even heretical. But the Tijaniyya also elicited criticism from Sufi leaders because of Ahmad al-Tijani's unusual claims. When, during the nineteenth century, al-Hajj Umar was endeavoring to extend the Tijaniyya way in West Africa, he encountered the full force of these criticisms. His major work, the *Rimāḥ*, was written in response to these attacks. The book is a polemic on behalf of Sufism in general and the Tijaniyya order in particular. In it Umar defends belief in the saints and encourages association with them. He castigates those who deny or even question the elevated role of these "friends of God" who, he claims, are not only superior spiritual leaders but also qualified interpreters of the law, preferable to the "legalists" whose ability and effectiveness are limited by their literal compliance to a particular interpretation of the written word. The saints (*awliyā'*), however, search for the truth wherever it leads them.[11] Mere association with the *awliyā'* is preferable to avoiding them, but better yet, according to Umar, every "intelligent person" should embark upon the quest which will bring him closer to God, because although God "opens" very few seekers, this level of spiritual attainment is possible for all Muslims. Umar's arguments are constructed in conformity with general Sufi concepts and rely for support on standard Sufi texts. Therefore when he turns his attention to the defense of Tijani doctrine, he points out that many Sufis have claimed to see the Prophet Muhammad in visions. He quotes one author as saying, "Everything has its distinguishing sign, and the sign of [spiritual] attainment by the worshipper is seeing the Prophet while awake."[12] Having established that visions of the Prophet are accepted among Sufis, the rest of the argument falls into place. The Prophet can appear to whomever he wishes and direct a person as he wishes. Consequently, if one accepts the basic Sufi premises of the argument, there is no logical rejoinder to al-Tijani's claims. (One could, of course, question his veracity.)

The Tijaniyya order was spread in West Africa during the nineteenth century largely though the activities of al-Hajj Umar. His efforts at proselytization fall into three broad categories. First was his attempt on returning from his pilgrimage to attract new adherents to the order in the Muslim centres of Borno, Sokoto, Masina and Futa Jallon. During this phase Umar directed his efforts primarily toward the more scholarly Soudanic community in order to form a group of Tijanis capable not only of attracting other followers, but also of defending the doctrines of the order against its detractors. The second aspect of his proselytization was in the influence of his many writings in which, as we have seen, he developed his own presentation of the new Sufi order. The third aspect was the influence of his *jihād* during which large numbers of people, directly affected by Umar's growing power, joined the Tijaniyya. The organization which grew up during Umar's *jihād* was as much political as spiritual. Each administrative centre in the new state (Dinguiray, Nioro, Segu, Bandiagara) was also a spiritual centre from where the leading *muqaddamūn* appointed under Umar's authority directed the spiritual affairs of the order. During these years of rapid expansion, the Tijaniyya therefore became associated with the social and political structure of a nascent Islamic state led largely by Futanke.

The fact that the Tijaniyya under Umar had spread in the wake of a *jihād* had considerable impact on the subsequent history of the order in West Africa. The spiritual essence of Tijani Sufism with which Umar had been endowed during his pilgrimage became increasingly obscured by the activities of warfare and the demands of political policy. Having begun with the *jihād* itself, this process of spiritual deterioration continued after Umar's death during the years of internecine strife among the various surviving leaders of his state, and if anything it intensified with the establishment of French colonial rule. The French conquest robbed the Tijaniyya of many of its leaders, who fled eastward to escape the invaders. Those who stayed behind were confused, not only as to how best to respond to the French presence, but as to what they should be most careful to defend: their social and political status, their personal spiritual authority or the religion of Islam in general. All of these were under attack, and there were strong differences of opinion about how best to respond. As we have seen, some resisted the invaders, others collaborated with them, and still others attempted in effect to ignore the entire situation, at least in the strict political sense. Cerno Bokar fell into this last category. He was neither uninterested in nor unaffected by the pressures and activities of life around him, but his primary concerns were religious and not political. A number of Cerno's discourses reflect his despair with the contemporary state of affairs, especially the condition of religious life. It was no doubt because of his extreme a-political stance that some of his followers considered him the true spiritual heir to al-Hajj Umar's teachings. Here was a man who was, in a way, untouched by the worldly accretions brought into the Tijaniyya through the course of the *jihād*.

The major problem facing West African Tijanis at the turn of the century was the absence of widely accepted spiritual leadership. The order itself was growing rapidly; people flocked to it (and to others as well, such as the Muridiyya in Senegal) in their search for religious protection against the turmoil and confusion of the times. Shaykh al-Tijani himself had proclaimed a rather pessimistic view of his own epoch, suggesting that it was no longer possible, as it had been in the early days of Islam, for man to avoid sin. But although trapped in this inescapable cycle of decline, al-Tijani offered an absolute guarantee of salvation for all those who joined his order, a guarantee which came from the Prophet himself.[13] This promise of salvation had strong appeal for many Muslims and operated as an important theme throughout the history of the order.[14] But the teachings of the order also emphasized the need for a *shaykh* from whom the adherents must receive guidance and direction as well as spiritual sustenance. Although Tijani literature described the qualities that a *shaykh* should possess, no formal institutions of selection and entitlement existed. Of course, the founder of the order, al-Tijani himself, was considered by all Tijanis to be its most elevated spiritual authority, but as the order grew it split into various factions, each claiming its own special relationship to him. The vast majority of West African Tijanis in the nineteenth and early twentieth centuries were linked to the founder through al-Hajj Umar, although this was not the only line. Umar himself had first become a Tijani through a *muqaddam* of a Mauritanian branch of the order, and by the turn of the century various other North African lines of initiation had been brought to West Africa by travelling *muqaddamūn*. But Umar's position was special; he claimed to have been named the *khalīfa*, or successor, of the founder for all West Africa. He was authorized to appoint sixteen *muqaddamūn*, each of whom was subsequently authorized to appoint four others. Through this original group of spiritual guides (in fact, he only appointed ten) al-Hajj Umar's line of the Tijaniyya order was spread in West Africa.[15] The authority by which the lesser *muqaddamūn* of this group appointed others is not clearly spelled out in the literature, but the order continued to expand and numerous additional *muqaddamūn* were appointed.

These *muqaddamūn* were the subordinate local authorities of the order, and several different ranks were included within this one title. Some *muqaddamūn* were authorized only to transmit the *wird* or litany of Tijani prayers to new members, others were authorized to transmit additional special prayers or spiritual exercises, and still others could appoint new *muqaddamūn*. These differences in role are not indicated by any additional title, and the modification of status of these officials was extremely fluid and not controlled by any central authority. The centres of authority which have existed tended to be localized, and these have constantly shifted in time and space. This is because authority within the Tijaniyya was exercised primarily through individuals rather than through institutions. Paul Marty had perceived this characteristic of the West African Sufi orders when he said that "it is not a common doctrine or idea which constitutes the close bond which unites the Africans, it is a man."[16] The centralization and widespread exercise of spiritual authority among the Tijanis depended on the appearance of a *shaykh* who received this title not from any appointment but through recognition by other Tijanis of his spiritual qualities. Theoretically these qualities had nothing to do with social or political status. Such a leader was required to possess a clear and pure spiritual link, through his *silsila* or chain of initiations, back to Ahmad al-Tijani. In addition, he was expected to reflect in his very presence the qualities of spiritual attainment appropriate to a spiritual guide, evidence of which was provided by his piety, religious devotion, ascetic inclinations and, not least, by the content of his dreams and visions.

Al-Hajj Umar possessed all these qualities. Although originally initiated into the Tijaniyya in West Africa through a Mauritanian branch of the order, he received a renewal and an improvement of his link to the founder from Muhammad al-Ghālī who had been appointed *muqaddam* by Shaykh al-Tijani himself. This made Umar a "third generation" Tijani. He also possessed the requisite spiritual qualities, which he described in the *Rimāḥ* and which were expanded upon by his followers.[17] He was appointed *khalīfa* on the authority of a vision in which Shaykh al-Tijani ordered al-Ghālī to give all the secrets of the order to Umar and to name him to this post. This vision was confirmed by other visions of Umar himself and of other leading Tijanis.[18] By the time of his death in 1865, he was considered not only a *shaykh* of the Tijaniyya order but a political leader of a *jihād* as well. His son Amadu, then in Segu, had been designated by Umar as his successor, but he never managed to win the unrivalled political loyalty of his father's followers, which resulted in his never being recognized as the sole spiritual authority for the West African Tijanis. After his flight from the region and his death, the lines of leadership became even more vague. By now no one individual could even make the claim that he was sole spiritual leader of the West African Tijanis. And in the minds of many the qualifications for this office had been modified; the idea was widespread that the members of the Taal family of al-Hajj Umar were the only legitimate claimants to such a title. Blood inheritance was not an essential qualification for Tijani leadership, but neither was it without precedent. Before his death Shaykh al-Tijani had named a companion, not a relative, as his successor, although he also provided for the future elevation of his own children.[19] In West Africa spiritual leadership was tending toward localization, and familial status was replacing spiritual qualities as the basis for selection. Muntaga b. Amadu in Segu claimed that his father had transmitted authority to him in a letter, which he was never able to produce.[20] In Nioro, Murtada b. Umar exercised some spiritual authority until his death in 1922. And outside the immediate region there were others: Seedu Nuuru Taal in Senegal, Madani b. Amadu in Hadejia (Nigeria) and Alfa Hashimi b. Amadu (son of Umar's brother) in the Hejaz. By the 1920s Cerno Bokar himself, as the great-nephew of al-Hajj Umar, was also considered a leading *muqaddam* in the order. During most of his adult life he was deeply concerned over the spiritual leadership of the order.

## *Shaykh Hamallah*[21]

Shaykh Hamallah emerged to prominence in the context of this search for spiritual leadership. Given different historical conditions, the movement which formed in his name would probably never have given rise to the political turmoil which surrounded it. But his attraction as a holy man was such that he became a catalyst for the release of the numerous social and political (not to mention, religious) tensions present in the western Soudan between the two world wars.

Two important contributions to the historiography of this movement have recently appeared, a doctoral thesis written at the University of Dakar by Alioune Traoré[22] and a revised version by Amadou Hampaté Bâ of his biography of Cerno Bokar.[23] Both these studies are sympathetic to Hamallah, representing as they do something of an inside view. However, they differ markedly from one another in emphasis, Hampaté Bâ's account relying mostly on oral evidence, and Traoré's largely on archival documentation, although he, too, conducted extensive interviews. Hampaté Bâ contends that most of the difficulties which surrounded Hamallah and his followers were the result of relatively minor personal jealousies and animosities blown out of all proportion by Hamallah's enemies and detractors.[24] Traoré places the blame for Hamallah's misfortunes more squarely on the French administration,[25] and he gently chides Bâ and Cardaire for not going further in 1957 in accusing "the tenants of the colonial system of partiality" in this affair.[26] But neither Hampaté Bâ in his recent book nor Traoré in his well-researched thesis reveal all that they know or suspect about the tangled politics which underlay the Hamallist affair, because even today the issue has not been drained of its emotionality. As a result of this fact, and as a barrier to more exhaustive research into the subject, the Hamallist files in the National Archives of Mali are still closed to the public.

The French sources which are available[27] tend to be openly hostile to the Hamallists,[28] and even when they are not they are almost always out of touch with African views of events. Only very rarely was the gulf which separated Frenchmen from Africans ever effectively bridged, especially on an issue as volatile as the Hamalliyya.[29] Not all attitudes were as extreme as those expressed in the following quotation, but it is a fair example of the flavour of French opinion about the origins of the Hamalliyya movement in particular and of similar movements in general:

> . . . departing from an orthodox foundation, the appearance of an enlightened mystic, ecstatic visions, a new revelation emanating from the Prophet or from the Angel Gabriel from which arises a new Way which immediately discovers its field of activity in a frustrated mystical population eager for miracles and always receptive to the madnesses into which the Shaykh would drag them. Possessing only the faintest colouring of Islam, practically illiterate and backward, this population is therefore incapable of judging the point at which this new Way resolutely embraces the most complete heresy.[30]

The emotional and pejorative language of this passage reveals the depths which misunderstanding and contempt could reach. Of course, in the Soudan of the period there were frustrated and gullible people for whom Hamallah had great appeal, but he attracted many other kinds of people as well: for example Muslim scholars, French-educated Africans, and level-headed merchants. Only in rare instances were the French able to grasp the nature of West African Islam and the internal dynamics of the Sufi brotherhoods. They saw Hamallah's movement as a threat, not only because of his broad-based support, but also because he would not openly defer to French authority.

The growth of Hamallah's movement and of opposition to him is complex and can be discussed here only in broad outline. The "Hamallists" became distinguished from other West African Tijanis for two fundamental reasons: first, they recited the *jawharat al-kamāl*, a prayer in the *waẓīfa* (part of the Tijani litany of prayers; see Appendix II), eleven times rather than twelve times (which was the common Umarian and Moroccan practice), and secondly, they venerated Hamallah as a *shaykh* and a *walī*, and some persons even claimed he was a *khalīfa*, or direct successor to Shaykh al-Tijani, and a *quṭb*, one who had attained the highest level of Sufi sainthood. In no other ways did Hamallists differ from other Tijanis on religious matters. These distinctive Hamallist characteristics also represent two of the very few facts about the movement on which all observers agree, which means that almost every other aspect of its origin and development are open to widely divergent interpretation. We are indebted to Hampaté Bâ and Traoré for their presentation of a generally accepted Hamallist view of the origins of the movement, but their evidence for this early period is based exclusively on oral material. Not one contemporary Hamallist written document has been produced which could substantiate the course of events as presented by the oral accounts. French documents can only corroborate certain external events; they say nothing about the thinking of either Tijanis or Hamallists. And the oral accounts themselves are not free of contradictions and anomalies.

The Hamalliyya was born in the first decade of the twentieth century. The most basic facts surrounding this event, on which all sources agree, are that in 1900 there appeared in Nioro an Algerian Tijani *muqaddam* named Sīdī Muḥammad b. Ahmad b. 'Abdallāh, known as al-Akhḍar. Al-Akhdar had been appointed *muqaddam* in Tlemcen (Algeria) by Shaykh Sīdī al-Ṭāhir Bū Ṭība,[31] a man who was considered by some to be a *khalīfa* in the order, having been very close to Shaykh al-Tijani himself. Shaykh al-Ṭāhir, and consequently al-Akhdar, recited the prayer *jawharat al-kamāl* eleven times. On his arrival in Nioro, al-Akhdar began preaching this version of the Tijani prayers, and not a few persons, the young Hamallah among them, accepted a renewal of their *wird* with him. Resistance and rivalry soon developed among other Tijanis who clung to the twelve recitations of the prayer. In 1909, with the death of al-Akhdar, Hamallah, then only about twenty years of age, was recognized as his successor as leader of the "*onze grains*" or "eleven beads" as this group came to be called. If not immediately, at least by the end of the next decade, Hamallah was being addressed as *shaykh*.

The Hamallist accounts fill out the bare bones of these facts in the following manner. They claim that the *zāwiya* of Shaykh al-Ṭāhir in

Tlemcen had preserved the purest form of Tijani practice in the entire order, due to al-Ṭāhir's close relationship to the founder; their continued recitation of the "eleven beads" was but one aspect of their special spiritual position. According to this account, al-Akhdar had been sent from Tlemcen on a special mission designed to re-establish the purity of Tijani practice in West Africa, which included more than the recitation of the "eleven," but also to identify a new spiritual leader to replace the declining fortunes of the Umarians, following the death of al-Hajj Umar and the flight of his son Amadu. The Tlemcen leadership had determined that a new *khalīfa* would appear in West Africa who would also be a *qutb al-zamān* (pole of the era), a very elevated *walī*. Al-Akhdar was instructed on the signs through which he would be able to recognize this new spiritual leader. After extensive travels, the itinerary of which varies from source to source, he discovered the person he was seeking in Hamallah, whom he indicated to his followers before his death.[32]

Perhaps this account is in some respects true; we are in no position to disprove it definitively. But neither is it very convincing in its totality when other facts are taken into consideration. In the first place, as indicated above, contemporary written evidence only supports the idea that al-Akhdar came to Nioro and proselytized his version of the Tijaniyya, the superiority of which he seems to have proclaimed. No Arabic documentation has come to light; and the French knew virtually nothing about the internal affairs of the order, so perhaps we cannot attribute much significance to their silence about Hamallah being discovered by al-Akhdar and named *qutb*. The closest we can come to any written support for this Hamallist claim is Paul Marty's statement that Hamallah "declared himself to be not a *muqaddam* but chief *shaykh* [*cheikh général*]."[33] Of course, it is entirely possible that al-Akhdar had encouraged Hamallah to proclaim himself as such, and he may well have done so for what he considered very good reasons. But the proposition that al-Akhdar had been sent on a specific mission to identify such a *shaykh* or *khalīfa* seems to be unique in the Tijani literature; there are many stories about the identification of *shuyūkh* by visions, but the idea that one man should be sent on a wide ranging voyage to find and identify one single *shaykh* seems most unusual.That he should have been sent from Tlemcen on behalf of the "mother houses" of the order in Algeria, as Hampatê Bâ states,[34] with the purpose of regenerating the West African Tijaniyya seems unacceptable without further documentary evidence, because Tlemcen and Shaykh al-Ṭāhir represented a dissident branch of the order in Algeria.

Al-Ṭāhir claimed to be Shaykh al-Tijani's sole successor as leader of the order.[35] That al-Ṭāhir was regarded as one of the leading *shuyūkh* seems to be beyond dispute,[36] but his claims to sole succession led to conflict with other Algerian leaders. The breach also widened into the broader political arena, because al-Ṭāhir condemned the policy of cooperation with the French which the majority of Algerian Tijanis pursued. Because of these internal political conflicts in the North African Tijaniyya, Traoré is careful not to make such broad claims as Hampaté Bâ about al-Akhdar's mission. Rather he emphasizes al-Ṭāhir's special position in the Tijaniyya and the desire of Tlemcen to maintain and spread the spiritual purity which they claimed was theirs. In presenting his case, however, Traoré glosses over the doubts which some Tijanis harboured about al-Ṭāhir's own claims.[37] For Traoré, al-Akhdar's mission was to encourage the rejuvenation of the flagging West African Tijaniyya and the return of its adherents to the pure form of doctrine represented by the "eleven beads." Why, one must ask, if Tlemcen was so important a center, and if al-Akhdar had been charged with identifying not only a *khalīfa* but a *qutb al-zamān*, did not he or indeed Hamallah find a place in the extensive biographical dictionary of the Tijaniyya written by one of its Moroccan *shuyūkh*, Ahmad Sukayrij?[38] Although Sukayrij's book is devoted primarily to descriptions of the companions of Ahmad al-Tijani, he gave considerable space to al-Hajj Umar whom he recognizes as a *khalīfa*. Why not to Hamallah, who was proclaimed not only to be Umar's successor as *khalīfa* but also to occupy the even more elevated position of *qutb*?

Of course, we are in no position to discuss how Sukayrij organised the contents of his book, but in raising this kind of question we can begin to perceive the different points of view which must have circulated about al-Akhdar, Hamallah and the movement which took his name. Sukayrij could not have been ignorant of Hamallah, but he must not have considered him so significant a figure as to mention him, even though Hamallists claim that their movement preserves the very essence of al-Tijani's spiritual teaching. We would suggest that the oral accounts cited above, although containing certain elements of fact, were elaborated into their present form relatively late in the history of the movement. We would like here to propose another interpretation of the origins of the Hamalliyya based upon an analysis of generally accepted facts in comparison with what we know of the structure and dynamics of the order itself. This view is largely hypothetical and requires the test of further research. Its major elements are that the Hamalliyya movement found its initial strength in Hamallah's exceptional religious personality, and that his following solidified into a powerful and significant movement primarily as a result of organized opposition to it from other Tijanis and from the French administration. This interpretation places a different emphasis on the role of the doctrinal dispute which characterized the early years of the movement, i.e. that Hamallists recited the *jawharat al-kamāl* only eleven times. It is true, of course, that al-Akhdar's proselytization of the "eleven beads" was opposed by some parties from the time of his arrival in Nioro. But we would argue that disputes over this matter would have remained local had it not been for Hamallah's extraordinary appeal, which was at first basically religious but later became politicized because of the actions of both his enemies and some of his followers.

The interpretation also reduces emphasis on the role of al-Akhdar and his Tlemcen connection by casting considerable doubt on the contention that he had been sent on a specific mission to identify a *khalīfa*. The idea that one man would be despatched on the vaguely defined mission to identify another previously unknown *shaykh* makes for a good story, but it is also tainted with the strong odor of *post facto* justification; furthermore, such a mission does not fit with general Tijani practice. One could accept that al-Akhdar, having met Hamallah and spent some time with him, became convinced that he was destined to become a *shaykh*. Perhaps he and Hamallah both had visions which convinced them of this fact, as the oral accounts aver. This pattern is widespread among Tijanis, for which al-Hajj Umar's appointment as *khalīfa* by al-Ghālī is evidence. The claim that al-Akhdar was on a specific mission is also placed in doubt by contradictions in the evidence. Hampaté Bâ has him travelling throughout Soudanic West Africa, having begun his journey in Egypt.[39] Traoré agrees with Marty that he arrived in Nioro after a lengthy sojourn in Mauritania.[40] Traoré claims that everywhere he went he announced his mission to identify a *qutb*; Hampaté Bâ implies that he kept this aspect of his work secret until he had identified Hamallah. In either case, could such a proclamation have escaped the attention of the French administration, and especially of Marty who was so pre-occupied with the affairs of the Sufi brotherhoods?

It seems much more likely that al-Akhdar's visits to Mauritania and the Soudan were part of a continuing effort by North African Tijanis to maintain links with their West African brothers. This activity was centered primarily in the Moroccan *zawāyā* of the order, which had much closer connections with West Africa than the Algerian ones. Movement between North and West Africa may have intensified at the turn of the century, but it was a long-established pattern going right back to al-Hajj Umar. Only a few years after Umar's death, his son Amadu was visited in Segu by two Moroccan Tijani *muqaddamūn*,[41] who seem to have played some role in Amadu's efforts to be recognized as successor to his father. The attraction of a North African initiation into the order was that it allegedly brought one into closer spiritual proximity to the founder of the order, Shaykh al-Tijani. The rapid growth of the Tijaniyya throughout West Africa during the colonial period was intimately associated with the development of these North

African relationships, and the pattern can be discerned throughout the region. One of the best examples is the branch of the order developed by Shaykh Ibrahim Nyass of Senegal, who gained adherents throughout West Africa. In 1937 he was appointed *khalīfa* of the order by Shaykh Ahmad Sukayrij in Fez.[42] The Tijaniyya in Kano, upon which Nyass was able to draft his movement, was based on a series of Moroccan initiations.[43]

Al-Akhdar's activities seem to fall within this pattern of spreading North African influence, but he was also in competition with the majority of North African *muqaddamūn* in that he was an advocate of the "eleven beads," apparently the only one in West Africa at the time. He certainly preached the superiority of this practice, and even chided local Tijanis, claiming that they had gone astray in reciting the *jawharat al-kamāl* twelve times. This was more than a subtle criticism of al-Hajj Umar and led to conflicts disturbing enough to have al-Akhdar deported to Dakar for a brief period.[44] Al-Akhdar thus planted the seeds of dissension in Nioro which were to grow into a bitter rivalry between the "elevens" and the "twelves," although the dispute itself did not reach maturity until some years later. Even when Marty wrote (his *Soudan* was published in 1920), he did not seem to consider the issue of *jawharat al-kamāl* to be particularly volatile. He judged Hamallah as potentially the most powerful Muslim leader in Nioro, but not to be a trouble-maker; he described him as reserved with the French but not an opponent. As for the political intrigues which by then had begun to surface among some of his followers, Marty explicitly absolved Hamallah of any part in them.[45]

The question of "twelve beads/eleven beads" is perhaps the most difficult aspect of the Hamalliyya movement for an outsider to understand. How could such a seemingly minor doctrinal point become a major issue of contention? It will be recalled that Shaykh al-Tijani received the litany of his order direct from the Prophet Muhammad in a vision. According to *Jawāhir al-Ma'ānī*, the *jawharat al-kamāl* should be recited as a part of the *waẓīfa* eleven times,[46] but late in his life al-Tijani added a twelfth recitation. Umar prescribed twelve recitations in the *Rimāḥ*,[47] and twelve certainly became the most widespread practice in the order. Why this modification was made has never been clearly explained, but one would suspect it resulted from a vision. In West Africa a popular explanation is that on one occasion Shaykh al-Tijani arrived late for the recitation of the *wazīfa* when those present had already recited the *jawharat al-kamāl* eleven times. The prayer was repeated once more in the presence of al-Tijani who did not object and therefore, it was argued, tacitly approved the twelve recitations.[48] This account is denied in North Africa; indeed, it would be surprising if a revealed litany of this sort could have been modified by such accidental means. Today most Tijanis, including many Hamallists, would argue that either eleven or twelve recitations is acceptable.[49] Hampaté Bâ takes this view and offers an esoteric, numerological explanation of the relative appropriateness of eleven or twelve recitations; he even has Shaykh Hamallah himself saying: "Once again, I declare that the 'twelve' is not an error."[50] Traoré, on the other hand, adheres more firmly to a strict Hamallist line; for him the modification of the original revelation of eleven recitations was a deviation,[51] although his view fails to accept any possibility of change within the litany, even for acceptable esoteric reasons, such as subsequent visions.

Today in West Africa the specific issue of "eleven beads/twelve beads" evokes relatively little emotion; and it seems never to have done so in North Africa. Indeed, the volatility of the question appears to have been directly related to the expansion of Hamallah's movement and its resultant political significance. Many Hamallists proclaimed the "eleven" as a symbol of their superiority and as a badge of their identity; their enemies employed the term as an epithet against those who, they claimed, had betrayed the spiritual teachings of al-Hajj Umar. Although the doctrinal aspects of this issue were debated by Tijani scholars, the sometimes violent mutual recriminations between rival groups which occurred in West Africa in the 1930s and 1940s seem a reflection less of fundamental religious difference than of the current social and political tensions.

We are arguing here that the activities of al-Akhdar might have caused no more than a slight ripple of upset among West African Tijanis had he not met Hamallah, whose religious persona was the essential ingredient giving life to the movement which later bore his name. We know little of his early life.[52] He was born about 1883 of a Moorish father and a Pullo mother, and both his father and grandfather were merchants who claimed *sharīfian* ancestry. Hamallah received a religious education, but reports concerning his scholarly endeavours are vague. Marty described him as well-lettered, with an abiding interest in books on mysticism; Traoré cites his extensive library as evidence of his learning.[53] But al-Akhdar had been impressed by Hamallah not because of his book-learning, but because of his mystical stature. At least that is the view given in all the oral accounts of how Hamallah was finally identified as *khalīfa*. The details of these accounts differ, which is not surprising since they can only be suppositions on transactions which took place between the two men in strict seclusion. But they agree on the main point, namely that Hamallah knew the "secret" or "Great Name" of God, which had appeared to him in visions,[54] and al-Akhdar took this as conclusive proof that Hamallah was the man he had been seeking. According to al-Hajj Umar, who devoted a brief chapter to the subject in the *Rimāḥ*, the "Great Name" of God was known only to "exceptional persons, such as prophets and *qutb* and the like."[55] One might therefore conclude that, since the "Great Name" had appeared to Hamallah in a vision, all al-Akhdar had to do was recognize him as *khalīfa*. But the matter was not so simple. The oral accounts also suggest that al-Akhdar was himself dispensing certain "secrets," and that some people felt that the possession of these "secrets" would qualify them to be *khalīfa*. The specific person most mentioned in this regard was Muhammad Mukhtar, a leading Tijani *muqaddam* in Nioro and one of Hamallah's former teachers.[56] He repudiated the "eleven" when Hamallah was named as al-Akhdar's successor, refusing to follow so young a man, and he consequently became a focus of opposition to Hamallah. So the question is: did al-Akhdar recognize the pre-existent fact of Hamallah's *khalīfa*-ship, or did he invest him with certain "secrets" which gave him the authority of office? Or should there perhaps be an affrmative answer to both questions?[57]

This is another of those questions which eludes clear answers. What seems more certain is that Hamallah was an extraordinary religious leader and that, whatever the means whereby he had come to his decision, al-Akhdar had made a wise choice. It also seems clear that the choice was fundamentally, and probably exclusively, a religious one. Al-Akhdar's affiliation with the anti-French *zāwiya* of Tlemcen had not escaped the attention of the local administration, but this caused little concern until the 1920s. Even the anti-Umarian thrust of the "eleven" did not at first seem very dangerous; not even the French were much concerned with the political implications of al-Akhdar's activities. Hamallah too was seen primarily as a mystic. For Hampaté Bâ and Traoré he was a contemplative, withdrawn spiritual teacher; for Marty he was an ecstatic:

> He has, so they say, ecstatic visions during which everything in heaven and earth passes before his eyes; he enters into direct communication with Allah and His prophet as he wishes. He receives abundant alms, most of which he redistributes. . . . [The *dhikr* sessions in his house each day] terminate most of the time with nervous crises and other well-known phenomena.[58]

Whatever judgment is made of Hamallah as a mystic or a religious leader, his widespread appeal in West Africa is indisputable. In so far as this appeal was religious, it was based on his personal qualities of asceticism, piety and humility, all characteristics which Muslims expected to find in saintly men. But there was also a political dimension to his appeal, and this seems to have been generated largely by the activities of his enemies, especially certain Umarians and certain officials in the French administration. The critical period during which the political force of the movement crystallized was from 1922 till 1924. Before 1922, official concern over Hamallah was muted; but in 1925 he was exiled from Nioro. The most interesting aspect of this dramatic transformation is that it had little to do with the personal activities of Hamallah himself, who was noted for his isolation and limited contact with the outside world. In the end, Hamallah was punished not for what he did but for what he failed to do. Some French sources do suggest that in the years immediately following the death of al-Akhdar, Hamallah actively proselytized on behalf of the "eleven," and that al-Hajj Malik Sy, a highly respected Tijani *shaykh* in Senegal, intervened to encourage Hamallah to desist from these activities.[59] The French averred that Hamallah replied "insolently" to the first of Malik Sy's letters (in 1911) and not at all to the second. In contrast to this allegation is the failure of the French authorities ever to implicate Hamallah directly in any of the increasingly violent outbursts later associated with the Hamallists. And there is Marty's observation, published in 1920, that in his judgement Hamallah was completely innocent of the "intrigues" which some of his followers were perpetrating; and that furthermore he considered that "the Moors submitted to [Hamallah's] obedience are those most amenable to our orders."[60]

In 1922 Malik Sy died, and some of the French thought they noted a subsequent hardening in Hamallah's attitude,[61] although there seems to be little justification for this interpretation based on Hamallah's known activities. The death of Malik Sy probably had more impact among the French than with Hamallah; Sy was considered a loyal subject of France and his activities were generally thought to be conciliatory.[62] One might more convincingly argue that the silencing of Malik Sy's voice gave scope to the influence of a more strident anti-Hamallist faction, which in the end managed to convince French officials of the danger which Hamallah supposedly posed to their rule.[63] This hypothesis is indirectly supported by other evidence, which implies that in 1922 Hamallah was beginning to gain widespread support among Tijani leaders. The relevant document will be discussed again below because it directly concerns Cerno Bokar.

> One of al-Hajj Umar's sons, called Murtada, was at Nioro; he died in 1922. Cerno Bokar of Bandiagara should have replaced him at Nioro as a Tijani *muqaddam* responsible to Muntaga [in Segu]. But there was a *sharīf* living in Nioro who never left his house. He is a very pious ascetic, whom the people of Nioro, due to his virtue and his piety, requested should be their Tijani *muqaddam*. Muntaga accepted this arrangement on the advice of his brother, Madani, in Hadejia [Nigeria] with whom he is in constant touch through pilgrims and *juulas* [merchants]. Madani even advised him to follow the indications of this *sharīf*.[64]

This isolated report, taken from an unnamed African informant, cannot be accepted as conclusive proof that certain well-placed Umarian

Tijanis were by 1922 prepared to accept Hamallah as a legitimate *muqaddam*. But neither can one fail to wonder where such a report might have originated had it not contained some grain of truth. We would argue that whether true or not, the report caused great consternation in Dakar.

Hamallah's enemies, both Muslims and French, were galvanized into action. Violent incidents occurred in 1923 and 1924 for which blame was laid at the door of Hamallah, although explicit proof of his complicity was never forthcoming. Indeed, the key to Hamallah's downfall, if his arrest and exile can be so described, was his studied aloofness from all the turmoil which surrounded him. In the end, the accusation which resulted in his punishment was that he had failed to intervene in a tangled and heated dispute over the succession to leadership of a Moorish group. The French charged that the dispute was kept alive by Hamallah's followers, who would have desisted had he ordered them to do so. But the report which, in the judgment of Traoré, led to Hamallah's condemnation was extremely wide-ranging; it accused him of unmitigated anti-French activity — not only failure to intervene in succession disputes (which, it should be added, were no concern of his), but failure voluntarily to visit French officials, failure to send his children to French schools, the fact that anti-French poems and tracts had been written by Hamallists (none of which was attributed to Hamallah), and, probably the most important, the presence of a growing number of committed Hamallists among the Africans working in the French administration.[65] The author of this report achieved his goal; Hamallah was condemned to ten years' exile, and in 1925 deported to Mederdra in Mauritania.

What the French wanted from Hamallah, and what he never offered, was a modicum of voluntary cooperation. Obviously, to have been able to point to Hamallah as a "loyal friend of France" would have been extremely advantageous for colonial policy. But whether Hamallah's failure to act in the manner preferred by the French was a conscious political decision or whether it sprang from other motivations, such as a religious penchant to isolate himself from worldly affairs, is impossible to say. He himself never spoke publicly on the issue. Certainly he refused to intervene in African affairs as much as in colonial ones. Hamallah's silence offered all parties the opportunity to portray him as they wished. The alleged injustice of his exile made him into something of a *cause célèbre* among certain French-educated politicians in Senegal. No less a figure than Lamine Guèye, then *conseiller colonial*, spoke out against the French decision.[66] He even wrote an article in the official journal *L'A.O.F.*, in which, while defending Hamallah, he gave his personal version of the *shaykh*'s meeting with the Governor-General of the Soudan, Terrasson de Fougères. This account, which tended to bring into relief the many French fears about Hamallah, must have also won him many new admirers among the critics of French policies, and further politicized the silent role he was to play, albeit perhaps unwillingly, in future events. After having been informed by the Governor-General that he was to be exiled, Hamallah, as reported by Guèye, replied in the following way:

> "I pay my taxes, I fulfill my obligations, I spread no sort of propaganda, neither oral or written, nor do I have on my conscience any act of hostility with respect to France or its representatives. If you know of any, tell me because I am prepared to submit to your punishment if my guilt is demonstrated."
> [The Governor retorted:] "Your children do not attend French school." [Hamallah replied that his children were too small, but the Governor asserted that Hamallah was also wrong not to intervene with his followers, to which he answered:]
> "Governor, Sir, I have already said that I have spread no sort of propagaganda. You are the personification of authority which you exercise effectively, having at your disposal soldiers, police and an army. As for me, I have only my rosary. When I have paid my taxes and fulfilled all the obligations imposed on a subject, my role is terminated. It is not for me to concern myself with those who upset the public order; would this not be to infringe upon your authority? Besides, you have never asked me to intervene with any Muslim or in any circumstances. Why not summon those you call my disciples and who are upsetting the public order? This is your right since they are transgressing your orders and acting contrary to your will; then you can chastise them in the manner they deserve."[67]

This article, addressed to an African public literate in French, reflected the current political mood of a significant section of the African population. The image of Hamallah firmly drawing the line between what he considered legitimate French authority and his own personal integrity was powerful stuff. And it may well be that a growing number of French-educated African Muslims were attracted to the Hamalliyya in the 1920s and '30s precisely because their association with Hamallah reinforced their personal integrity as Muslims at a time when concern over the contamination of becoming "Europeanized" must have been profound. The French had made it no secret that one of the aims of their educational policy was to render Muslims less "fanatical." The growing numbers of *évolués* (as the French-educated, French-speaking Africans were patronizingly called) in the Hamalliyya may have brought to their attention the first hard evidence that this policy was not working. One of the major concerns expressed in the Descemet report of 1925 was that Hamallah's influence over African employees in the colonial service had reached alarming proportions; two teachers had even resigned from the service rather than accept new postings away from Nioro (ordered, it should be added, with the specific aim of removing them from Hamallah's influence).[68] However, French opinion on what was happening was not unanimous. Even as late as 1939, the Governor of Soudan in his annual political report was prepared to argue that the Hamalliyya in fact aided French policy because "in simplifying to a great extent religious practices and in shortening prayers and rosaries, it permits its adepts, while not compromising their faith, to devote more of their time to their work and diverse occupations." The report goes on to observe that the attraction of youth and *évolués* to this supposedly "tepid" religious practice is perfectly normal since the Hamalliyya, breaking as it does with older-established religious practice, contributes to the ability of the youth "to liberate themselves from the grip of their families and from ancestral customs."[69] No general surveys exist which could document the motivations of persons who joined the Hamalliyya at this time, but the few interviews with Hamallists made in connection with this study would suggest that, whatever their associated interests, these persons at least were seeking to reaffirm their personal religious commitments, for which they were prepared to make considerable sacrifices. Descemet was correct in expressing concern over the dangers which the movement represented to French interests, if resurgent Islam was indeed such a danger.

The "eleven beads" had come a long way from those early years in Nioro when al-Akhdar had gained a large portion of his support among Wolof and Marka merchants. Hamallah had attracted a wider range of adherents, especially among the Moors; and the movement began to develop a diverse and geographically extensive membership representing a cross-section of social, ethnic, and occupational groups. Not a few scholars sought renewal of their *wird* with Hamallah.[70] By 1922 some well-placed Umarians had offered him at least tacit support. And the 1920s and '30s witnessed a growth in membership among *évolués*. At no time in its history could this movement as a whole be justifiably described as the "frustrated mystical population" which some Frenchmen imagined, although its membership was not free of extremist and even bizarre elements. The greatest fear harboured by the French, despite a few dissenters, was the prospect of a unified party of Muslim *évolués* agitating for social and political change. The security of the French presence relied on the continued political division of African society. Hamallism could never have provided widespread political unity, but the increasingly violent nature of the incidents perpetrated in its name was disturbing to the French as well as perhaps inspiring to anti-French Muslims. The profoundly political nature which the Hamallist movement developed in the 1930s and '40s is emphasized by its relatively rapid demise as a political force with the appearance of legitimate political parties after the Second World War.[71]

In 1930 there was a violent incident in Kaedi (southern Mauritania), directed in part against the local colonial administration, which resulted in twenty-seven deaths. The French felt that they saw Hamallah's influence in this affair and moved him from Mauritania to Adzopé in southern Ivory Coast where he served the ramaining five years of his exile. The idea was to isolate him, and all Moors were barred from entry to Ivory Coast during this period. But other merchants continued to find their way to him, and he continued to initiate people into the "eleven." During this period of his exile Hamallah modified his prayers to an abbreviated form permissible when one is either travelling, in a dangerous situation or in war. Charges were made that some of his more fervent followers had begun facing west in their prayers (the direction from which they expected him to return) and also blasphemously putting his name in their prayers ("There is no god but God, and Hamallah is His prophet"). The extent of such practices has yet to be demonstrated, but their existence reflects the extremely emotional nature of the situation.[72]

Hamallah's exile ended in 1935. He returned to Nioro in January 1936, but he continued to pray the abbreviated prayer until well into the next year, when he was dissuaded from doing so by Seedu Nuuru Taal of Senegal. A high-powered delegation visited Nioro for just that purpose, including not only Seedu Nuuru, but the Governor-General of French West Africa and the Governor of the Soudan. The entire affair is described in a letter from Shaykh Hamallah to Cerno Bokar. Seedu Nuuru was sent to treat with Hamallah privately, and Hamallah explained to him that he had adopted the abbreviated prayer because he feared for his safety. Seedu Nuuru suggested that the French might be willing to offer a pledge of security if Hamallah would return to the normal form of prayers. This was all agreed, to the great relief of the French, who "prepared a great feast for which they expended much money; they rejoiced and were extremely happy."[73] The French also offerred Hamallah a monetary reward for his cooperation, which he refused; the sum was given over for the repair of the local mosque. Seedu Nuuru was given a medal and allegedly some money. Hamallah was then visited by his local enemies and detractors, whom he refers to in his letter as the "rejecters," (that is, those who rejected his teaching, although describing them thus is almost equivalent to calling them unbelievers). There was a semi-public display of reconciliation, which did not particularly impress Hamallah. He concluded his letter to Cerno Bokar: "That is what occurred between us and the Europeans and the 'rejecters;' but it is all a ruse which they are plotting."[74]

Whether a ruse or not, Hamallah and his followers were yet to experience their most serious trials. In 1938 a violent repression of Hamallists in Bandiagara was triggered by Cerno Bokar's submission to Shaykh

Hamallah. But in 1940 a long-festering animosity between some of Hamallah's followers (including his sons) and certain hostile Moorish groups erupted into a violent confrontation in which there were some 400 deaths. Although Hamallah broke his usual silence and publicly condemned this horrible outburst, he was nonetheless arrested, along with over 700 of his followers. He was deported to Algeria and thence to France, where he died in January 1943.[75] The movement which bore his name did not die with him, although after the war it gradually surrendered its political significance to legitimate political parties.

## NOTES

1. Until a relatively late date, men were not allowed to bring their wives to the Soudan, but according to accepted practice, many of them had an African mistress. Occasionally the offspring of these unions were educated in France, but more usually the women and children were abandoned when the official was posted elsewhere.
2. For a semi-fictional account of a colonial career, see M. Delafosse, "Les États d'âme d'un colonial," *L'Afrique Française: Bulletin du Comité de l'Afrique française et du Comité du Maroc*, 1909, pp. 62, 102, 127, 162, 200, 240, 288, 311, 338, 373, 414. See also, T.C. Weiskel, *French Colonial Rule and the Baule Peoples: Resistance and Collaboration, 1889–1911* (Oxford, 1980), 214–5.
3. ANM, Fonds ancien, 1-D-49, Monographie du Cercle de Mopti, "Organisation politique et administration des groupes indigènes du Cercle de Mopti avant l'occupation française."
4. "La Politique indigène," *L'Afrique Française*, 1909, Supplement, 348–9.
5. "Circulaire de William Ponty, du 30 août 1910," *L'Afrique Française*, 1910, 341.
6. See G. Hardy, *Une Conquête morale. L'Enseignement en A.O.F.* (Paris, 1917).
7. See L. Kaba, *The Wahhabiyya*.
8. *Ibid*. One of the most successful examples of the combination of Western curricula and teaching methods with traditional Islamic subjects is to be found in the *madrasa* school of al-Hajj Sa'ad 'Umar Touré in Segu, Mali. The language of instruction is Arabic, and all modern subjects are taught as well as the religious ones. The school at present has more than 1,000 students.
9. JM, I, 51.
10. For a detailed history of the order, see Jamil M. Abun-Nasr, *The Tijaniyya* (London, 1965).
11. *Rimāḥ*, I, 88ff.
12. *Ibid*., I, 200, quoting al-Dabbāgh.
13. Abun-Nasr, *The Tijaniyya*, 42–4.

14. Aḥmad Sukayrij, *Kashf al-Ḥijāb* (Morocco, 1961), 329–30, writes about Muhammad al-Kansūsī who claimed to have left the Qadiriyya in favour of the Tijaniyya because in his opinion God had chosen to create it as a force against the corruption of that epoch. Al-Kansūsī's ideas were important in West Africa because he entered into debate with leading West African Qadiris in order to justify his conversion. See Sukayrij and Abun-Nasr, *The Tijaniyya*, 168ff.
15. For a discussion of Umar's appointments of *muqaddamūn* see J.R. Willis, *Al-Ḥājj 'Umar b. Sa'īd*, 196.
16. P. Marty, "L'Islam en Mauretanie et au Sénégal," *Revue du Monde Musulman*, 31 (1915–16), 378.
17. See for example M.A. Tyam, *La Vie d'el Hadj Omar, qasīda en poular*, translated by Henri Gaden (Paris, 1935).
18. *Rimāḥ*, I, 192.
19. Abun-Nasr, *The Tijaniyya*, 23.
20. P.-J. André, *L'Islam noir. Contribution à l'étude des confréries religieuses islamiques en Afrique occidentale* (Paris, 1924), 65.
21. His full Arabic name was Sīdī Aḥmad Ḥamāhullāh b. Muḥammad b. 'Umar al-Ḥasanī al-Tijānī al-Tishītī, but I have used the form of the name as it was usually pronounced by my informants.
22. Alioune Traoré, *Contribution à l'Étude de l'Islam. Le Mouvement tijanien de Cheikh Hamahoullah*, Thèse de 3° cycle, Université de Dakar, 1975.
23. VE.
24. See for example, VE, 72ff.
25. Traoré, *Contribution*, 144ff.
26. *Ibid*., 142.
27. Traoré employed extensive documentation available in Senegal and Mauritania.
28. But not always; Marty's account of Hamallah is rather favourable, *Soudan*, IV, 218ff.
29. A notable exception is Amadou Hampaté Bâ who befriended Marcel Cardaire of the Bureau des Affaires Musulmanes, an agency charged with the surveillance of Muslims, and with whom he wrote *Tierno Bokar, le Sage de Bandiagara*.
30. Ct. Rocaboy, "L'Hamallisme," CHEAM 1153.
31. For Shaykh al-Tāhir see Sukayrij, 414–5. Nothing about al-Akhdar or the Hamallist movement appears in Sukayrij.
32. VE, 57ff; Traoré, *Contribution*, 43ff.
33. Marty, *Soudan*, IV, 220.
34. VE, 58–9.
35. Abun-Nasr, *The Tijaniyya*, 96.
36. See Sukayrij, 414–5 and Traoré, *Contribution*, 46.
37. His translation of a portion of Sukayrij's brief biographical entry on al-Tāhir is misleading. Traoré (p. 46) translates: "In spite of such gifts and qualities as these, some men have tried, but in vain, to tarnish his reputation." I translate it as: "However, I have seen some of the brothers (may God improve their affair and mine) who deny the majority of what is attributed to him, but only God knows the truth of that." Sukayrij, 414–5.

38. *Kashf al-ḥijāb* was published in 1961.
39. VE, 59–60.
40. Marty, *Soudan*, IV, 211; Traoré, *Contribution*, 48–9.
41. BN, Arabe 5713, f. 59a-b; the visit occurred in 1868–9.
42. M. Hiskett, "The 'Community of Grace' and its opponents, the 'Rejecters': a Debate about theology and mysticism in Muslim West Africa with special reference to its Hausa expression," *African Language Studies*, XVII (1980), 103; John N. Paden, *Religion and Political Culture in Kano* (Berkeley, 1973), 97–8.
43. Paden, *Religion and Political Culture*, 82–3; 86–7.
44. Marty, *Soudan*, IV, 219.
45. *Ibid.*, 222.
46. JM, I, 124.
47. *Rimāḥ*, II, 82.
48. VE, 58.
49. Traoré, *Contribution*, 82.
50. VE, 58 and 94.
51. Traoré, *Contribution*, 87ff.
52. *Ibid.*, 53–6.
53. *Ibid.*, 60–3; Marty, *Soudan*, IV, 220.
54. TB, 48 and VE, 68; these two versions differ in interesting respects. Traoré, *Contribution*, 51.
55. *Rimāḥ*, I, 195.
56. See VE, 63–4; Traoré, *Contribution*, 112–3; Marty, *Soudan*, IV, 217–8.
57. "Secrets" were an important currency among the *shuyūkh* of the order; see Paden, *Religion and Political Culture*, 98, quoting Ibrāhīm Nyass, *Riḥlat Ḥijāziyya*.
58. Marty, *Soudan*, IV, 220.
59. F. Quesnot, "L'Evolution du Tidjanisme sénégalais depuis 1922," CHEAM 2865 (1958), Ch. IV. See also Abun-Nasr, *The Tijaniyya*, 151–2.
60. Marty, *Soudan*, IV, 222.
61. Quesnot, "L'Evolution," 25.
62. See Marty, "L'Islam en Mauretanie et au Sénégal," 369ff.
63. P. Alexandre argues in this way in "Hamallism, an Islamic Movement in French West Africa," in R.I. Rotberg and A. Mazrui (eds), *Protest and Power in Black Africa* (New York, 1970), 497–512.
64. ANM, Fonds récent, 4-E-18, Affaires Musulmanes, Mission du Capitaine André, 1923. André's reports must be treated with care since he often got his facts wrong.
65. Traoré, *Contribution*, 295–300, quotes a lengthy excerpt from the Rapport Descemet, Archives Nationales de Mauritanie, Série E 2/33, 1925.
66. Traoré, *Contribution*, 144.
67. *Ibid.*, 150–1, quoted from l'*AOF*, 28 janvier 1926; this passage is also quoted in A. Gouilly, *L'Islam dans l'AOF*, 139–40, where he gives the title of the article as "Comme au pays des mille et une nuits." Hampaté Bâ gives a different account of this meeting in VE, 79–80.
68. Traoré, *Contribution*, 297.
69. ANS, 2 G 39/8, Soudan, Rapport Politique Annuel, 1939.

70. Traoré provides a detailed discussion of supporters and enemies of Hamallah.
71. Alexandre, "Hamallism," 507, who claims many Hamallists entered the RDA.
72. See Traoré, *Contribution*, 186ff.
73. A copy of this letter was held in the library of Baba Thimbely, Bandiagara; a microfilm copy is now held in CEDRAB, Timbuktu, Mali, and in the MAMMP Collection, Yale University Library.
74. *Ibid*.
75. Traoré gives a detailed description of these events up to Hamallah's death.

Part II

# THE RELIGIOUS HERITAGE AND SPIRITUAL SEARCH OF CERNO BOKAR

The preceding chapters have explored certain aspects of the general social and political conditions in which Cerno Bokar lived. As we turn to the man himself, our attention must shift to a much more specialised field of investigation, the indigenous West African traditions of Islam from which Cerno Bokar developed his own thought and teachings. This exploration will lead us into subject-matter vastly different from that already discussed; we will be examining the rich fabric of West African Islamic belief and practice with the purpose of understanding Cerno Bokar's personal interpretations of his religion and his mysticism. These chapters may often give the impression that religious preoccupations insulated Cerno Bokar from a concern about the conditions which surrounded him, but this would be misleading. It would be more correct to say that Cerno's response to the contemporary malaise was religious rather than political; he did not look for political solutions to man's contemporary problems because he did not view them as political problems. His primary concern was to establish Islamic principles firmly within his community, because he believed that man's highest priority should be his personal salvation.

From a political perspective, the few documented comments Cerno Bokar offered about the French reflect inconsistency and even naiveté. He feared, for example, that West Africa's own cultural heritage might be lost through an "infatuation" with foreign manners and mores: "We see our Sudanese children becoming more or less inexact copies of Arabs or Europeans, depending on their training."[1] He encouraged people to respect and meditate on their own traditions, implying by this term not only the Islamic *ḥadīth* of the Prophet, but also that corpus of local oral literature which is imbued with moral and spiritual content.[2] However, he seemed to welcome technological innovation as evidence of what man can achieve when he draws upon "divine strength."[3] In addition, and perhaps more surprisingly, Cerno did not, in principle, oppose attendance in French schools by young Muslim children. As evidence on this issue we have Amadou Hampaté Bâ's account of his own entry into French school. In the first decade of the twentieth century many Muslims saw French schools as insidious institutions: "to go to French schools was to become an unbeliever."[4] Hampaté Bâ was initially placed in school against the wishes of his mother, who subsequently sought to get him out by offering a payment for his release. But Cerno allegedly intervened, advising her not to interpose herself "between Amadou and his God." Cerno does not seem to have perceived that both modern technology and Western schooling would be major factors in undermining the very traditions which he hoped to preserve.

But even if Cerno Bokar's perception of his world was inconsistent, he could never be charged with swerving from the principles he set for himself. He consistently refused to engage in political confrontation even when, after his submission to Shaykh Hamallah, his enemies were intent on destroying him. The issue for him was not winning a political battle but clinging to the principles of his faith. His personal religious considerations had led him to the conclusion that Hamallah was his spiritual superior and that Tijani doctrine dictated submission to him. That decision thrust Cerno Bokar into the political arena, but all his life had in a way been a preparation for this tragic dénouement. Being the man he was, with the status he enjoyed, he could not avoid pronouncing a definitive opinion about the crucial issue of Tijani leadership. His willingness to endorse Hamallah and thereby invite the extreme displeasure of both French and African authorities was entirely consistent with the direction his life had taken. Cerno Bokar was the great nephew of al-Hajj Umar; he was therefore a Futanke and a Taal, a member of the leading Tijani family in West Africa. But the conditions of his childhood and youth had separated him from the mainstream of Futanke social and political development in Bandiagara. Cerno Bokar's future was committed to traditional religious scholarship rather than to the French schooling received by many of his relatives early in the twentieth century. When he later became a *muqaddam* in the Tijaniyya order he performed the duties of his office as he saw fit, refusing to conform to contemporary practices which he considered deviations from Tijani doctrine. His insistence rankled with some other *muqaddamūn*, but this issue was minor in comparison to his submission to Hamallah, which elicited extreme and immediate reactions.

# 3

# THE EARLY YEARS

## *Conditions in Bandiagara*

Cerno Bokar was probably born in the early 1880s in Segu. We cannot establish the year of his birth with certainty, and dates have been proposed as early as 1875[5] and as late as 1886. Amadou Hampatê Bâ stated categorically in an interview that the 1875 date, published in *Le Sage de Bandiagara*, is incorrect;[6] he argued that the date should be 1886 because Cerno Bokar was one year younger than his cousin, Seedu Nuuru Taal of Dakar, who was born in 1885. However, no means has been found to confirm the date of Seedu Nuuru's birth, and in his recent publication, *Vie et Enseignement de Tierno Bokar*, Hampatê Bâ again proposed that the date was 1875. French estimates of Cerno's birth date range from 1878 to 1883.[7] Eleven years is a long time in the life of a child, and events in Cerno Bokar's childhood would undoubtedly have had a very different impact on him according to his age. For example, his father fled from Segu at the time of the French conquest of the city (1890), never to rejoin his family.[8] If Cerno Bokar had been born in 1875, he would have been a young man of fifteen at the time of the French attack; but if he had been born in 1886, he would have been no more than four years old. Of course, even if we knew his exact age at the time of his father's departure, we would still have no way of judging his reaction to this separation. But this example clearly illustrates the difficulty we have in seeking to portray Cerno Bokar's childhood. We tentatively suggest a birth date in the early 1880s on the basis of scanty circumstantial evidence. Had he been fifteen years old at the time of the conquest, he might well have accompanied his father in flight; at that age he would have been considered a young man, and expected to fend for himself in many ways. However, he remained with his mother throughout this period, which suggests that he was somewhat younger.

Cerno apparently began his Qur'anic studies in Segu with Abdullahi Jire, a former student of his maternal grandfather, al-Hajj Seedu Hann. Study of the Qur'an would probably have begun at about six or seven years. When Cerno Bokar's father left Segu, Abdullahi Jire assumed responsibility for those in the family who remained there, including Cerno Bokar, his siblings and his mother, aunt and grandmother. When during the reinstatement of Bambara authority by the French in 1891, Segu became unsafe for the Futanke, Abdullahi Jire removed the family to a Somono village for their protection.[9] He also seems to have been responsible in part for convincing Cerno's mother, Aissata, to take her children to Bandiagara in 1893 after Agibu's installation there by the French. One might assume that such a move would have been logical, considering conditions in Segu; and many Futanke were joining Agibu in Masina at this time. Perhaps Aissata also entertained hopes of being reunited with her husband. But one account, probably apocryphal, suggests that the decision was taken at least indirectly because of Cerno Bokar himself. It seems that one day Abdullahi Jire[10] discovered Cerno playing in the streets wih his friends; he had a Bambara drum tied round his waist which he was beating avidly. Jire went immediately to Aissata to report this irreligious behaviour; he said that although he was able to care for all the family, he felt they should join Agibu in Bandiagara. Otherwise, he feared the children would "become Bambara."[11] We cannot place too much emphasis on this story, but it does add at least some weight to the suggestion that Cerno Bokar was a young child during this period, perhaps seven or eight years old.

Cerno Bokar was named for his grandfather, Bokar Seedu (Arabic: Abū Bakr b. Sa'īd) al-Hajj Umar's older brother.[12] The elder Bokar acquired the scholarly title of *cerno*, and the grandson received his names in memory of his grandfather, and not because he had himself earned the title of *cerno*. Cerno Bokar was therefore the great-nephew of al-Hajj Umar, and it would be difficult to overstate the influence on his life of his paternal heritage. It was an influence which was pervasive and yet profoundly ambivalent. Cerno Bokar was born during the twilight years of the Umarian state. His father Saalif (Arabic: Ṣāliḥ) is remembered more as a scholar than a warrior and as a close companion to Amadu, Umar's son and successor in Segu. He felt compelled to flee before the advancing French, perhaps more out of loyalty to the Futanke leadership than from fear of the advancing armies.[13] His decision to leave his family under the protection of Abdullahi Jire was possibly motivated by the desire to protect them from the uncertainty and anticipated hardships of the future. He may also have felt that Jire, a Somono of local lineage and not a Futanke, might have been less vulnerable to French oppression or Bambara revenge. We have already seen how Jire first removed the family from Segu and then how he may have been influential in convincing Aissata to take her family to Bandiagara where she might settle in the relative security of Futanke society. However, the reality of conditions in Bandiagara was far different from what had been anticipated. Agibu was preoccupied with securing his own personal position in relation both to the French and to the people he now governed. The Futanke were divided among themselves, not only because of old disputes, but also because of deep differences over Agibu's collaborationist policies. For whatever reasons,

Aissata did not join the circle of Agibu's close associates. Oral accounts claim that this was because Agibu neglected her and her family and treated them almost as enemies.[14] But it is also possible, although no explicit documentation exists to support this view, that Aissata decided on her own account to dissociate herself from Agibu and his retinue.

At issue here is not only Aissata's husband, Saalif, but also her father, al-Hajj Seedu (Arabic: Sa'īd) Hann. Saalif is reputed to have been very close to Amadu; if the oral accounts are at all accurate, he abandoned Segu with Madani, Amadu's son who had been left in command there, after the French Conquest of that city in 1890. The remnants of this defeated army later joined Amadu in Nioro, where another unsuccessful stand against the French was staged. Amadu and his army then moved to Bandiagara, whence they fled further eastwards in 1893. Traditions state that Saalif accompanied Amadu in his flight from Bandiagara; we do not know any of the further details of his fate, but his possible survival of the rigours of Amadu's emigration and his subsequent failure to return to Bandiagara with those who later deserted Amadu may have given rise to Agibu's coolness toward Aissata, or indeed to her own second thoughts about accepting his hospitality.

Aissata was also closely associated with Amadu through her own father, al-Hajj Seedu Hann, a Pullo (or perhaps Futanke) scholar who had probably first met al-Hajj Umar in Sokoto and had been initiated into the Tijaniyya order through him. Al-Hajj Seedu did not accompany Umar when he left Sokoto and did not participate in the *jihād*, but came to Segu after the Umarian conquest of that city.[15] He was one of the ten *muqaddamūn*, or spiritual leaders, directly authorized by al-Hajj Umar in West Africa to transmit the prayers and teachings of the Tijaniyya order,[16] and as such he exercised considerable influence in Segu. His leadership seems to have been largely religious and spiritual, but he actively supported Amadu's claims to succession as Commander of the Faithful after the death of Umar and was therefore clearly associated with Amadu's political goals. Al-Hajj Seedu composed a letter in which he severely criticised those "covetous brothers" who were opposing Amadu's succession; he also asserted that not only had al-Hajj Umar named Amadu *muqaddam*, but also that he had gathered all the leading Futanke in Masina in order to proclaim to them that Amadu should succeed him. He then went on to cite numerous authorities and precedents for Amadu's succession including examples from 'Uthmān b. Fūdī and Muhammad Bello in Sokoto, al-Mukhtār al-Kuntī in the Qadiriyya Sufi order and Ahmad al-Tijani, the founder of the Tijaniyya order.[17] It seems unlikely that Agibu was one of the covetous brothers referred to in this letter since it was written sometime during the late 1860 or early '70s when he was still very close to Amadu. But their subsequent rift, and Agibu's collaboration with the French in order to depose and replace Amadu, could not but have created some distance of feeling between him and the woman who was not only al-Hajj Seedu's daughter but also Saalif's wife.

Aissata therefore arrived in Bandiagara without husband or close kin to support her; either she was snubbed by Agibu, or she purposely avoided him, and was consequently forced to rely on her own devices to find the means to maintain her three children and her sister, who had accompanied her. She was not completely without friends and acquaintances. She found some assistance in the small Hausa commercial settlement in Bandiagara, to which she was drawn by the connections of her own parents with Hausaland. But a much more sustained source of support came from Amadu Ali Cam, a man who was to exert considerable influence upon Cerno Bokar. He took an interest in raising the young Cerno and in directing his education. Cerno became a close friend of Amadu Ali's son, Tijani, and ultimately married his daughter, Nene.[18] But most important may have been the influence on Cerno Bokar of the relative position of the Cam among other Futanke. The Cam were a family of caste origins in Senegal; islamized over the centuries, many of them responded to al-Hajj Umar's appeals to join the *jihād*, and one of their number was appointed *muqaddam* by him in the Tijaniyya.[19] Despite their religious commitment and contributions to Umar's military campaigns, some of their Futanke comrades refused to forget their caste origins; they were at times disparaged and generally set apart. We will discuss below the possible implications of this fact for Cerno Bokar.

Notwithstanding the assistance Aissata received from Amadu Ali Cam and from the Hausa, her new life was difficult, and there is some suggestion that the family subsisted for a time on the edge of poverty. She was reduced to selling prepared food or milk in the market, and until the time Cerno Bokar had begun teaching and consequently was able to command a labour force large enough to construct some mud brick buildings, the family lived in dwellings of straw.[20] Aissata had been given some land to farm in Bandiagara, but there is no record of how productive the fields might have been, and there seem to have been no slaves or servants to help work the land. These conditions were far different from what Aissata had known in Segu where, as the daughter of a respected leader in the Tijaniyya brotherhood and the wife of a member of Amadu's court, she had probably never been required to provide for her own sustenance. Nothing suggests that Aissata felt particularly resentful or humiliated by her new circumstances, but they could not have been easy. Indeed, she is credited by some sources as instilling in her children a respect for the dignity of labour.[21] Cerno Bokar learned several productive skills including the weaving of straw mats,[22] tailoring and especially embroidery,[23] a métier at which he was particularly talented. Economic necessity dictated this kind of work, but at the same time Aissata refused to ignore her children's religious education. That Muslim parents with Aissata's background should have insisted on a religious education for their children was by no means unusual, but it must be remembered that an extended scholarly preparation implied economic consequences for the family. Aissata stood to lose a certain portion of the economic productivity of her sons as a result of their studies, a loss which apparently she could ill afford. We know nothing of the possible extent of her sacrifice in this regard, but Cerno Bokar was well aware of it. He is reported to have said that his mother "nourished me with her milk and then with her sweat."[24]

## *The influences of family*

The pattern of Cerno Bokar's familial relationships is now rather more clear: abandoned by his father and distanced from his father's family, he was raised by his mother to whom he became extraordinarily devoted. These circumstances can be interpreted as having considerably influenced Cerno Bokar's later life.

Although in Bandiagara Aissata herself on the margins of Futanke ruling circles, her sons nonetheless bore the name Taal. Name alone did not provide a guaranteed passage to prominence and influence, but it did carry a certain social weight in and of itself. The combination of Cerno Bokar's sound scholarly and religious training with his kinship to al-Hajj Umar made it almost inevitable that he should become one of the more widely recognized leaders of the Tijaniyya Sufi order in the western Soudan. The belief among many West African Muslims that the *baraka*, or spiritual grace, of a holy man could be inherited led many people to enter or renew their relationship with the Tijaniyya through Cerno Bokar. Not only was he felt by blood to be "closer to al-Hajj Umar," but his scholarship and piety were seen as proof of his spiritual inheritance. His visibility and reputation among Tijanis consequently increased, primarily due to his position in the Taal family. However, his prominence owed little to most of his relatives, or to most of the Futanke in Bandiagara, who after Agibu were becoming increasingly associated with French colonial interests, in terms of both education and politics. Cerno Bokar was not without allegiance to them (mutual relationships were not completely severed until near the end of his life), but in matters of religion he took very little notice of their views, opinions or advice. For guidance in this domain he looked to his own mentors and to his own conscience. So far as religion was concerned, Cerno Bokar's opinion was that most of the Futanke, as well as many of his own family, had gone astray. This independence of conviction was one of the primary reasons why he was able to submit to Shaykh Hamallah in 1937 in spite of what he knew would be extreme reactions from many members of his family. Cerno Bokar's submission to Hamallah was based on a number of specific religious imperatives (which are discussed below), but his freedom to act on his personal convictions must have sprung from the social conditions in which he grew up. Cerno had been isolated from the mainstream of Futanke social and political development in Bandiagara and from the growing alliance with French interests. His closest associations were with the Cam family, a faction who in general felt themselves somewhat ostracized by other Futanke; the Cam of Segu were among the first Tijanis to join Hamallah. Futanke and Taal opposition to Hamallah centered in part on his alleged usurpation of the spiritual position of al-Hajj Umar. Cerno Bokar considered these claims to be based on misinterpretations (or ignorance) of Tijani doctrine and upon misplaced family loyalty. He is reported to have observed:

> Faith and truth, in that they are connected with God, are not the prerogatives of one individual, nor one race, nor even one country. One who believes that these virtues are the privilege of his family is as foolish as one who might say, "The sun shines only for my family; the rains fall and the streams flow only for my people."[25]

Such a statement would be completely understandable in the wake of events following Cerno Bokar's submission to Hamallah; but in fact they were spoken several years earlier, well before he knew what price his own family would force him to pay for his personal religious convictions.

The interpretations presented here, given the nature of the evidence before us, can be little more than suppositions. But even if one can accept the probability that the social distance between Cerno Bokar and other Futanke, combined with his subsequent elevated rank as a Tijani *muqaddam*, contributed to his particular brand of independent religious attitude, this tells us nothing about why and how he became a contemplative mystic. Here supposition can easily fade into fantasy, because even the circumstantial evidence is vague. In subsequent chapters we will trace the mystical traditions to which he was exposed, but none of these appears on the surface to be quite so introspective and personal as Cerno Bokar's own form of mysticism. Of course, a contemplative tradition is not absent from Islam, but evidence for it in West Africa is very slender. With respect to Cerno Bokar, this question is largely unanswerable, but oral accounts tempt one to look to Aissata as a significant influence. Cerno was extraordinarily devoted to his mother, which he revealed in often unusual ways. Even as an adult, he personally laundered her clothes in a local stream.[26] Her counsel and advice were cherished by him, and at her death his grief was severe and extended. He isolated himself for days and reacted as if some of his own vital force had been carried away; friends and family became increasingly concerned about him.[27] Eventually he emerged from this crisis and nothing more is known about its after effects, except that in the wake of his loss some say he considered setting out on the pilgrimage to Mecca. Although this episode well illustrates the intensity of Cerno's relationship with his mother, it gives little insight into what specific religious influence she might have exercised. Local traditions imbue her with a certain piety, as well as a degree of formal religious training, which she had received from her father, Seedu Hann. And judging from her insistence on the education of her own children, it might not be unjustified to suggest that she had nurtured a spiritual quality in Cerno Bokar which became central to his own religious understanding, an interpretation implied in oral accounts. More than this, however, one cannot say.

It is from this brief and sketchy background that we must turn to an examination of the religious traditions into which Cerno Bokar was educated. In the complexity and detail of some of the explanations which follow, we might temporarily lose sight of Cerno Bokar himself, but it should be remembered that these were the sources upon which he drew in the development of his own ideas and teachings.

## NOTES

1. TB, 91; VE, 185; Monod, "Homme," 153.
2. Discourse 44.
3. Discourse 6.
4. Amadou Hampaté Bâ, interview of 4 May 1978.
5. TB, 18; VE, 22.
6. Amadou Hampaté Bâ, interview of 2 May 1978.
7. ANM, Fonds Récent, 1-G-198, Statistique des Écoles Coraniques, Cercle de Bandiagara, 1921–24; Fiche de Renseignement sur Tierno Bokar, 20 juillet 1937.
8. TB, 21; VE, 25.
9. TB, 22; VE, 26; Amadou Hampaté Bâ, interview of 2 May 1978.
10. Jire is not mentioned by name in this story, but the narrator identifies the person in question as a former student of al-Hajj Seedu Hann, Cerno's grandfather.
11. Sori Hamadun Bala, interview of 30 September 1977.
12. The French agent, Mage, met Bokar Seedu in Nioro during his travels; he commented on his lack of influence in the local political hierarchy; A.E. Mage, *Voyage dans le Soudan occidentale, 1863–66* (Paris, 1868), 643.
13. TB, 18–21; VE, 25.

14. Interviews with Amadou Hampaté Bâ, 2 May 1978 and Sori Hamadun Bala, 30 September 1977.
15. See Murray Last, *The Sokoto Caliphate* (New York, 1967), xxxix-xlii, for a discussion of al-Hajj Seedu.
16. Willis, "Al-Ḥājj 'Umar . . . and the Doctrinal Basis . . .", 196.
17. BN, Arabe 5561, ff. 66b–69b; this letter is undated but appears to have been written after 1868–9, when Amadu formally received the title Commander of the Faithful, since Al-Hajj Seedu addresses him in this manner. (See BN, Arabe 5713, f. 59a-b, for this date.) The letter was written specifically in response to questions addressed to him by Amadu. This letter was brought to my attention by David Robinson.
18. TB, 28–30; VE, 35; interviews with Sori Hamadun Bala, 30 September 1977 and with Dauda Maiga, 29 September 1977.
19. Willis, "Al-Ḥājj 'Umar . . . and the Doctrinal Basis . . .", 196; the person referred to was Tafsir Ali Cam.
20. Sori Hamadun Bala, interview of 30 September 1977.
21. Theodore Monod, "Homme de Dieu," 150.
22. Sori Hamadun Bala, interview of 30 September 1977.
23. TB, 30; VE 30–1.
24. TB, 28; VE, 36.
25. Discourse 18.
26. Dauda Maiga, interview of 30 September 1977.
27. TB, 40–1; VE, 50–1; with respect to Cerno Bokar's relationship to his mother, it is interesting to note a remark by E. Caron in *De St. Louis au Port de Tombouctou* (Paris, 1893), 181, about Tijani in Bandiagara, whose mother had been retained in Dinguiray:

    In the Soudan, the natives treat their mothers with great deference and believe themselves dishonoured if they are not near them; as a chief, Tijani suffered even more acutely the absence of his own mother, as much from filial sentiments as from his pride.

# 4

# RELIGIOUS HERITAGE: CERNO BOKAR AS STUDENT AND TEACHER

As with so many aspects of Cerno Bokar's life, we are able to provide only few details of his religious training. This dearth of information is especially frustrating because the influences on his religious thinking were not simply those of the standard texts which were studied by all West African scholars. Cerno Bokar had certainly studied these, but he was not particularly attached to "book learning." He was a contemplative man, much given to seeking his own interpretations and finding his own personal path to understanding. As we have suggested in the previous chapter, perhaps his mother had nurtured these characteristics in him; certainly the oral accounts of her would have us believe this. Nonetheless, the teachers and the teachings with which he came into contact must also have been profoundly significant in this respect. We can say much more about the teachings than we can about the specific teachers who worked with Cerno Bokar. In the next chapter we trace the development of his interpretations of Tijani Sufism, not only from the basic writings of this religious order, but also through the men who seem to have been his spiritual masters. In this chapter we examine the nature of his formal religious education, but we also explore the influence upon him of a particular teaching in dogmatic theology (Arabic: *tawḥīd*) called *kabbe* in Fulfulde. Although based on written Arabic texts, the *kabbe* was transmitted orally; it developed through several stages of increasing complexity, and concluded with an "initiation" into a body of esoteric religious knowledge.

Although we cannot confirm the precise channels through which Cerno Bokar came into contact with this theological teaching, its influence on his own thought seems to have been profound. His personal version of an Islamic catechism in theology, which came to be known as the *mā 'd-dīn* (Arabic for "What is religion?") was also taught orally in Fulfulde, proceeded through several stages of increasingly complex interpretation, and concluded with an esoteric initiation. The esoteric dimensions of both the *kabbe* and the *mā 'd-dīn* were based on numerological analyses of words and letters, while at the same time emphasizing the essential and predominant role of the intellect in developing an understanding of one's religion. Sufism, on the other hand, while not anti-intellectual, tended to emphasize an experiential spiritual development which was acquired through prayers, recitations and various spiritual exercises. The great Sufi masters, such as al-Hajj

Umar, taught that the understanding gained through these experiences transcended any gained by any other means.

We can therefore identify at least three discrete elements in the learned traditions of Islamic West Africa, the Sufi or mystical, the literate-intellectual (formal academic study) and the non-literate intellectual (memorized texts, like the *kabbe*). Of course, these elements constantly interacted and few Muslims would have seen them as completely separate, but it is useful for us here to examine them individually so as to see more clearly their separate contributions to Cerno Bokar's thought.

## *Formal studies*

Cerno Bokar's early studies probably followed the pattern predominant in the western Sudan at that time. We have already suggested that he began Qur'anic studies at the age of six or seven with Abdullahi Jire in Segu. The number of years devoted to study of the Qur'an varied with the ability and interest of students. Those with particularly prodigious memories would memorize the entire Qur'an, which some might accomplish in their teenage years, although many would proceed to other studies without achieving this task. Arabic was not the mother-tongue of most West African students, and initial Qur'anic studies proceeded by the rote memorization of sections of the Qur'an without translation or comment; hence, recitation of the Qur'an was learned without any understanding of its content. Comprehension of the Arabic language began only in later years when the student began to study "books." Only the more capable and interested students advanced to this second level of study; most would leave school having only learned to recite some verses of the Qur'an as well as how to perform their required prayers and rituals, such as ablution.

The study of books began with relatively small and simple volumes, usually on the subject of *tawḥīd*, the doctrine of the unity of God. If the Qur'an, the revealed word of God, formed the foundation of Muslim religious study, *tawḥīd* was the essential second step during which basic Islamic principles were studied. With the study of "books" began the formal study of Arabic language as well, for at this stage texts were translated and explained. Lessons proceeded as follows: a section of text was copied out of the book by the student who then read it back to his teacher to make sure that any errors were corrected. The teacher would then explain and comment on the text, which the student would repeatedly go over until he fully understood it. Only then would he proceed to copy another section of the book being studied. All books studied formally with a teacher were approached in the same way, no matter how advanced a student might become. This method of learning, so similar in approach to that used during the years of Qur'anic recitation, is responsible for the high degree of memorization which attended these traditional studies. Many students memorized large portions of all the texts they studied. At the same time, however, this teaching method was also responsible for the perpetuation of a great deal of unimaginative teaching in West Africa. In most cases, there was no supervisory control over the content of oral explanation and commentaries on books studied. Anyone who could read and write Arabic could set himself up as a teacher, and a great number of these apparently had little real understanding of, or sensitivity to, the material they taught. For them teaching was a dry, mechanical process of writing out and reciting one section of text after another, with little attention being paid to whether the student really understood the import of what he was supposed to be learning. Unfortunately, a large number of teachers were of this kind, and the low opinion which Europeans held of Muslim education in the Western Sudan was based on the great numbers of unqualified teachers.

Of course, many Africans were themselves well aware of the shortcomings of this system. Few formal mechanisms existed for testing the qualifications of a prospective teacher, and none of these was controlled by a central authority. Nor was there any institution which could directly prevent a person from teaching. Any person who could attract students could teach; and conversely, the only means to insure that one did not teach was to deprive him of students. In the twentieth century the French tried to institute controls over Muslim schools by requiring schoolmasters to be licensed. But the pre-colonial system was controlled only by the laissez-faire process of the students' choice. Whereas this system may not have been very effective in eliminating the less competent teachers, it did allow for some rudimentary religious training to be widely available to the population, and it did not prevent the academically competent from pursuing their own training as far as they wished. The choice for parents placing their young children in Qur'anic training may have been limited — a local school would invariably be selected — but for the more advanced students the choice was considerable, and the style and emphasis of teaching might vary considerably, primarly because of the intensely personal nature of Islamic academic training in West Africa. The sources of this diversity require some explanation.

The primary aim of all Muslim scholars and teachers was the preservation and transmission of the Islamic religious tradition, as expressed in the Qur'an, the *ḥadīth*, and in various standard religious texts. If some scholars in their teaching placed primary emphasis on preserving the tradition, as they understood it, trying in their explanations never to stray far from the written text, others were more concerned with the efficacy of transmission, and these experimented with various methods of facilitating their students' comprehension. Since the religious tradition itself was not subject to change, the possibilities for innovation and experimentation lay in the transmission of knowledge, in commentary and in explanation. Some of these commentaries were committed to writing, and became standard texts, but the bulk of them were oral and they were often put into verse to make them easier to memorize. Indeed, Muslim education was in effect the oral transmission of the written word. No student, however competent he might be in Arabic, was considered qualified to teach a particular text unless he had studied it with a teacher. This was because all the texts were seen to require explanation and commentary. Consequently, a teacher's understanding of a given text was composed first of the commentary of his teacher, and secondly, if he was so inclined, of his own personal interpretations.

But the personal nature of the relationship between student and teacher went much further than the transmission of commentaries. Becoming the student of a particular teacher meant almost total submission to him. The teacher could become the most fundamental and pervasive influence in the student's moral and personal development. This relationship is not to be understood as the side-effect of a particular system of religious training; for many Muslims it was the central feature of the educational process. The selection of a teacher might therefore be subject to a wide range of considerations: his piety and religious personality, his reputed expertise in a particular discipline, or his teaching ability. Of course, his family and political relationships might also be a matter of concern. Some students travelled great distances in order to work with a given teacher; indeed, those students who set out in this way to search for knowledge were held in particularly high esteem.[1] The advanced student might study the various subjects of his curriculum under one teacher, or under several different specialists. In general the curriculum continued from *tawḥīd* into other subject areas such as law, grammar, advanced Arabic language, theology, the *ḥadīth*, and commentary on the Qur'an. Only the most dedicated students would touch on all these subjects. The majority ended their schooling after some study of *tawḥīd* and the law. Depending on his own ability and on his teachers, the student might eventually become completely literate in Arabic and be able to speak the language as well.

Cerno Bokar seems to have followed this normal course of study as a child and as a young man. After his arrival in Bandiagara he may have continued with the Qur'an for some time, but he soon undertook the study of "books." No evidence exists to suggest that he memorized the entire Qur'an, nor do we know much about his intermediate studies of "books," but he did become extremely competent in Arabic, which enabled him to pursue advanced study. Information about his early teachers is scanty,[2] but the one person with whom he studied the longest and who probably had the greatest influence upon him was Amadu Tafsiir Bâ, a Pullor scholar who had become blind by the time Cerno came to him.[3] Cerno remained under the guidance of Amadu Tafsiir for about eight years and seems primarily to have studied books on Sufism with him. Whether they read any other subjects together is not clear, but the Sufi dimension of their relationship is attested to in several sources. Amadu Tafsiir was a Tijani Sufi and the student of a student of al-Hajj Umar — a scholarly pedigree carrying prestige. He is reputed to have taught Cerno Bokar a number of major Sufi texts, including books by al-Ghazālī and Ibn 'Arabī, as well as the two most important Tijani treatises, the *Jawāhir al-Ma'ānī* by 'Alī Ḥarāzim and the *Rimāḥ* by al-Hajj Umar.[4]

Informants also trace Cerno Bokar's personal spiritual development to his relationship with Amadu Tafsiir: "He studied with Amadu Tafsiir until he was able to bring together the truth (*ḥaqīqa*) and the law (*sharī'a*). He was 'opened' [by God]."[5] This kind of description is designed to attribute to Cerno Bokar very high spiritual attainments. The language is derived from the Sufi vocabulary: to be "opened" by God refers to an individual's ability to comprehend the hidden, esoteric reality (truth or *ḥaqīqa*) which underlies the manifested, exoteric world of sensual perception. According to Muslims, the religious law (*sharī'a*) which is based upon God's revelations (the Qur'an), has been given to man in order to direct his activities in ordinary life. Sufis believe that some persons, with the aid of God, are able to perceive the hidden realities and to comprehend their relationship to the manifested world and to the revealed word of God.[6] Such persons are considered to be "friends of God" (Arabic: *walī*), often loosely called "saints" in European literature of the subject. The informant quoted above, one Koola Sidi, a favored disciple of Cerno Bokar, clearly wished to attribute saintly characteristics to him. Of course, we cannot make any judgments about Cerno Bokar's spiritual achievements; certainly he does not seem himself to have claimed any of the accomplishments here ascribed to him. At the same time, this quotation is a fair statement of the goals to which he aspired. He described mysticism as the "consequence . . . of a lived experience in which the intuition might be activated as a result of a lengthy meditative observation by an individual predestined for the divine light."[7] He advised his disciples:

> Observe everything with the eyes of your profound intelligence and in the light of the law of analogy which connects the events and elements of the three kingdoms of nature with one another [the animal, vegetable and mineral kingdoms]. Once you have discovered this secret mechanism, it will aid you in implanting within yourself the truth of divine matters which are situated

beyond the letter of the Qur'an. Then you will know the significance of the verse: "[He] teacheth man that which he knew not." (XCVI, 5)[8]

Although we cannot confirm Koola Sidi's spiritual attributions to Cerno Bokar, one can understand why he might have assumed such accomplishments in a man who spoke thus. But the question before us here relates not to whether Cerno Bokar had been "opened" by God, but to the content of the religious training which led him to think in the way he did.

The influence of Amadu Tafsiir is attested by another source. Amadou Hampaté Bâ claimed that Cerno was "initiated" into the secrets of Sufism by him.[9] The word "initiation" should here be understood in a rather technical sense; it is the translation of the Arabic "*talqīn*," which means giving instruction, often implying secret instruction. Sufi literature uses the word *talqīn* to indicate the process of instructing new disciples in the recitation of special prayers, as well as of authorizing the recitation of them. This procedure is often referred to in European languages as initiation; it is an event to which considerable import is given by the Sufis, and, it will be discussed in greater detail in the following chapter. This is not the initiation to which Hampaté Bâ here refers; Amadu Tafsiir was not Cerno Bokar's initiator in this sense. What seems to be in question here is the transmission of rather specific secret knowledge. That West African Sufis communicated "secrets" among themselves is not in doubt; numerous references to them occur throughout the oral and written literature. Hampaté Bâ claims that Amadu Tafsiir initiated Cerno into the science of numbers,[10] and sometimes he speaks of these secrets as if they were specific formulae or even physical objects.[11] Classical Sufi sources give a very different connotation from this one to the word "secret" (Arabic: *sirr*). One authority translates the term as "mystery" rather than secret; another describes it as "the innermost part of the heart in which the divine revelation is experienced."[12]

Cerno Bokar may have been heir to both kinds of secrets, and perhaps he was initiated into both by Amadu Tafsiir, although we have no conclusive proof of this. Cerno refers in the above quotation to the "secret mechanism" of observation and meditation through which one can seek "the truth of divine matters." This comment could be interpreted as referring to either of the kinds of secret we have just discussed: the knowledge of an esoteric science of numbers to probe the deeper meanings of written texts, or the development of an inner capacity to receive "divine revelations." But one should be clear that these two "secrets" are of a very different nature: one results from an intellectual exercise, the other from a spiritual exercise. In Cerno Bokar's religious thought and practice we find evidence of both forms of exercise;

whether they were also part of one single initiation is difficult to say. Certainly a considerable segment of his thought is traceable to an identifiable Islamic pedagogical tradition among the Fulbe: the *kabbe*. We must now examine the content of this particular tradition.[13]

## *The kabbe*

*Kabbe* is the Fulfulde equivalent of the Arabic word *'aqīda*, meaning "article of faith;" both words derive from roots which mean "to tie." The *kabbe* was that part of the religious studies curriculum in which the Fulbe introduced students to the basic fundamentals of *tawḥīd*, the doctrine of the unity of God. Early French administrators recorded the existence of the *kabbe* in the late nineteenth and early twentieth centuries among Fulbe of both Futa Jallon and Upper Volta. However, antecedents to this form of teaching go back to the seventeenth century, and the *kabbe* as the French found it may have been the last remaining vestige of this much older tradition, or it may have been one particular part of a still active and widespread form of teaching. Because the basic characteristics of the *kabbe* are so close to those of Cerno Bokar's *mā 'd-dīn*, we conclude that he was deeply influenced by this particular teaching. As we mentioned at the beginning of this chapter, both teachings were transmitted orally in Fulfulde, both proceed from explanations of the elements of *tawḥīd* through levels of more sophisticated interpretations, and both conclude with an "initiation." In spite of these congruences and other more specific ones which will be explained below, we cannot assert with certainty that Cerno Bokar had received a *kabbe* initiation, nor even conclusively demonstrate that he had come into direct contact with the *kabbe*. On the other hand, even if he never learned the *kabbe* itself, he could not have been ignorant of the broader traditions of which it was a part.

The content of the *kabbe*, although containing different elements in its variant forms, was based on a classic treatise on *tawḥīd* written by the fifteenth century North African scholar, Muḥammad b. Yūsuf al-Sanūsī. This tiny book (extending only to ten small pages of printed Arabic) was entitled *al-'Aqīdat al-Ṣughrā* (*The Lesser Dogma* or *The Lesser Catechism*) and often called *Umm al-Barāhīn* (*The Source of Proofs*).[14] It became a standard text in North and West Africa and was the subject of numerous written commentaries. A brief introduction to the more important elements of this text will be helpful in tracing its influence in West Africa.

The *Aqīdat al-Ṣughrā* opens with the following statement:

'Know that rational judgment consists of three parts: the necessary, the impossible and the contingent. The necessary is that which cannot be conceived by the intellect as not existing. The impossible is that which cannot be conceived by the intellect as existing. The contingent are those things of which the existence or non-existence is acceptable to the intellect. And it is incumbent upon every legally competent adult that he know what is necessary, impossible or contingent with respect to our great and powerful Master [God]. It is also incumbent to know the same with respect to the prophets.[15]

Al-Sanūsī then describes and discusses the proofs of the twenty necessary, the twenty impossible and the countless contingent attributes of God, as well as the three necessary and the three impossible attributes of God's Messengers. The treatise concludes with an explanation of how the Muslim testimony of faith, "There is no god but God, and Muhammad is the Messenger of God," contains all these concepts within it. He then says:

The intelligent person should recite [this testimony of faith] often, while calling to mind that which it contains from the articles of faith until it, with its meaning, mingles with his flesh and blood. Then, if God wills, he will behold some of its boundless secrets and wonders.[16]

The book therefore contains a rational explication of the attributes of God and of His Prophets, as well as an injunction to repeated recitation, which through an experiential process may bring one into touch with "secrets" and "wonders." These two strands run through the entire tradition of the *kabbe* in West Africa.

The *'Aqīdat al-Ṣughrā* may have acquired its prominent position in religious curricula as much because of the veneration in which its author was held as because of the contents of the treatise itself. Al-Sanūsī was considered a great Sufi saint; after his death one of his disciples wrote a biography of the master describing his mystical attainments and surveying his scholarly writings.[17] This book was subsequently abridged by the great Timbuktu scholar, then resident in Marrakesh, Aḥmad Bābā,[18] who also wrote a commentary on *al-'Aqīdat al-Ṣughrā*.[19] Aḥmad Bābā, on his return to Timbuktu in 1607, was therefore probably one of the channels through whom the work and teachings of al-Sanūsī was spread to West African scholars. Since his own commentary on the *'Aqīdat* is not extant, we do not know his interpretations of the text, but his abridgement of al-Sanūsī's biography suggests that he accepted the mystical view of the man put forward by its author. Two passages from Aḥmad Bābā's book seem worthy of mention here. Both concern deceased scholars who have appeared in visions to still living former companions. One reported in the vision that he had been seriously reprimanded after his death by Munkar and Nakīr (the angels who examine the dead as to their faith) for not having read the *'Aqīdat*. The second was seen, in the vision, teaching the *'Aqīdat* in paradise, which he claimed to be unequalled in value as a text.[20] Visions of this sort exercised great influence among mystically oriented Muslims and were accepted by some as virtually unassailable indications of divine will. Undoubtedly, the *'Aqīdat al-Ṣughrā* derived much of its venerated status from this kind of testimony.

By the later seventeenth century some Fulbe scholars were teaching commentaries of the *'Aqīdat* in their own language. One of these was translated into Arabic by a Pullo scholar called Muḥammad al-Wālī b. Sulaimān (fl. 1688–9) under the title "The Peerless Method, concerning the knowledge of the science of *tawḥīd*" (*al-manhaj al-farīd fī ma-'rifat 'ilm at-tawḥīd*).[21] This translation, as well as other works on *tawḥīd* by Muhammad al-Wālī, were widely distributed in West Africa. "The Peerless Method" contains all the elements of the Sanūsī tradition already mentioned: the entire text of the *'Aqīdat* is effectively quoted in full and elaborated upon; and there is a section on the saintly attainments of al-Sanūsī. The indications in this text are not only that *tawḥīd* is the most fundamental of all subjects which one can study, but that the *'Aqīdat* is essential for all those embarking on the mystical path: "Know all those who desire to enter the company of the friends of God, you will find in the *'Aqīdat al-Ṣughrā* a body of considerable knowledge which will inform you of the tenets of faith necessary for you before learning *tafsīr*, *ḥadīth* and *fiqh*. Do not abandon it after studying it."[22] Indeed, the mystical and esoteric dimensions of this commentary are rather striking. Considerable discussion is devoted to the relationship between the outer, manifested world (Arabic: *ẓāhir*) and the inner, esoteric, hidden spiritual realities (Arabic: *bāṭin*). An interest is also revealed in the science of letters (Arabic: *'ilm al-ḥurūf*), or the esoteric interpretation of their meaning. For example, explanations such as this are given for the letters in the name Muhammad, as well as for those in the word *shaykh*.[23]

Whether this connection between the esoteric sciences and the Sanūsī tradition of *tawḥīd* was first established in West Africa is not clear, but Muhammad al-Wālī is a definite link in the chain of transmission of *'ilm al-ḥurūf* in this region. Muhammad b. Muhammad al-Fulānī al-Kashnāwī, the Katsina scholar who wrote a treatise on this subject,[24] established the authority of his book on a dual *isnād* (Arabic: chain of authority) passing first through one Muhammad b. Muhammad al-Fulānī Bindū, a Borno scholar still remembered in local oral traditions. The *isnād* then splits into two lines: the first directly to the father of Muhammad al-Wālī, Sulaimān b. Muhammad al-Fulānī al-Māsinī, and the second to Aḥmad Bābā al-Tinbuktī via two other scholars, Muhammad b. Wākār (?) al-Wankarī and Ahmad b. Ahmad al-Tinbuktī.[25] Muhammad al-Wālī is also mentioned in the early nineteenth century Arabic literature of the Sokoto Caliphate where his writings on the esoteric sciences (magic squares, astrology, and the science of letters and numerology) are implicitly criticized for having contributed to a pre-occupation with them by some scholars at the expense of the more orthodox religious sciences. Shaykh 'Uthmān b. Fūdī composed an angry poem on the subject in which he castigated those practitioners of the esoteric sciences who used their knowledge for personal worldly gain:

> They call it secret knowledge, but they lie.
> It is not secret, but evil, knowledge.
> Whereas the secret is in the sciences spread by
> The friends of God, the possessors of discrimination.[26]

Shaykh 'Uthmān's feelings about the alleged misuse of certain kinds of knowledge were an important factor in his efforts to reform Islamic practice; in this passage he reveals his concern about what constitutes a valid and legitimate "secret." A similar issue would attain significance for Cerno Bokar: how to identify a legitimate Sufi *shaykh*.

The "Peerless Method" seems to have been a direct antecedent of the *kabbe* as it existed in the late nineteenth and early twentieth centuries. The only oral text of the *kabbe* presently available for consultation and comparison was collected in south-western Niger among the Gaobe Fulbe.[27] This version of the *kabbe* is by no means a complete reiteration of the "Peerless Method," but the major themes, and even the language of some passages, seem to be derived from it. Al-Sanūsī is nowhere mentioned by name, but his influence is pervasive:

> Knowledge of the *sharī'a* is obligatory for every legally competent adult, and they must know what is necessary, impossible and contingent with respect to God Almighty, and they must know these things with respect to the Prophets (Blessings and peace be upon them). This is so the competent adult will become a believer who has the certitude of his belief and whose heart can see into his religion.[28]

The attributes of God, and their rational proofs, are presented in a manner very reminiscent of the "Peerless Method." There seems little doubt that the *kabbe* as recited in the twentieth century is a part of the tradition of theological teaching which began with al-Sanūsī.

In the early years of their occupation, the French encountered the *kabbe* in Futa Jallon, Masina and Upper Volta. Initial French reports were unclear about the precise contents of the *kabbe* itself, but they provide important information about the characteristics associated with its transmission. One of the earliest published French accounts of the *kabbe* appeared in 1899 in a general study of West African Islam.[29] It is worth quoting in full:

> It remains to call attention, in Masina, to the existence of a curious Muslim sect, the center of which is in the village of Sassa. Its founder, Khair al-Dīn, who still

leads it, had sought to simplify Islam and to purify it through a progressive initiation and through the exclusive teaching of three books which summarize all the principles of the faith and which are assigned to threee categories of adepts. Children are allowed to read only the first, which is apparently the Qur'an; knowledge of the second, a summary of the *ḥadīth* is the privilege of older men. The third, which appears to be the explication of a particular Sufi doctrine, is confided only to *talibes* ([Sufi] seekers) or to disciples who aspire to become such and are considered worthy of it. Only these last perform the entire prayer, the other two categories of faithful being reduced to an abbreviated version of the obligatory prayers.

Some years later another French author, offered a much fuller discussion of this "sect" and its history. He spoke of the "rites of the *kabbe*" in which "religion is reduced to the meditation of the mysteries of Divine Unity."[30]

This sect was born in Futa Jallon among the Fulbe. During the time of al-Hajj Umar the grand master of this knowledge in this country was Alpha Mahmadou Hella. The conqueror [al-Hajj Umar] ordered him and his disciples to refrain, under pain of death, from persevering with their dangerous doctrines, but they went into hiding and their propaganda did not diminish. One of their number, a native of Labe who knew neither how to read nor write, since these skills are useless for the predestined, set out for the pilgrimage. He stopped among the Fulbe of Jelgooji (in the region of Djibo [Upper Volta]) and married. The power of this initiate was such, so they say, that he could kill an ox simply by pronouncing the name of Allah in front of it; the meat of this ox, although it had not been slaughtered according to Muslim ritual, was nonetheless permissible [for eating] because God himself had killed it.

When this man departed, he confided the mysteries of *tawḥīd* to his wife, and she taught them to others who were distinguished by their austerity and by their ardent piety. One of these was called Khair al-Dīn, of the Diallo family who lived in Ouro Saba in the canton of Jelgooji. To the meditations on Unity, he added the book of Shaykh Sanūsī, *al-Burhān*, which, translated into Fulfulde under the name *kabbe*, became, thanks to him, one of the holy books of the sect. In this way Fulfulde[31] became, after Arabic, a sacred language of Islam. The dogmas of *tawḥīd* translated into this language were learned word for word by the pastoral Fulbe, and were then commented upon in a series of extremely abstract deductions.

Before commenting on these two passages, it would be useful to include one more quotation, this one in connection with the recorded *kabbe* text which has been consulted for this study. Boubou Hama, who collected this version in Niger in the 1960s, attributes the origin of *kabbe* to one Alfa Issa who had studied in Jelgooji where he became a specialist in Islamic law:

This venerated marabout had no male children, but only two daughters who learned the Qur'an and Arabic. Faced by the ignorance of his people, Alfa Issa drafted, in Fulfulde, a treatise on the laws of Islam intended for those of his compatriots who did not have the opportunity to learn the Qur'an and Arabic. The treatise was called "kābi-tawidi" (the book of the knowledge of God). The word "kābi" is the root of "kabankobi," the term by which the Issabe (the Fulbe of the group of Alfa Issa) are called. The "kābi" is still employed today and the young Issabe may marry only after having assimilated its teaching.[32]

Several other traditions about the origins and nature of the *kabbe* exist, but they corroborate the general pattern which emerges from the three quoted here. First, it is extremely interesting that these accounts attribute the origin of the *kabbe* to local scholars of the recent past. Even in the cases where the teaching was viewed as being introduced to an area from outside, it is not presented as a widespread or ancient text.[33] The basic theme which is promoted is that it was invented by a learned marabout either to "purify" or to "simplify" the basic teachings of Islam or to make these more accessible to non-literate Muslims. Also interesting is the role which women were seen to play in its transmission; on this aspect of the *kabbe* one can only offer the speculation that perhaps women were attracted to this teaching since literate scholarly training was not readily available to them. Another striking feature of these accounts is the sectarian qualities with which the *kabbe* is described. These seem to be closely associated with the initiatory nature of the teaching, proceeding as it did through three stages. For many practitioners, memorization of the text became a prerequisite for general acceptance as a "full-fledged Muslim." These sectarian practices, although condemned by the majority of Muslim scholars, were undoubtedly justified by the partisans of the *kabbe* by al-Sanūsī's own injunction in the *'Aqīdat* that the knowledge of the attributes of God and His Prophets were "incumbent upon every legally competent adult." The point is elaborated further in the *kabbe*: "This [knowledge] is so the competent adult will become a believer who has the certitude of his belief and whose heart can see into his religion." Such concepts led to the conviction among some Muslims that only the masters of *tawḥīd* (the *kabbenkoobe*) were "true believers," as well as to various sectarian practices: that only the *kabbenkoobe* recited their prayers in full; that only they were qualified to slaughter animals;[34] that their members were buried in a cemetery separate from other Muslims; and that persons were not qualified to marry until they memorized the text of the *kabbe*.[35]

These sectarian practices provide yet another clue to the long history of the *kabbe*. The same teaching, with similar sectarian tendencies, apparently flourished in Hausaland in the latter eighteenth and early nineteenth centuries. Shaykh 'Uthmān b. Fūdī, the leader of the Sokoto *jihād*, had himself devoted much energy to combating these teachings. To whom else but local *kabbenkoobe* could the following reference have been made?

They spread among the people the idea that whoever did not devote himself to *tawḥīd* in the manner in which they themselves had determined was an unbeliever, and that the common Muslims were not legally qualified to slaughter animals, nor could they marry if they did not know *tawḥīd*.[36]

Shaykh 'Uthmān campaigned against the sectarian tendencies of the *kabbenkoobe* and against their exclusivity. But it is doubtful that he would have opposed the mere teaching of a book like the *'Aqīdat al-Ṣughrā*, even if some of its Fulfulde commentaries bordered on the questionable discipline of scholastic theology. What he opposed was the elevation of these discourses to a central place in one's religious life and the imposition on others of any particular interpretation. Al-Hajj Umar had probably opposed the *kabbe* in Futa Jallon later in the nineteenth century for much the same reasons.[37]

That the *kabbe* was sometimes taught in a manner more in accord with orthodox belief is evidenced by Paul Marty's description of it in Futa Jallon.[38] By the time Marty wrote, considerable excitement concerning the *kabbe* had been stirred up by French administrators who felt because of its initiatory aspects that it represented some form of Pullo mysticism or secret society. Marty firmly disagreed with these assertions; according to him "the *kabbe* is very simply the Fulfulde translation of the Arabic word *tawḥīd*," which was taught at a particular stage in the educational curriculum. Its supposed mystical and numerological aspects were dismissed as the mere "intellectual recreations" of those scholars who had acquired an arcane knowledge of the dogma. We will discuss the initiatory and esoteric aspects of the *kabbe* in the following section; here let us examine what Marty saw in Futa Jallon around 1920 as a rather more academically respectable face of the *kabbe*.

According to Marty the *kabbe* was taught in Futa Jallon within the section of the curriculum called *firugol*, which means "translation" or "commentary." He implies that the *firugol* was an intermediate course of study preceded by Qur'anic recitation and the fundamentals of reading and writing and followed by *funūn*, which he described as higher studies. *Funūn* comprised the study of such subjects as jurisprudence and Arabic language and grammar. *Firugol* began with the study of *tawḥīd* (the *kabbe*) and Qur'anic exegesis and continued with the study of various West African works written in Fulfulde[39] and also included the study of certain Sufi books, mainly the writings of al-Hajj Umar and the *Jawāhir al-Ma'ānī* of 'Alī Ḥarāzim, a major Tijani text. Since it is extremely unlikely that one would undertake the reading of these Sufi texts before studying Arabic language and grammar, it seems more probable that the "stages" of *firugol* and *funūn* were undertaken concurrently and were in some fashion intermingled. The distinction between them was not level of study but linguistic emphasis: *firugol* was aimed at training students to become literate in Fulfulde, whereas *funūn* was advanced studies in Arabic. Marty comments on the Fulbe attitude to their own language:

The study of the *kabbe* is accompanied by *tafsīr*, or exegesis and interpretation of the text of the Qur'an. For a long time the Fulbe have asserted that their language was a holy language, coming it is true after Arabic, but preceding many of the idioms of the peoples, more often fetishists than Muslim, who surrounded them. One knows that the Qur'an can conserve its sacred character only by maintaining its Arabic form. Translation would modify its sense and composition . . . Nonetheless, for some time the Qur'an has been daily translated into Fulfulde, either orally or in writing. Several versions, remarkable for their precision and their elegance, circulate even today among the *karamoko* [teachers] of Futa. It is with the aid of these translations and interpretations that the Fulbe give their students training perhaps less based on memory and more intelligent and more analytical than what one finds in other black countries.[40]

We know from local sources that religious instruction was given in Fulfulde at least in part for strict pedagogical reasons; Fulbe scholars in Futa Jallon believed that students would be better able to learn and understand religious concepts in their mother tongue.[41] And high value was placed on literary competence in Fulfulde; the course in *firugol* concluded with a public examination during which the student was expected to translate and comment on a verse of the Qur'an in Fulfulde.

Marty, then, saw the *kabbe* as a respectable part of the religious studies curriculum taught in Fulfulde. Certainly in the context here described, it was but one small part of a very broad course of study. His description suggests that the *kabbe* taught in this manner might have avoided any sectarian tendencies, which only flourished where it was the sole form of instruction, as among the Jelgoobe pastoralists. At the same time, Marty played down the mystical and numerological aspects of the *kabbe* which were certainly present in Futa Jallon. These can be better discussed in connection with the *mā 'd-dīn* of Cerno Bokar, to which we now turn.

## *The mā 'd-dīn*

This lengthy examination of the history of the *kabbe* was precipitated by our discussion of Cerno Bokar's relationship with one of his most influential teachers, Amadu Tafsiir Ba. As already mentioned, we cannot prove conclusively that Cerno Bokar had learned the *kabbe* itself, but all the circumstantial evidence suggests that he was familiar with this particular tradition. There is certainly a likelihood that he learned it from Amadu Tafsiir, since it was he who is said to have initiated Cerno into the secrets of Sufism. But many other opportunities also existed to learn of the *kabbe*. The French discovered it being taught very near to Bandiagara, in Thioy, Barani, and Ouankore. These villages are all located in the alluvial plain below the Bandiagara cliffs, not far from Louta, the residence of the Cam family where Cerno Bokar lived for a brief period around the turn of the century. If he did not learn of the *kabbe* from Amadu Tafsiir, he would have been able to do so in Louta.

The most convincing proof of Cerno Bokar's knowledge of the *kabbe* tradition is his own theological teaching, known as the *mā 'd-dīn*, Arabic for "What is religion?" The *mā 'd-dīn* was the second part of an introductory Islamic catechism composed by Cerno Bokar and taught orally to students in his own school as well as to adults, especially those who could not read and write Arabic. Quite a number of women as well as older men sought this instruction,[42] which must have been very welcome to many Muslims in Bandiagara who had neither the time, inclination nor ability to learn Arabic but who wished to improve their knowledge of Islam. This teaching was therefore a significant contribution to the continuing task of all Muslims to protect and extend their religion. The *mā 'd-dīn* was not, strictly, a version of the *kabbe*, but the two teachings have so many characteristics in common that one must conclude that there was some relationship between them. Both were introductory teachings in *tawḥīd* taught orally in Fulfulde; both were initiatory by nature, leading from a basic to an esoteric teaching based on numerology. The text of Cerno Bokar's catechism was his own, as apparently were the mnemonic patterns of lines and dots which he designed to be traced in the sand in order to aid his students in remembering the texts. The concepts themselves were those of Islamic dogma and Sufi doctrine.

However, important as this teaching among Muslims might have been, local Bandiagara accounts refer to a different motivation for its introduction: the proselytization of Islam among the Dogon. The introductory section of Cerno's catechism is developed around a story about the instruction of a Dogon convert in certain fundamental Islamic principles. This narrative asserts that Cerno Bokar invented this teaching specifically in order to instruct the new convert, so that whatever was the actual pattern of learning the catechism in Bandiagara, whether among young students or illiterate adult Muslims, in the minds of many people it was a teaching connected with the proselytization of Islam. The following version of this story was collated from two interviews in Bandiagara.[43]

A Dogon became aware that the fetishes of his religion varied one from another. The fetishes which were placed between two villages and those in each compound were different from each other. Even those of his mother and his father were not the same. He could not understand this. He then investigated Islam. He asked someone to write the *fātiḥa* [the first *sūra* of the Qur'an] for him. He then erased it and went to another teacher and asked him to write the *fātiḥa*. He did so and what had been erased reappeared. The Dogon found that it was the same. He erased it again and went to another person, one who had recently become a Muslim, and asked him to write the *fātiḥa*. As he began to write, the same *fātiḥa* appeared. "This is the truth," exclaimed the Dogon, "not the fetishes." He decided to search for a teacher who could help him to understand this religion. Someone advised him, "If you are seeking religion, go to Sisse in Bandiagara; his only concern is the religion of Allah."

Now it happened that this teacher had recently taken a new wife, a woman who had been given to him. [Women were often given in marriage to religious teachers as a pious gesture.] Just before the Dogon arrived, Sisse had asked his new wife, Hannatu, what she understood about her religion. She became upset and retorted, "Are you saying that my mother and father are unbelievers?" Sisse was unable to calm Hannatu's agitation before the arrival of the Dogon, who announced himself by saying "*as-salām 'alaikum*," peace be with you [a Muslim greeting]. Hannatu was silenced when she heard these words!

The Dogon said, "I am searching for my religion; I was told to come to Sisse whose only concern is helping one to understand." He said he had never prostrated himself before God, not even once; nor could he read. Sisse told him that if he was persistent he could accomplish something; his intelligence would aid him. He told the Dogon to bring some sand, which he smoothed out on the earth between them. But he realized the Dogon could not grasp the Arabic letters he traced in the sand. Sisse pondered about what he might do, how he might teach him something of *tawḥīd*. Sisse remembered an Arabic proverb he had heard: "Don't tell your Bambara slave to take down the *shahāda* in writing; it is with his tongue that he will learn it." So Sisse decided he might teach by making points in the sand, the pattern of which the Dogon would not forget. He explained everything without writing and the Dogon understood.

This fascinating account can be analysed from several perspectives. To what extent are its assertions literally true? What is the nature of the thinking which underlies this particular presentation of events? And what light does this account throw on Cerno Bokar himself? As we have said, this story appears in Cerno Bokar's oral catechism as part of the introductory section to the theological teaching itself. Most informants consulted believe that the Sisse in this story is Cerno himself and that the Dogon was a man who became his close friend, Ancamba Nandigi. Whether Cerno actually composed his teaching, along with its innovative mnemonic pattern of lines and dots, specifically in order to instruct Ancamba is not clear. But the fact that the origin of this teaching is placed in the context of teaching to converts is important. During this period the Dogon were converting to Islam in growing numbers, and Cerno seems to have exercised considerable influence among them. But even if Cerno had been motivated to produce his catechism by the need to teach new converts, this account is somewhat misleading in suggesting that the idea came to him from a rather derogatory proverb about teaching Bambara slaves. Similar to the traditions about the *kabbe*, no suggestion is made that the catechism might have been based on an old and established form of religious teaching, which it most certainly was.

The basic theme of this story is not, however, the invention of the teaching; it is how the proper use of the intellect leads to true religion. The Dogon, through his own observation, reaches a conclusion about the "truth" of Islam; Sisse subsequently tells him that "his intelligence would aid him" in understanding his religion. Indeed, Sisse's "*only* concern is helping one to understand." This emphasis on the importance of the intellect in leading one toward Islam recalls the significance which al-Sanūsī placed on it in the study of *tawḥīd*. Here the intellectual theme is directed toward the issue of conversion, providing an Islamic view of why and how people are drawn to their religion. Perhaps it would be more appropriate to say that this is Cerno Bokar's view. What we know of him from informants and from his own discourses suggests a man who was constantly in search of a deeper understanding of Islam through his own observations and personal meditations; and he encouraged those around him to pursue a similar search. One of his disciples recalls that Cerno counselled that everyone must "understand his religion. . . . How can one follow what one does not understand? . . . Through understanding one is able to follow one's religion with integrity."[44] And what is reported about Ancamba Nandigi by Bandiagara informants suggests that a close relationship developed between him and Cerno because they shared a deep intellectual curiosity:

> [Ancamba] possessed a profound knowledge of medicinal plants. From the time he met Cerno Bokar the two of them began to cure people together, Cerno from the Arabic perspective, and Ancamba from the Dogon perspective, with his knowledge of plants. They joined the two approaches to cure quite a few illnesses. In the end this Dogon converted completely and he even gave Cerno Bokar his oldest son [for religious schooling].[45]

According to Hampaté Bâ, the informant who provided this account was himself cured of leprosy by Ancamba Nandigi![46] Hampaté Bâ was also able to elaborate on this medical collaboration:

> Whenever Ancamba brought a plant, Cerno would search for its analogous Qur'anic verse. It was a kind of medicine at once physical and mental. Ancamba was incredible! And of course it was because of this that he became a Muslim; he had surpassed the ordinary level of things. He was constantly in contact with plants, constantly in contact with nature . . . constantly busy searching, meditating, examining. He would follow the animals [to observe them] in their different activities. Because African healers, in addition to the fundamental instructions they received, augment their knowledge by their personal observations."[47]

Ancamba Nandigi became one of Cerno Bokar's closest companions and was one of the few people with him when he died. Certainly we would like to know much more about their relationship and collaboration. But even the information we have offers some insight into the nature of Cerno Bokar's active mind and creative involvement with the world around him. His approach to knowledge was not based on concepts of the exclusivity of Islam, even if he accepted it as being the "true religion," but on a desire to understand the lessons to be found in the diversity of God's creation. Properly understood everything that existed, and every event could offer to man a religious lesson. Cerno's discourses reveal the extent to which he developed this ability. His relationship with Ancamba Nandigi shows how this same attitude could encourage him to seek Muslim analogies for the non-Muslim cures of Dogon healers. No doubt this attitude accounts in part for Cerno's popularity among the Dogon as well as among other Muslims.

Let us now turn to the text of the catechism itself; it consists of three parts.[48] The first, called the Primordial Pact, is presented as a closely argued appeal to devote oneself to religion. Its premises are taken from the Qur'an and the *sunna*, and its argument is that man has been endowed by God with a precious possession, the power of reason or intellect (Arabic: *'aql*) which if properly employed can aid him to find his salvation. The specific advice given to one who has decided to tread the religious path is rather minimal: to learn eleven short *suwar* of the Qur'an, "to learn the concepts of theology [*tawḥīd*], which is none other than the esoteric meaning of the *shahāda*; this knowledge is indispensable and is largely sufficient;" to learn prescriptions of purification, and to become initiated into Sufism: "this initiation will cause you to know the true face of our Lord Muhammad." These brief prescriptions are highly reminiscent of the *kabbe*; they represent the basic essentials of Muslim practice centered upon a knowledge of *tawḥīd* and culminating in a Sufi initiation. The primary emphasis is on the use of one's intellect for gaining an initial understanding of religion.

The second section of the teaching is that called *mā 'd-dīn*, deriving its title from the first question of this religious catchism: "What is religion?" It is the heart of the teaching in which are described the basic tenets of Islam as well as the attributes of God and of the Prophets. The logical proofs of these attributes are not elaborated here as in the *kabbe*, but Cerno Bokar's debt to al-Sanūsī and to the *kabbe* is clearly indicated in his assertion that these attributes constitute the "hidden teaching" of the *shahāda*: "There is no god but God, and Muhammad is the Messenger of God." And like al-Sanūsī, who recommended that every "intelligent person" should recite the *shahāda* often, Cerno said:

> . . . the spoken recitation of the first formula of faith is . . . considered the best mental devotion one can perform in order to please God, whose primordial attri-

bute is Being-Oneness. . . . This formula exalts the emanations of the creative entity; it establishes the differentiation of the essence and plunges the soul into communion with the source of all existences in God. Being is One. The Creative Entity is endowed with anteriority, with eternity, with plenitude and with originality. Differentiation establishes that life, wisdom, hearing, sight, will, speech, and creation belong to the Being-Oneness. Meditate on the following verse:

> He is the First and the Last, and the Outward and the Inward; and He is the Knower of all things. (LVII, 3)[49]

The third part of Cerno's teaching (called "synthesis of the esoteric teaching") was an initiation into an esoteric body of knowledge. As presented by Hampaté Bâ[50] this was a Sufi initiation concerned with an understanding of Sufism in general and of the Tijaniyya order in particular. These aspects of the initiation were undoubtedly important to Cerno Bokar, and we will discuss them in the following chapter. Here we will examine another aspect of this initiation which seems to have been an essential part of the *kabbe* tradition: numerological analysis. Another quotation from Paul Marty on the *kabbe* provides an excellent introduction to this discussion. Marty was greatly disconcerted by the numerological aspects of the *kabbe*, and in fact he quoted the following passage in order to debunk them. No doubt he would have been able to cite numerous half-educated marabouts who employed numerology to mystify their less learned fellow-Muslims. But many scholars attached a profound significance to the study of numbers, which were seen as a medium for understanding the relationship between the inner and outer meanings and manifestations of the created world.

> God has revealed 104 books to man, but 100 are unknown to us at the present time. The four which we possess are: the Pentateuch of Moses, the Psalms of David, the Gospel of Jesus, and the Qur'an of Muhammad. Moreover, the doctrines of the 104 revealed books are condensed into these last four. The last four are contained and summarized in the Qur'an.
>
> The Qur'an is entirely contained in the *Fātiḥa*, which is its first chapter. The *Fātiḥa* is entirely contained in its opening formula, "In the name of Allah, the Merciful and Compassionate." This formula is condensed into the name, Allah.[51] The numerical value of the letters which compose the name Allah [in Arabic] is 66 (*alif*: 1; *lām*: 30; *lām*: 30; *hā'*: 5). This number 66 is a sacred number which contains all the attributes of God (50) and of the Prophet (16). The divine attributes number 25 positive [i.e., necessary] namely: existence, eternity, immutability, etc., and 25 negative [i.e., impossible] namely: non-existence, contingency, changeability, etc. There are 16 similar prophetic attributes. Immediately after the Qur'an, children assimilate these teachings which are considered an introduction to the *kabbe* and which are absolutely necessary, say the teachers, in order to know how to conduct oneself in life.[52]

This passage is significant for several reasons. The first section of the quotation appears in a sightly different form in *The Peerless Method* of Muhammad al-Wālī b. Sulaimān, thus establishing a link between the seventeenth- and nineteenth-century versions of this teaching in *tawḥīd*. However, the more recent version of the *kabbe* is not identical to the seventeenth-century one. Muhammad al-Wālī, closely following al-Sanūsī, lists forty attributes of God (twenty necessary and twenty impossible) and six for the prophets (three necessary and three impossible). Whereas here we have a total of fifty attributes of God and sixteen of the prophets, totalling sixty-six, the numerical equivalent of the name Allah. Somewhere along the line of its transmission, al-Sanūsī's list of attributes was expanded into a total of sixty-six, thus conforming to a numerological analysis of God's name. Cerno Bokar's *mā 'd-dīn* is organized in the same manner; indeed, it is more complex. The total number of points in the *mā 'd-dīn* (excepting points $A^{7-19}$ and $A^1$, $B^1$ and $C^1$) is ninety-nine, corresponding to the ninety-nine names of God. These are subdivided into thirty-three points of religious doctrine plus fifty attributes of God and sixteen attributes of the prophets.

This kind of numerological manipulation derived from well established Islamic concepts. Seyyed Hossein Nasr in his *Introduction to Islamic Cosmological Doctrines* claims that in Islam the idea of unity or *tawḥīd* overshadows all others "and remains at every level of Islamic civilization the most basic principle upon which all else depends." The goal of all Islamic sciences and methods, he claims, was "the demonstration of the interrelatedness of all things."[53] In his discussion of the *Ikhwān al-Ṣafā*, the tenth-century Islamic encyclopaedists, Nasr describes this "interrelatedness of all things" as a chain of being connecting God with all creation:

> The chain of being essentially means that all beings in the Universe exist according to a continuous hierarchy which is ontological as well as cosmological. A particular entity has a position in the great chain of being depending upon the degree to which it participates in Being and Intelligence; or one might say, upon the degree to which it possesses the perfections and virtues which in the absolute sense belong only to Pure Being, or God, who is transcendent with respect to the chain. [. . .] Everything exists for a purpose, the final purpose of the cosmos being the return of multiplicity to Unity within the heart of the saints.[54]

Similar cosmological ideas had of course been assimilated by West African scholars, as the quotation from Marty indicates. That brief passage desribes a hierarchy of the revealed word of God; moving "upward" (or inward) through this hierarchy there are the 104 books revealed to mankind, the four books of the so-called world religions, the Qur'an, the *Fātiḥa* (the first *sūra* of the Qur'an), the phrase "In the name of Allah," and finally the name Allah itself. Each successively higher level brings one closer to what might be called the pure word of

God, His name, Allah. Viewed from the opposite perspective, i.e. in its "downward" (or outward) movement, the name Allah is seen as the creative source of the revealed word of God in all its various manifestations. This concept should not be unfamiliar to Christians; the Gospel of St John begins: "In the beginning was the Word." This hierarchy of the revealed word of God, then, is an expression of the chain of being described by Nasr. But it also asserts an analogical relationship between the hierarchical order of the revealed word and the hierarchical order of all creation, which was believed to proceed from God through different levels of spiritual reality to visible, manifested creation.

What interests us here is not so much the various hierarchies in the chain of being, but the principle of analogical analysis which was employed in their study. The methodology of analogical analysis and demonstration was a logical derivation of the Muslim hierarchical vision of the cosmos: all existence is interrelated because it shares a common source in God, the Creator. Similarly, the principles which govern, for example, the observable forces of nature are related to the principles which govern the unobservable reaches of the cosmos. By studying what is observable and by employing the principles of analogy one can gain greater understanding of what is not observable. During the classical period of Islamic scholarship almost all the natural sciences were studied from this perspective, but the one discipline which seems to have gained and retained prominence among Muslim scholars in West Africa was numerology, because of its fundamental importance to all the other sciences. Its numerological applications were derived in part from Pythagorean mathematics, according to which numbers not only represent quantity but possess qualities as well. We can discern these aspects of numerology in the following quotation from Hampaté Bâ, in which he describes the number one as being analogous to God:

> It is the source; all numbers come from 1, but the 1 does not come from any other number. It is the symbol of supreme purity. It does not accept multiplication, $1 \times 1 = 1$. God does not emerge from His secrecy except through revelation, that is, addition. Thus, $1 + 1 = 2$, $1 + 2 = 3$, $1 + 3 = 4$, and so on up to 9, and on to infinity.[55]

The number 9, on the other hand, represents imperfectible materiality because it cannot change. No matter what number is multiplied by 9, if one adds the digits of the resultant number they will always equal 9.[56] For example, $9 \times 542 = 4878$; $4 + 8 + 7 + 8 = 27$; $2 + 7 = 9$. Hampaté Bâ's comments were offered to me in illustration of the numerological concepts taught in the *kabbe*, but they conform closely to the views of the *Ikhwān al-Ṣafā*,

> Know, brother, that the Creator, most exalted, created as the first thing from His Light of Unity the simple substance called the Active Intellect, as 2 is

generated from one by repetition. Then the Universal Soul was generated from the Light of the Intellect as 3 is generated by adding unity to 2. Then . . . [matter] was generated by the motion of the soul as 4 is generated by adding Unity to 3. Then the other creatures were generated from . . . [matter] and their being brought to order by the Intellect and the Soul as other numbers are generated from 4 added to what went before it.[57]

Following the same principles of analogy, many Muslims placed great emphasis upon the symbolism of letters, especially those placed at the beginning of certain *suwar* of the Qur'ān.[58] Numerology became associated with this study because each letter in the Arabic alphabet was said to have a numerical equivalent. Consequently, words could be transposed into numbers and analyzed for analogical and allegorical meaning through the application of numerological methods. A brief example follows. The Qur'anic verse, "Say, He is God" (*Qul huwa Allāh*, CXII, 1) can be translated into a numerical formula: say, 11 is 66. We have seen above that the numerical equivalent of Allah is 66. *Huwa* equals 11 because *hā'* is 5 and *wāw* is 6. But how could this statement be true? A numerological manipulation in which the progressive digits from 1 to 11 are added together claims to prove it: $1 + 2 + 3 + 4 + 5 + 6 + 7 + 8 + 9 + 10 + 11 = 66$.[59]

These few examples give some indication of numerological practice; the possibilities are endless. Of course, certain applications of numerology were considered illegal by scholarly Muslims, and all of it was seen as superstitious by unsympathetic European observers. But despite the abuses to which this science may have been subjected, we should now be able to understand why it assumed a central role in West African scholarship. Numerological as well as other forms of analogical analysis were effective tools in teaching and demonstrating certain relationships and concepts contained within the doctrines of *tawḥīd*. Another important factor, which should not be overlooked, was that mastery of the principles of analogy offered a scholar the possibility of independent intellectual enquiry which was not usually acceptable in the religious sciences of the day. No West African scholar was going to set out to develop a "new" Islamic theology; the question probably never arose. The task to which creative thought *could* be applied was in the understanding of how one could better transmit the received theology so that Muslims could truly comprehend it and incorporate it into their lives.

Cerno Bokar's *mā 'd-dīn* was a teaching with these same aims of transmission. Like the *kabbe*, the *mā 'd-dīn* provided a student with a basic understanding of Muslim theology and, through its initiation, with the methodological tools which could enable him to continue his personal religious search throughout his life. The study of *tawḥīd* is a study without end, because no one can ever fully understand the

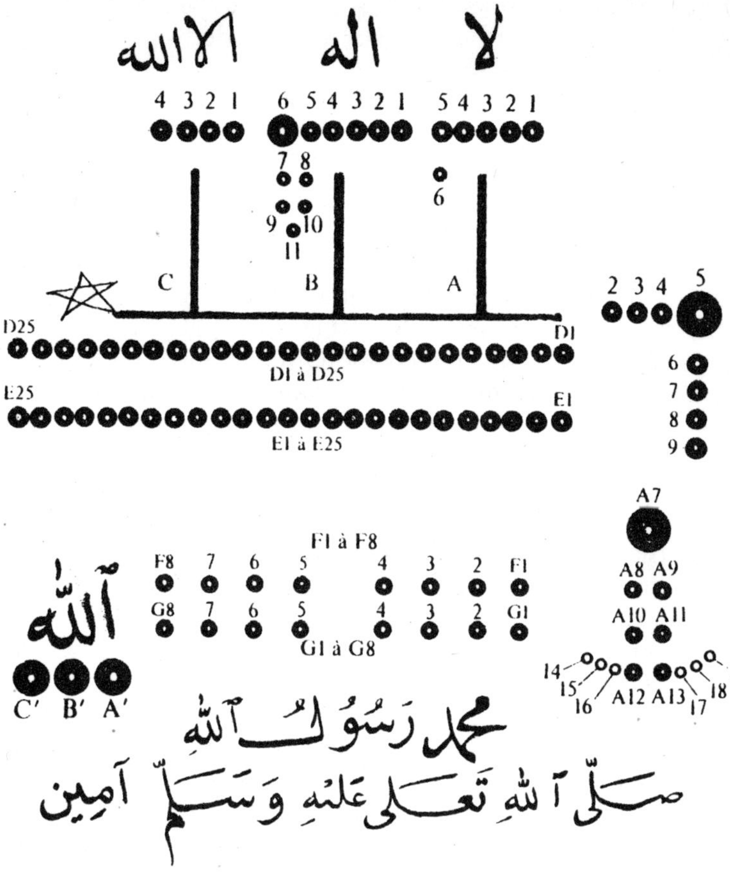


The *mā 'd-dīn*.

relationships which exist between the multiplicity of manifested existence and the unity of God. Initiates were apparently free to modify the format of the teaching based upon their personal understanding, their meditations and their numerological calculations. This is presumably what Cerno Bokar did when he composed his *mā 'd-dīn*, to which we now return in order to illustrate some of its numerological and analogical dimensions. (The following paragraphs should be read with reference to the table above.) Cerno's catechism is presented as a conversation between Sisse, the marabout, and Ancamba, the new convert; the *mā 'd-dīn* therefore proceeds as a series of questions and answers. The first point is actually number 9: Ancamba asks, "What is religion?" and Sisse answers, "Religion is a way or a road." The points then continue:

8 How many ways have there been? There have been seventy-three.

7 What is their condition? The first seventy-two are ways of error.
6 Only the seventy-third is the path of rectitude.
5 The unique attaining to God.
4 From our father Adam until our Lord Muhammad all have followed the same path.
3 It is called *Islām*.
2 It is the path of deliverance.
1 It is the way of salvation, the Hanifiyya way.[60]

It is not without significance that this entry into theological discussion moves from point 9 to point 1, from a number representing extreme materiality to one representing the unity and spirtuality of God. At the same time, these nine numbers form the basis of all numerological calculations and are consequently the fundamental elements to be employed in any subsequent esoteric study of theology. The vertical lines A, B, C, are the three basic pillars of the Hanifiyya way: *Islām*, submission to God, *Īmān*, faith, and *Iḥsān*, comportment in the sense of upright behavior. Each of these pillars is elaborated in a number of conditions or requirements. The points under D and E represent the attributes of God; F and G represent the attributes of the prophets. All these points were of course explained in detail; they constituted the elementary teaching of the *mā 'd-dīn*.

The three points in the lower left of the diagram (A', B', C') are the beginning of the Sufi teaching which introduces the student to an esoteric understanding of Islam. They are: *sharī'a*, the Law, *ṭarīqa*, the Sufi way, and *ḥaqīqa*, the Truth. These concepts are an expression of the Sufi hierarchy of religious experience. In the strictest dogmatic sense Islam demands nothing more of its adherents than outward conformity to the *sharī'a*; no Muslim need do more to achieve salvation. The religious experience of most Muslims, according to Cerno Bokar, would fall into this category. These are the Muslims "attached to the letter." However, more is possible, and some Muslims — a minority — enter the Sufi way. Entry to the Sufi way is allowed only to those who have demonstrated their comprehension of and conformity to the law. If the religion of the law can be said to be directed outwardly, the religion of the Sufi way is directed inwardly: one learns esoteric interpretations of Islamic principles and one strives to apply these principles to one's inner life. The experience of *ḥaqīqa*, the Truth, was reserved to very few indeed, "an élite within the élite" according to Cerno Bokar. They were the saints of Islam who "adore God in truth." Cerno Bokar said very little about this level of attainment; he did not consider himself to have achieved it.[61]

Both the *kabbe* and the *mā 'd-dīn* were taught in a manner which conforms to this Sufi view of Islam. In its elementary form it was taught to children in the early stages of their educational formation or to

Muslim converts or to illiterate Muslim adults. The esoteric interpretations and numerological manipulations were taught only to specially selected individuals, presumably those who showed promise in terms of both religious devotion and intellectual acumen. These persons were called "initiates;" not only could they initiate others, but they were also free to adapt their teaching as they saw fit, always of course protecting the received theology itself from change. The principles of analogical reasoning offered a creative mind almost unlimited possibilities to enrich and embellish this teaching. Cerno Bokar was a master at finding the analogical religious significance of almost every object or event which came to his attention. He may have been exceptional in this regard, but the point is that the form and structure of this teaching enabled and even encouraged marabouts to activate their minds in just this way and consequently to enliven their religious teachings. But most important of all, initiation offered an individual the wherewithal to continue his mystical journey to its highest reaches, to the perception of ultimate Reality.

Cerno must have received this sort of initiation from Amadu Tafsiir, or from someone else, because he subsequently initiated seven other persons into the esoteric sciences of analogical and numerological analysis.[62] Unfortunately we know nothing about how he selected these persons nor about the precise procedures of initiation. It should be noted, however, that this initiation, although it included material about Tijani Sufism, was accomplished outside the established Tijani hierarchy itself. The Tijani hierarchy of *muqaddamūn*, or spiritual guides, will be described in the next chapter, but here we should briefly point out that the authorizations or "initiations" which they transmitted within the Tijaniyya order itself were a separate line of transmission to the one here under discussion. Amadu Tafsiir was a Tijani *muqaddam*, but he was not Cerno's *muqaddam*. For Cerno, other than being one of his academic teachers, he was probably an initiator into the *kabbe* tradition described here. Cerno Bokar himself became a Tijani *muqaddam*, and as such he appointed four other *muqaddamūn*; but none of these four figure among the seven persons whom he initiated into this esoteric body of numerological knowledge. This apparently curious separation of roles may simply reflect an attitude among Muslims that the *kabbe* and Tijani Sufism represented two separate, although related, traditions. Cerno Bokar participated in each tradition, although in somewhat different capacities. Indeed, considerable understanding of Cerno Bokar can be derived from an analysis of the various roles he performed in Bandiagara as teacher, initiator, and Tijani *muqaddam*. The site of all his activities was his compound; a description of what went on there may aid us in discerning the relationships between the various aspects of the man.

## *The teacher and his school*

Cerno Bokar began teaching in about 1908, apparently after considerable hesitation.[63] We do not know the reasons for his uncertainty; perhaps he was struggling with the implications of his mother's advice that one must first be capable of caring for oneself before presuming to care for another. Perhaps he was considering the pursuit of a metier other than teaching. Some years earlier, he had spent about a year in Bobo Dioulasso (Upper Volta) working as a tailor and embroiderer,[64] at which he was particularly skilled. In any case, by about 1908 he was teaching Qur'anic studies to a few young children in his compound. The school grew slowly over the years and by the early 1930s was a flourishing institution offering instruction in the full breadth of the Muslim curriculum. Estimates of the numbers of students in attendance are widely divergent. Hampaté Bâ states that at the height of its activities in the mid 1930s the school boasted almost 200.[65] This number seems exaggerated, but we do not know what categories of "student" might be included in it. On the other hand, French official estimates were always very low, and we do not know how they were obtained. Three archival references to Cerno Bokar's school appear during the period 1921–4 estimating between fourteen and seventeen students in attendance.[66] There are no references for the 1930s until the Hamalliyya crisis when no figures were given. If we consider as "students" all those persons who looked to Cerno Bokar as a "teacher," in the broadest sense of these terms, then something like Hampaté Bâ's estimate is probably more accurate.

The activities of Cerno Bokar's compound were somewhat broader than what a Western reader might understand by the term "school." Instruction was offered in all levels of study from introductory Qur'an to advanced Sufi studies. Cerno directed the advanced studies himself, while elementary work was delegated to a younger man, Momadu Taalel, a relative whom Cerno raised as a kind of adoptive son. They were the only two instructors. The teaching schedule itself was organised into specific "class" times for morning and evening instruction with time off from Wednesday to Friday afternoons. However, the goals of any actual course of study tended to be dependent upon the interests and motivations of the individual student, and for the youngsters, upon the demands of his or her family. Certain benchmarks of accomplishment were formally recognised, such as the memorizing of a section of the Qur'an, or the completion of a particular book, but these were of course individual achievements. One did not proceed even through the early years of school by grade or class. The "student body" tended to be fluid, with individuals entering and leaving the school at different times of the year. This high turnover occurred without much impact on the continuity of study since the nature of the instruction was largely tutorial.

The activities of the school went far beyond the formal teaching of Muslim studies. Like most traditional West African religious schools, Cerno's students paid only minimal fees, if they paid any at all. However, they compensated their teacher by working for him. They collected firewood, fetched water and performed other household chores; more important, they also farmed his land. During the times of planting and harvesting, instruction was given in temporary shelters adjacent to the fields. These activities, especially the farming, not only fed Cerno and his family, but also provided the economic wherewithal to maintain the school. A number of students actually lived in the compound; these were often, but not always, students from outside Bandiagara and were almost completely dependent upon their teacher for their food. Cerno also had to be prepared to offer hospitality to visiting scholars or to others who might come to Bandiagara seeking his counsel. These callers would invariably bring gifts and thereby also contribute to the economic wellbeing of the school.

The child or young adult in school was therefore not isolated from the daily demands of life; students participated in household and other work much as they would do in their own homes. In many ways the teacher became a kind of substitute parent; the student was expected to be completely obedient to him, and the extent of dependence of a student upon a teacher was often extreme, particularly in the case of the student coming on his own from another town or village, who would often arrive with nothing more than the clothes on his back; nor would he even have the assurance that he would be accepted as a student. Once accepted he would be expected not only to work for his teacher but to treat him with extreme deference and respect. This state of dependence, although occasionally exploited by teachers, was an essential element in the educational formation of children in Muslim schools. It emerged not only from the traditional relationships which prevailed between parent and child, but was reinforced by religious teachings on humility. One was expected to learn how to be humble toward God from being humble towards one's parents, one's teachers and one's elders in general. It was in the relationship between the Sufi *shaykh* and his disciple that these rules of deference were most clearly articulated, but they were reflected in the rules of behaviour for students and children in general.

If the daily demands of life were not eliminated from school, a distinct separation nonetheless existed between the activities inside and outside the confines of Cerno Bokar's compound. This difference resided not only in the nature of the activities themselves, but in the approach and attitude taken toward them. Cerno often alluded to this difference in his discourses, in which he called his compound a *zāwiya*, or Sufi study center. He also referred to it as a "sanctuary of love and charity,"[67] as a place to which one comes "hoping to find the tranquility which is lacking in one's heart,"[68] and as a centre "for the praising of God."[69] Although only Sufi disciples would have been expected to approach Cerno's compound with some understanding of what was implied in these allusions, every person attending the school of no matter what age was unquestionably affected by the commanding presence of the teacher from whom these kinds of statements proceeded. The young children may have had little direct contact with Cerno; the older students of "books" may have been deeply engaged in their studies, but none of them could have completely escaped the influence of the humble search for religious understanding in which their teacher engaged because it pervaded every aspect of activity in the compound.

Cerno's primary concern was to influence those around him, whether student, disciple, relative or acquaintance, toward undertaking the spiritual search to which he himself had been called. He was not heavy handed or insistent over this, but nor did he miss any opportunity to confront people with their own attitudes and actions. The following story illustrates his exceptional ability at seizing upon chance events to bring fundamental questions to the attention of his students. One day Cerno was speaking to a group of advanced students when a baby sparrow fell from its nest. No one moved to the aid of the squealing bird; for one thing it would have been highly disrespectful to interrupt the teacher. However, after a time Cerno Bokar halted his presentation and called for the bird to be brought to him. Concluding that it was not injured, he climbed up on a stool to inspect the nest and discovered it had become dislodged. He secured the nest, returned the bird to it and, resuming his place, said to the group:

> I must speak to you of charity, for I am distressed to see that not one of you is adequately possessed of this true kindness of heart. And such a blessing it is! If you had a charitable heart it would have been impossible for you to continue listening to a lesson when this miserable little creature was crying out to you for help and soliciting your pity. But you were not moved by his despair; your heart did not hear his appeal. In truth my friend, the knowledge of one who commits to memory all the theologies of all the religions will be but worthless baggage if one does not have charity in his heart.[70]

The younger students in Cerno's school would not have been expected to face up to the question raised on this occasion, but undoubtedly they would have heard the story.

In addition to the formal training of students, Cerno received in his compound a wide range of persons who came to him for different purposes: adults who were learning his catechism, those Tijani adepts who looked to him as their *muqaddam*, those who were being initiated into the esoteric sciences, and ordinary inhabitants of Bandiagara seeking advice or support. On Thursdays, when no formal classes were held, a group of scholars and teachers generally gathered in his compound for the reading and discussion of various books, usually the major Tijani texts, which were commented upon by Cerno himself. Rather than lectures, these were discussions, and occasionally rather heated ones.[71] The frequenters of Cerno's compound, then, included a wide range of people from all walks of life, from various ethnic groups and with differing interests. Each of them had a personal relationship to Cerno which derived from their particular orientation, as student to teacher, as Tijani adept to *muqaddam*, as disciple to spiritual guide. But these various categories of people were not strictly segregated from one another even if they did not participate in the same activities. Non-scholars might sit in on a Thursday discussion; younger students might be present during an advanced lesson; informality would have been the order of the day. The only exception to this would have been the initiations and transmission of "secrets" which took place in private. This meant that Cerno Bokar's attitudes and ideas pervaded the atmosphere of the compound and influenced everyone present. Although his discourses may have been directed to more advanced students and to Sufi disciples, they would have been heard by anyone who happened to be present. Their guidance and their encouragement were available to anyone who desired to listen.

## NOTES

1. Baba Thimbely (in an interview of 25–1–1977) quoted the following couplet from a Fulfulde poem about the value of travelling to complete one's studies:

   He who does not work will be poor, he will have difficulties even in finding his dinner.

   He who does not pack his baggage will be prevented [from success] and will only find distress.
2. ANM, Fonds Récent, 1–G–198 (1921), and interviews with Amadou Hampaté Bâ, 2–5–1978, and Koola Sidi, 20–3–1978.
3. TB, 28–30; VE, 33–5.
4. The *Rimāḥ* has been briefly described above, pp. 41–2, and is more fully discussed in Chapter 5. *Jawāhir al-ma'ānī* is a biography of Shaykh al-Tijani which contains extensive material on the doctrine of the order.
5. Interview with Koola Sidi of 20–3–1978: "Omo jannga do Amadu Tafsiiru faa . . . mo reentinii hakkunde hakiikata e sariaata. mo laatii omtaado sanne."

6. Most studies of Sufism would discuss these concepts. Two recent publications by 'Abd al-Qādir as-Sūfī are particularly interesting from this point of view: *Indications from Signs* (Atlanta, 1979); and *The Hundred Steps* (Norwich, 1979).
7. Discourse 36.
8. Discourse 8.
9 TB, 29; VE, 34; interview with Amadou Hampaté Bâ of 2–5–1978.
10. Interview with Amadou Hampaté Bâ, 7–7–1981.
11. "Cerno Bokar was in Niger where his father had left some secrets for him which he had gone to look for." Interview with Amadou Hampaté Bâ, 1–7–1980.
12. Annemarie Schimmel, *Mystical Dimensions of Islam* (Chapel Hill, 1975), 192; see also J.S. Trimingham, *The Sufi Orders in Islam* (Oxford, 1971), 211.
13. Amadou Hampaté Bâ claims that numerology was associated with all forms of Sufism in West Africa, and he does not connect Cerno Bokar's initiation specifically to the *kabbe* tradition. Interview, 7–7–1981.
14. Translated into French by J.O. Luciani (Algiers, 1896). John Hunwick, in a personal communication, suggested that *umm* here implies "the firmest or most convincing" of proofs.
15. *Ibid.*, p. 1 Arabic; p. 5 French.
16. *Ibid.*, p. 10 Arabic; p. 17 French.
17. Muhammad b. Ibrāhīm al-Mallālī, *al-Mawāhib al-qudsiyya fīl-manāqib al-Sanūsiyya*.
18. M.A. Zouber, *Ahmad Bābā de Tombouctou (1556–1627): sa vie et son oeuvre* (Paris, 1977), 103–5, where he summarizes Ahmad Bābā's *al-La'ālī al-sundusiyya fī l-faḍā'il al-Sanūsiyya*.
19. *Sharḥ al-ṣughrā*, *ibid.*, 121–2; no copies of this work are extant.
20. Bibliothèque Générale et Archives, Rabat, D984, fol. 125.
21. Two versions of this text have been consulted in the Bibliothèque Nationale, Paris, Arabe 5541, fols. 130–151, and Arabe 5650, fols. 111–130, the latter being incomplete at the end.
22. BN, Arabe 5541, fol. 135a.
23. *Ibid.*, fols. 131b, 132a; also 145a.
24. *Bahjat al-āfāq wa-īḍāḥ al-labs wa'l-ighlāq fī 'ilm al-ḥurūf wa'l-aufāq*. School of Oriental and African Studies Library, London, MS 65496.
25. *Ibid.*, fol. 11a. See also A.D.H. Bivar and M. Hiskett, "The Arabic literature of Nigeria to 1804: a provisional account," *Bulletin of the School of Oriental and African Studies*, XXV, Part 1 (1962), 135–7.
26. Muhammad Bello, *Infāq al-Maisūr* (London, 1957), 5–6.
27. Recorded by Boubou Hama in Tera *cercle*; neither the date nor the name of the reciter is given with the tape. See B. Hama, *Contribution à la Connaissance de l'histoire des Peul* (Paris, 1968), 330–1. Amadou Hampaté Bâ has collected numerous versions of the *kabbe* in Upper Volta, and has now collated them into a single long version, written in Fulfulde, but I have not been able to consult this work. Several brief versions of the *kabbe* are to be found in the Bibliothèque Nationale, Paris; see Arabe 5671, 79b–80b and Arabe 5684, 185a–186b.

28. A copy of this taped version of the *kabbe* was kindly furnished by Boubou Hama in Niamey. Copied through the kind assistance of Dioulde Laya, Director of CELTHO, Niamey, the text was transcribed and translated with the asistance of Almamy Malik Yattara, Bamako.
29. A. Le Chatelier, *L'Islam dans l'Afrique occidentale* (Pàris, 1899), 287–8.
30. R. Arnaud, "Islam et la politique musulmane française en A.O.F.," *L'Afrique française: Bulletin du Comité de l'Afrique française. Renseignements coloniaux et documents*, 1912, 14–5.
31. In his text Arnaud uses the term Poular, the language of the Futanke of Futa Toro, but I have used Fulfulde here so as not to confuse the general reader; in any case the language in use in Jelgooji was not Poular.
32. Hama, *Contribution*, 330.
33. Amadou Hampaté Bâ, in an interview of 2–5–1978, attributes the origins in Jelgooji to a marabout from Futa Toro; an archival report from the Jelgooji region itself attributes its origins to another outsider, but claims he invented it himself in order to teach the illiterate Fulbe pastoralists: ANS, AOF Série G, 15–G–186, "Islam dans la Résidence de Dori," 31 July 1899.
34. See Arnaud, "Islam et la politique musulmane."
35. This statement by Boubou Hama was confirmed in an interview with Diallo Aboubakar, Niamey, 5–6–1980.
36. Muhammad Bello, *Infāq*, 43. Shaykh Uthman made a similar attack in his *Naṣā'iḥ al-ummat al-Muḥammadiyya*; this reference was given me by John Hunwick.
37. See Arnaud, "Islam et la politique musulmane."
38. P. Marty, *L'Islam en Guinée* (Paris, 1921), 349ff.
39. Marty mentions works by several local scholars including Mouhammadou-Samba Mombeya, for whom see Alpha Ibrahim Sow, ed., *Le Filon du Bonheur Éternel* (Paris, 1971).
40. Marty, *L'Islam en Guinée*, 353–4.
41. Sow, ed., *Le Filon*, 30.
42. Interview with Dauda Maiga, 30–9–1977, and with Baba Thimbely, 1–10–1977.
43. Interviews with Baba Thimbely, 1–10–1977 and 21–1–1978. Published versions can be consulted in TB, 96–7 and VE, 195–8. The story forms part of the first lesson of Cerno Bokar's teaching.
44. Interview with Dauda Maiga, 30–9–1977.
45. *Ibid.*
46. Interview with Amadou Hampaté Bâ, 2–5–1978.
47. *Ibid.*
48. The full text of Cerno Bokar's catechism can be consulted in TB, 96–120, and VE, 195–239.
49. Discourse 5.
50. In both TB and VE, and in interviews.
51. This same passage, with some slight modifications, appears on the first page of *The Peerless Method*.
52. Marty, *L'Islam en Guinée*, 352–3.
53. S.H. Nasr, *An Introduction to Islamic Cosmological Doctrines* (London, 1978), 4.

54. *Ibid.*, 68, 72.
55. Interview with Amadou Hampaté Bâ, 3–5–1978.
56. *Ibid.*
57. Translated from *Rasā'il Ikhwān al-Ṣafā*, I, 28 (Cairo, 1928) in Nasr, *Introduction*, 46, note 12.
58. Schimmel, *Mystical Dimensions*, 411–25.
59. Interview with Amadou Hampaté Bâ, 2–5–1978.
60. See the full text of the *mā 'd-dīn* in Appendix I. Some of my comments are derived from interviews with Amadou Hampaté Bâ.
61. The Sufi way itself was subdivided into three stages or degrees which were themselves analogous to the Law, the Sufi way and the Truth. (Triads abound in this esoteric teaching.) They were *taqlīd*, or behaviour based upon imitation of the Sufi *shaykh*; *naẓar*, or comprehension of the inner meaning of religious principles; and *dhawq*, or the actual subjective experience of these principles. See VE, 226.
62. According to Amadou Hampaté Bâ (3–5–1978) the initiates were Koola Sidi, Samba Fouta, al-Hajj Cambal, Modibbo Karakinde, Ibrahim of Jelgooji, a young Mossi whose name was forgotten, and Hampaté Bâ himself.
63. TB, 30; VE, 36–7.
64. Interview with Koola Sidi, 20–3–1978.
65. VE, 37.
66. ANM, Fonds Récent, 1–G–198, 1921, 22, 24.
67. Discourse 1.
68. Discourse 3.
69. Discourse 4.
70. Monod, "Homme," 154–5; also related in TB, 84–5; VE, 160–1.
71. Interviews with Dauda Maiga, 30–9–1977; Amadou Hampaté Bâ, 2–5–1978.

# 5
# THE SPIRITUAL SEARCH

Sufism (Arabic, *taṣawwuf*) is often descibed as Islamic mysticism, which Cerno Bokar defined as "imparting the knowledge of God to the human spirit."[1] Mysticism, for him, was an interaction between God's revelation and man's efforts to absorb this revelation into his own understanding, an effort which he described as "a lived experience in which the intuition might be activated as a result of a lengthy meditative observation."[2] We explored in the previous chapter one aspect of Cerno's meditations, his search for analogical and numerological relationships between manifested existence and ultimate reality (*ḥaqīqa*). As we noted, this is fundamentally an intellectual discipline, based on the acquisition of certain specific knowledge, in this case the knowledge of *tawḥīd* and the science of numbers. The second and perhaps more central ingredient in Cerno's mysticism was derived from the Tijaniyya Sufi order; this was much more experiential than intellectual and focused on various spiritual exercises, especially the repeated recitation of certain prayers. Cerno's Sufi ideas came primarily from two Tijani books, the *Rimāḥ* of al-Hajj Umar and the *Jawāhir al-Ma 'ānī* of 'Alī Ḥarāzim. Both books are filled with quotations from classical Sufi authors offering a reader a broad selection of generally accepted Sufi ideas, as well as detailed information on Tijani doctrine. Cerno Bokar's discourses as well as the content of his catechism suggest an intellectual and spiritual debt to these two works, which must have been the basic sources of his religious teaching.

West African Sufism was founded upon the complementarity of intellectual and spiritual disciplines. The very first pages of the *Jawāhir al-Ma 'ānī* provided an explicit link between Sufism and the study of *tawḥīd*:

> Know that God Almighty has attributed to all things both an external and an internal or hidden [aspect]. The soul of man has both an external and internal [aspect] because it is included among [created] things. That which man comprehends with the external aspect of his soul is interpreted by it through image, imagination and the senses; these are not comprehended by his inner soul at all. That which is comprehended by the internal aspect of the soul is knowledge which is communicated directly to the internal soul and is distinguished by sound experiences and the secret of gnosis and the secret of *tawḥīd*. . . .
>
> The manifestations of God Almighty through His hidden name to the internal soul bring about perceptions through the eye of discernment and not through thought or theorizing. He who perceives through the eye of discernment is a knower of truths and of hidden meanings. No outward forms remain

with one of what is perceived by the eye of discernment. Nor is there any suffering connected with it; one is relieved from the difficulty of thought. With the arrival of these revelations in his inner soul one masters the divine sciences, and the sciences of the secrets of internal (hidden) meanings and of that which is related to the hereafter, and of direct knowledge of the unity of existence and the denial of anything which might be equated with God. And the secrets of *tawḥīd* and of gnosis appear to him.[3]

This passage is a philosophical elaboration of the major theme in Cerno Bokar's religious thought and practice: the search for a hidden reality which he called "the truth of divine matters," or "the real and eternal beauties."[4] According to this passage, knowledge of what Cerno Bokar called the *ḥaqīqa* could be attained through the direct methods of gnosis, without "thought or theorizing." The suffering which attends the comprehension of lower forms of written knowledge is not a part of gnosis. But the Tijani books are careful to insist that all Sufism is built upon the Qur'an and the *sunna* which are the starting point of all mysticism. "The knowledge of *taṣawwuf* will emerge from the essence of the *sharī'a* only if one probes deeply into the knowledge of the *sharī'a*."[5] According to this view, all Sufis must first "suffer" through the trials of academic religious studies in order to reach the point of beginning mystical training. The *mā 'd-dīn* and the *kabbe* were structured in this way, even if these curricula had reduced the essential academic training to a minimum. Some aspects of Tijani doctrine implied that even this training could be completely eliminated and that mere adherence to this Sufi order was a guarantee for entry into paradise.

This point illustrates one of the more complex aspects of writing about Sufism: the diversity of its interpretation and application. An individual became a Tijani by being authorized by a properly appointed *muqaddam* to recite the special litany (*wird*) of Shaykh al-Tijani. Organizationally the order included people from every social level of the society in which it existed: political leaders, highly trained religious scholars, farmers, merchants, and so forth. These people related in many different ways to the mystical teachings of the order. Theoretically, spiritual development as a Tijani depended upon personal devotion and efforts expended in spiritual exercises. In fact, the leaders of the order in West Africa were almost always either very highly trained scholars or prominent members of the leading political families, or both. And on the few occasions when the theory of spiritual development became a fact despite established social norms, there was trouble. No matter how radical an institution the Tijaniyya may have been under al-Hajj Umar in the mid-nineteenth century, by the early twentieth its leaders were generally conservative, seeking to protect their social and political positions. By comparison, Cerno Bokar's attitude was relatively radical in that he clung tenaciously to the gnostic goals which he understood to be at the heart of the Tijaniyya. Politically, and even socially, he refused to act out the role of a prominent Futanke which others expected of him.

Although Sufi organisations were profoundly affected by their social milieu, mysticism as a discipline is extremely personal. The structure of the order, as well as the transmission of its teachings and the training of acolytes, was articulated through a network of personal relationships. And status within the hierarchy shifted through a combination of appointments by superiors and of personal mystical experiences, such as visions and dreams, which were themselves understood as indications of one's spiritual development. The entire structure was extremely fluid, and in the end there were no external standards by which objectively to judge the spiritual status of any individual within it; the acolytes themselves decided to whom they would attach themselves on the basis of their own personal judgment of the merits of any particular leader.

Tijani doctrine was highly controversial during the era of its expansion in West Africa which resulted in heated disputes with non-Tijanis. By the early twentieth century these particular disagreements had faded in significance, although many studies of the Tijaniyya have focused on these doctrinal issues in a way which overemphasized their importance in the overall history of the order.[6] There has also been a tendency among scholars to look at the spread of the Tijaniyya as a military movement under al-Hajj Umar.[7] These views of the Tijaniyya are justifiable: the order did spread in West Africa in its early years due to a *jihād*; and the doctrinal disputes were real and significant. But the essence of the Tijaniyya was devotional and mystical. If Cerno Bokar had never read any Sufi book other than the *Rimāḥ* and the *Jawāhir al-Ma'ānī* he would have had ample material to justify and even direct his own mystical inclinations; these works are filled with profound observations and commentaries about the Sufi quest. The contentious doctrines of Shaykh al-Tijani were also there, but Cerno Bokar never had to defend these in his lifetime. Nor did he have to fight a *jihād*; indeed, he spoke firmly against such undertakings.[8] Even this point of view could be justified by what al-Hajj Umar wrote in the *Rimāḥ* about the "greater *jihād*" against one's own moral shortcomings as opposed to the "lesser *jihād*" of the sword against the unbelievers.[9] The emergence of a contemplative mystic like Cerno Bokar from within the Tijaniyya should therefore not be at all surprising. He may appear to be unique in West Africa not because there were not others like him, but because few studies of African Sufism have been made from this particular perspective.

## *Cerno Bokar as muqaddam*

In keeping with the pattern common among Tijanis, Cerno Bokar was appointed and re-appointed *muqaddam* many times. The informal, private ceremony of appointment is in fact one of authorization. According to Tijani doctrine, none of their prayers is to be recited without proper permission, and a *muqaddam* is a person who has been designated to grant these permissions; some senior *muqaddamūn* are also authorized to appoint other *muqaddamūn*. Cerno Bokar may well have originally received the *wird* as a child while still in Segu.[10] Hampaté Bâ claims he was even appointed a *muqaddam* as a child,[11] not in the sense of possessing full authorization to transmit the *wird* but so that he would be constantly trained and oriented toward the role which he would eventually play as an adult. We cannot confirm this practice among West African Tijanis, but Shaykh Ahmad al-Tijani seems to have treated his own sons in this way, naming them as future spiritual leaders when they were still young.

Cerno's early appointments as an adult were made by *muqaddamūn* outside the Taal family. The first of them came through the spiritual line of al-Hajj Salmoye of Jenne,[12] a Marka who had performed the pilgrimage to Mecca several times and who had received his own appointment as *muqaddam* in Fez. During the later nineteenth century he was responsible for spreading the Tijaniyya in Jenne, especially among the Marka.[13] But he departed for the pilgrimage yet again in 1894 never to return to Jenne, so it is unlikely that he personally appointed Cerno Bokar. Nonetheless, the influence on Cerno of this line of appointment may have been considerable, as we will see below. The second line of appointment by a non-Taal was through Nyaaro Karamoko who belonged to a *sharīf* family (descendants of the Prophet) that had settled and intermarried in West Africa. Nyaaro Karamoko may have become *muqaddam* through Amadu b. al-Hajj Umar,[14] but in any case this line was certainly Umarian. Later Cerno "renewed" his appointments from both Muntaga Taal of Segu and Seedu Nuuru Taal of Senegal.[15] The spiritual significance of these two renewals is difficult to comprehend. Both Muntaga and Seedu Nuuru were grandsons of al-Hajj Umar, and the former claimed to have received an authorization as ultimate spiritual leader from his father, Amadu b. al-Hajj Umar. Some evidence suggests that Cerno received these renewals from his cousins out of respect for their status in the family, but that he never accepted them as personal spiritual guides.[16] Other sources claim that Cerno functioned as a *muqaddam* under the authority of Muntaga. The confusion on this issue reflects the complexity, as well as the vagueness, of the matter here under discussion. But the likely conclusion seems to be that although Cerno expressed considerable deference toward Muntaga because of his status in the Taal family, it is doubtful that he regarded him as a superior in religious or spiritual matters, especially because he was unlettered in Arabic.

By the early 1920s Cerno Bokar himself was widely recognized as a leading *muqaddam* of the order. In Bandiagara his position was unrivalled,[17] even by Tijani Agibu, now *chef de subdivision* and ranking Taal in the local political hierarchy. Cerno's influence also extended into the surrounding region; for example, Alfa Umar Dow, the premier religious teacher of Mopti at the time, had renewed his *silsila* with Cerno Bokar.[18] Alfa Umar Dow, a Pullo, was born about 1850 in Hamdullahi; he later lived and studied in Bandiagara during the rule there of Tijani Amadu, from whom he received the *wird* and was appointed *muqaddam* of the Tijaniyya. Of particular interest is the fact that Alfa Umar, like al-Hajj Salmoye, had also renewed his initiation from a *muqaddam* from Fez, Moulay Fadl Allah, in about 1898.[19] But by the 1920s he apparently looked to Cerno Bokar as his spiritual guide. It may be about this time, during the early 1920s, that the question of leadership within the Tijaniyya order became a crucial issue. A 1923 French report included the following observation, obtained from an unnamed African informant:

> One of the sons of al-Hajj Umar, called Murtada, was at Nioro and died in 1922. Cerno Bokar of Bandiagara was to have replaced him in Nioro as a Tijani *muqaddam* under the authority of Muntaga (in Segu). But there was a *sharīf* living in Nioro who never went out of his house, a very pious ascetic. Because of his virtue and piety, the people of Nioro requested that he be made Tijani *muqaddam*. Muntaga accepted this proposal on the advice of his brother Madani, in Hadejia (Nigeria), with whom he is in constant contact via pilgrims and Juula [merchants]. Madani even advised him to follow the prescriptions of this *sharīf*.[20]

This report, which was quoted above in our discussion of Shaykh Hamallah, indicates Cerno Bokar's high status in the Tijaniyya order by the 1920s. The *sharīf* referred to, of course, is Shaykh Hamallah, who as we have seen also received his Tijani initiations and appointments via a North African *silsila*. Therefore, by this date at least some West Africans felt that the spiritual status of Hamallah had been accepted by a number of leading Umarian Tijanis; Cerno Bokar's acceptance at this point may have been tacit, but according to this report that of Madani and even Muntaga was much more explicit. Not all the Umarians agreed with these arrangements following the death of Murtada, and this situation may well have helped to set the stage for the unsettling events which followed, when many Umarians tried to undermine the growing appeal of Hamallah.

We must now attempt to analyse Cerno Bokar's conduct as *muqaddam*. The functions of this office can be divided into two major aspects. The first, which we have already described, is that of "granter of authorities": the *muqaddam* authorizes persons to recite Tijani prayers and he appoints other *muqaddamūn*. His second function is that of spiritual guide; the *muqaddam* directs the spiritual development of his disciples. In practice of course these roles might be so completely intermingled as to be almost indistinguishable from one another; one would expect the disciple to receive various authorizations directly from the person who was guiding his spiritual development. But from our information concerning Cerno Bokar, it seems that these roles might be performed by quite separate individuals. Much of Cerno's own spiritual training has been attributed to Amadu Tafsiir Ba who, although a Tijani *muqaddam*, never played any role in Cerno's various appointments and renewals within the order. Cerno himself initiated six persons into the "secrets" of Sufism, in the tradition of the *kabbe* discussed in the previous chapter. But he also appointed four Tijani *muqaddamūn*, about whom we know little more than their names;[21] none of these four received the esoteric initiation of the *kabbe* from him. Little is known as to why such a split should be present and any suggestions put forward here should be considered somewhat speculative. There are, however, a set of indigenous concepts which might explain this situation. In the *Rimāḥ*[22] Umar quotes a Sufi authority to the effect that there are three different kinds of *shaykh*, each of whom is capable of providing a different kind of religious guidance. There is the kind who imparts the knowledge of books (*shaykh al-ta'līm*), those who can aid one's spriritual development through association and companionship with him (*shaykh al-tarbiya*), and the kind who can transmit spiritual benefits and blessings (*baraka*) through the medium of a personal meeting (*shaykh al-tarqiya*). Individuals are attracted to any one of these kinds of *shaykh* on the basis of their own personal inclinations.

Although in practice it might be difficult to classify specific Muslim personalities into any one of these categories, it seems clear that this kind of distinction did function within Islamic society. Cerno Bokar was an academic teacher, but he was not considered the most prominent scholar of Bandiagara; he was, however, felt to be the leading Tijani *muqaddam*. He himself is reputed to have received spiritual training from Amadu Tafsiir, who was not his own *muqaddam*. As we have seen, the pattern of *muqaddamūn* relationships was designed not only to transmit authorizations to recite Tijani prayers, but also to bring one closer to the spiritual benefits which flowed from Shaykh al-Tijani, by improving one's relationship (*silsila*) to him. We have no evidence to suggest that Cerno Bokar ever spent any considerable length of time with any of his own *muqaddamūn*. These kinds of relationships might be described as *tarqiya*, those considered spiritually beneficial to an individual even through brief contact. The more lengthy association of *tarbiya* was perhaps similar to that between Cerno Bokar and Amadu Tafsiir, or between Cerno and some of his own disciples.[23] Indeed, from what we know of him, Cerno Bokar seems to have preferred to develop relationships of *tarbiya* between himself and his disciples, which is evident in the manner in which he is said to have transmitted the *wird* to new members of the order. His attitude was strict, and he did not make it easy for those who wished to join. One Tijani, a school teacher at the time of his entry into the Tijaniyya, recounted his experience on this occasion with Cerno Bokar and his own personal views about the procedure:

People would come to [Cerno's] house and ask to be given the *wird*. He kept some of them waiting a long time. I can take myself and my two friends as an example; we waited more than three months. Even then he had not completely decided to allow us to practice [the wird]; he did not permit us to enter the order. One of us asked him his reasons, and finally he said, "Yes." As *muqaddam* he would not accept just anyone; he wanted to have confidence in the individual. . . . He wanted to determine that the person was truly in need of [the *wird*], and that he would retain it. First of all he would teach the person how to practice his religion: how to pray and how to perform both the major and minor ablutions. When he was confident that the person knew all this, he would permit him to take the *wird*. Without learning these things it was not worth the trouble, because prayer precedes the *wird*. Because if you do not have the *wird*, you are not prevented from entering Paradise, whereas if you do not pray, you will not go to Paradise. However, if you know how to pray, and you have the *wird*, and if you perform it appropriately, that can only increase your advantages.[24]

Another informant provided a more sophisticated explanation of the same procedure:

[Cerno Bokar] was different from all the others who gave the *wird*, because only if he saw in the person the sign of his faith would he give it. . . . Some people came only so it would be said they had the *wird*. . . . But the *wird* is only a branch; the trunk is to be found in Islam, which must be understood first. The *wird* is a kind of decoration, he said, but Islam is that which truly augments one. When the trunk is well established, the beautiful branches will come.[25]

In view of what has been said above about the origins of Sufism in the Qur'an and in the *sunna* (quoting from al-Hajj Umar), and of what we have learned about the structure of Cerno Bokar's *mā 'd-dīn*, there should be nothing suprising about the procedures described here: a knowledge of Islam necessarily precedes the practice of Sufism. But in fact, Cerno's rigorous screening process was very unusual, and it was resented by some Tijanis. Complaints were apparently submitted to Seedu Nuuru Taal during one of his early visits to Bandiagara (1928 or earlier) who felt called upon to express his own disapproval of Cerno Bokar's practices.[26] Conditions for membership in the Tijaniyya, of course, included obedience to the *sharī'a*, but Shaykh al-Tijani had also stated that the *wird* should be given to anyone who requested it.[27] Many West African Tijanis had come to accept minimal requirements for admission to the order, and some leaders were perhaps also concerned lest the strength of the order and even what they considered its principles be modified by an overstrict policy of admission.

Seedu Nuuru's disclaimer probably had little effect on Cerno Bokar; but the interesting question remains as to why Cerno should have adopted an approach so seemingly out of line with what appears to have been the predominant Umarian practice. We would suggest that he was motivated to these kinds of practices by his personal preference for the kind of spiritual and religious training which was demanded by the relationships of *tarbiya*, the progress of a disciple through lengthy association and companionship with his teacher. Having said that Cerno's strict attitude toward new members in the order was unusual, we must add that it was not unique to him. He may well have adopted the practice as a result of his early association with Jenne, whence he received one of his first Tijani appointments as an adult. Paul Marty had noted that the Jenne Tijanis were also strict in the matter of new admissions to the order:

> The *muqaddamūn* do not authorize the *wird* on the first request. They subject the postulant to a certain novitiate, designed to test him, or rather to increase his desire for an initiation which is all the more valuable for not being squandered.[28]

This description could well apply to Cerno Bokar; we cannot say for certain whether he adopted his procedures based on this Jenne precedent, but his attitude reflects his determination to pursue his religious obligations as he saw fit despite external pressures.

## *Cerno Bokar as spiritual guide*

Cerno Bokar's role as a spiritual guide is more difficult to describe. Spiritual guidance concentrates not on the transmission of specific authorizations or knowledge, but on the nurturing in the adept of his own personal spiritual search. The ultimate goal is nothing less than the transformation of the individual's entire state of being so that he might move closer to the presence of God. The mystical quest and its attendant transformations are discussed at some length in the Tijani literature, although not usually in any analytical depth. The descriptive idioms and metaphors are often profoundly evocative, although any clear understanding of how specific methods work, or precisely when they are suggested to disciples, remains elusive. Yet, from a survey of the Tijani writings along with material from his discourses, we can derive an outline of the conceptual system which underlay Cerno's approach to spiritual guidance, and a few indications of its application.

In the most general terms, the Sufi concept of spiritual quest can be described as follows: the aspirant, under the direction of his guide (*murshid*), seeks to bring himself into a certain condition (*maqām*) in preparation for the *possibility* that God *might* transform his state of being (*ḥāl*). Man's own efforts, although absolutely necessary, are seen as tentative and transitory; permanent transformation comes only as a gift from God. The role of the spiritual guide is to assist the disciple in preparing himself for this possible transformation, which is seen to proceed through a number of stages.[29] Al-Hajj Umar called this lengthy process of spiritual preparation *tarbiya*:

> The intention of *tarbiya* is the cleansing and purification of the essence from any slackness, so that it will be capable of bearing the burden of the secret (*sirr*). This is not possible unless wrongdoing is eliminated from it, and unless vanity and falsehood are prohibited from coming into contact with this objective. When for a time these are separated from it, [the essence] exists with only the attributes of its true nature, and God Almighty might purify it without any intermediary.[30]

For Umar, as for most Tijanis, spiritual development required both moral change (elimination of wrongdoing, vanity and falsehood) and psychological change (purification from internal slackness). The *murshid* could aid an aspirant in this process only through lengthy and intimate association, in other words as a *shaykh al-tarbiya*.

Most discussions of Sufi spiritual transformation contain both moral and psychological overtones. Perhaps the most moralistic of the metaphors employed by al-Hajj Umar in his description of spiritual quest was that of the *jihād al-nafs*, or struggle with the carnal soul. This allusion to *jihād* (struggle, or "holy war") is derived from both the Qur'an and the *ḥadīth*. In a lengthy chapter on *jihād* in the *Rimāḥ*, Umar quotes the Qur'anic verse: "As for those who struggle towards Us, We will guide them in Our paths, for truly God is the Light of the doers of good" (xxix, 69). He also quotes the following *ḥadīth*, pronounced by Muḥammad on returning from battle against those who opposed his Muslim community. He said,

> "We have returned from the lesser *jihād* to the greater *jihād*." And they said, "What is the greater *jihād*, O Messenger of God?" He said, "The struggle with the carnal soul and with the passions."[31]

The *nafs*, or carnal soul, sometimes referred to as the lower soul, can be described as those parts of man which he shares with the animals, including all natural functions and appetites as well as one's debilitory habits and passions. Indeed, the Sufis often describe the *nafs* with the characteristics of certain animals:

. . . the covetousness of the crow, the greed of the dog, the pride of the peacock, the baseness of the calf, the unruliness of the lizard, the malice of the camel, the restlessness of the cat, the ferociousness of the lion, the wickedness of the snake, the shyness of the mouse, and the frivolity of the monkey.[32]

Although the *nafs* can be the host to all these sinful attributes, and be "more evil than seventy Satans," one is cautioned against rejecting it entirely. "Rather one must accept it as his companion, through which he will manage his struggle and his flight [from evil passions]."[33] Bringing the *nafs* under control is often likened to training an animal (in the following passage either a camel or a horse):

. . . beat it with the whip of the Book [Qur'an], bind it with the halter of reproach and judgment, set limits upon it with conscientious rebuke and reprimand, and place the saddle of firm intention upon it with the girth of determination. Then mount it with the profession of the *sharī'a* and ride it into the fields of Truth [*al-Ḥaqq* ].[34]

Cerno Bokar spoke in a similar vein when he described one's efforts to control the *nafs* as a shepherd seeks to control his sheep:

When sheep become agitated, the shepherd is no longer able to guide them. Then one sees him doing everything to prevent them from scattering. What is true for the temporal shepherd is also useful for the spiritual shepherd. Each of us is a shepherd for his passions. Certainly it is necessary to master them; they are just another kind of sheep. We must avoid the possibility that they will leap over our heads, overrun us and drag us into a moral abyss, a valley where neither the soul nor the spirit can survive.[35]

The taming, training and control of the *nafs* is man's major task in his spiritual search; he begins with this and probably is never able to abandon it. He is able to carry on this struggle because, although the *nafs* constitutes a great part of his functioning life, man also possesses other constituent parts which are relatively independent of it. These include the intellect (*'aql*), the heart (*qalb*), and the spirit (*rūḥ*); additional attributes to these might be included in discussions by various Sufis.[36] Cerno Bokar never presents a systematic discussion of how all these parts of man fit together and interact,[37] but we can derive some understanding of his views from his discourses. He believed that the human spirit (*rūḥ*) was a particle of the Divine Spirit entrusted to man via Adam at the time of his creation. This idea is taken from the Qur'an: "And when I have fashioned him and breathed into him of My Spirit, then fall down before him prostrate" (XXXVIII, 72).[38] One of the goals of the Sufi quest for Cerno was to achieve a state in which "the spirit is constantly occupied with reciting the name of the Lord."[39] Many Sufis would claim that the natural propensity of the spirit is to move toward God, from which it is hindered by the evil ways of the *nafs*. The heart (*qalb*) does not figure much in Cerno's discourses. Many Sufis consider it to be the seat of faith; Cerno's view may be very close to this, for he sees the heart as the source of a certain internal energy which can transform one's faith to a higher form. He speaks of a black material which God has placed in each human heart, which can be ignited through "prayer, love and charity" and maintained at high heat through the recitation of *dhikr* (special Sufi prayers). Should this fire be extinguished and the material be allowed to grow cold, it can poison the "spiritual organism."[40] This idea of internal heat can also be found in the *Rimāḥ* where Umar discusses the conditions for reciting *dhikr*. One is prohibited from drinking water either during or immediately after the recitations because "the heat of the *dhikr* attracts illuminations, revelations and 'mystical experiences' . . . but drinking water stifles this heat."[41]

Although in this view both the spirit and the heart are separate from the *nafs*, neither of these parts of man is seen to possess the capacity to stand completely alone against the *nafs*. The properly trained intellect (*'aql*), however, can actively direct and control the *nafs*. Umar quotes one of his Sufi authorities to the effect that in the *jihād al-nafs* one must rely on the "prohibitive [faculties] of the intellect and of one's self-will [*mulk*]."[42] These are the commanders in one's internal war against the spiritually debilitating qualities of the *nafs*. The intellect, then — so central in Cerno's thought as man's most important possession in his initial understanding of religion — continues to play a vital role during his spiritual search. His concept of the role of the intellect is close to that described by Muhammad al-Ghazālī in his *Alchemy of Happiness*.[43] He likens man's constituent parts to a kingdom in which the sovereign is the heart and the prime minister is the reason. Reason administers the kingdom, and should some subject rebel, "following his own passions," then this is reported to the heart so that the disorder can be be controlled. The concept of the intellect as a kind of watchdog and adviser to a sovereign heart, which is compassionate in the exercise of its authority seems much closer to the Sufism of Cerno Bokar than the metaphor of *jihād* and warfare, which al-Hajj Umar pursues at length in his writings. Cerno endorsed the *jihād al-nafs*, the aim of which he saw as "the vanquishing of our faults: egoism, exaggerated love of self, scorn for one's fellow man, and so on."[44] But he consistently spoke of his own method as one of love and charity. The faults of the seeker must be overcome, but the methods employed by Cerno were rather more indirect than those suggested by some of the authorities whom al-Hajj

Umar chose to quote. As we have already seen, Cerno believed the intellect gave man the capacity to understand his position in life, his relationship to God and therefore the necessity to pursue his religion. Through the intellect man could also understand the values to be derived from "initiating" oneself into the Sufi way. Once embarked, the intellect would continue to serve as an internal guide. Indeed, man had been endowed with intelligence for precisely this purpose:

God has no need of reason nor of human intelligence. He gave them to us for use in this life. We are not therefore to bring them untouched to the grave, that is, to live and die without meditating on and drawing spiritual profit from the events which happen to us and from the things which we ascertain.[45]

In the pattern of Cerno Bokar's spiritual search, then, the faculties of the intellect are directed more toward perception and direction than toward punishment and prohibition. This approach seems more gentle than some of the harsh directives which Umar quoted in his description of the *jihād al-nafs*, and yet in another section of the *Rimāḥ* he defines the Tijaniyya as a "way of thankfulness," or a "way of gratitude and love" *as opposed to* a "way of struggle."[46] This statement is not the contradiction it might at first seem; Umar is not suggesting that Tijanis do not engage in the *jihād al-nafs*, but rather that they do not tend to employ some of the more extreme or physically demanding spiritual exercises endorsed by some Sufi groups. Tijanis concentrated on the recitation of prayers and sought "the attachment of one's heart to the Truth [God]." But other exercises were also employed, precisely which ones and when they were suggested was left to the discretion of the *murshid*. One might, for example, be directed into isolation (*khalwa*), or to fast, or to recite certain *dhikr*. The following passage briefly indicates how these kinds of exercises were seen to aid the adept in the struggle with the evils of the *nafs*, not by direct confrontation but indirectly through the effects of the exercises themselves:

In isolation one is cut off from those bearers of falsehood who number among the lifeless; in performing *dhikr* one must abandon the speech of error, desire and nonsense which is [normally] on his tongue; by reducing the intake of food one reduces the vapour in the brain and thereby lessens the carnal appetite so that the intellect can return to its devotion to God and His Prophet.[47]

Cerno Bokar may have employed all these kinds of exercises in guiding his own disciples, but, judging from his discourses, he placed greatest emphasis upon the recitation of the prescribed Tijani prayers (the *wird* and the various *adhkār*) and personal meditation, especially of Qur'anic verses. Recitations of prayers were recommended specifically for the purpose of assisting a disciple in his struggle to overcome those habitual propensities which hindered his movement toward God. The emphasis placed on such recitations was in no way unique to the Tijaniyya; it pervaded Sufi Islam. It will be recalled that al-Sanūsī in his *'Aqīdat al-Ṣughrā*, for example, had enjoined the frequent recitation of the *shahāda* until its meaning "mingled with one's flesh and blood."[48] Although the recitation of these prayers was believed to impart spiritual benefit from mere repetition, many leading Sufi thinkers also felt that the actual manner of recitation was of critical importance to the effectiveness of the prayer. Al-Sanūsī had said that the *shahāda* should be repeated "while calling to mind that which it contains from the articles of faith." Al-Hajj Umar, in a passage very reminiscent of al-Sanūsī, counsels that during the recitation of the *shahāda* one should "banish everything from his heart which might take the place of God Almighty so that the phrase 'There is no god but God' will exert an influence upon the heart and so that this influence can spread to other parts of the body."[49] He also said that when reciting the *dhikr*, "one should bring its meaning into his heart each time [he repeats it], and he should pay attention to his heart, evoking the meaning until his heart is reciting the *dhikr* and he is listening to it."[50] In other words, prayers were not to be recited mechanically but with an intense concentration of attention so that their meanings might come to life within the disciple's own body.

This internal reordering constitutes the spiritual transformation which is the goal of the Sufis, and one can now begin to comprehend that for all its moral overtones, its profoundest impact is psychological. To achieve a state in which, as Cerno Bokar said, "the spirit is constantly occupied with reciting the name of the Lord" requires considerable change within the individual. The language of Cerno's discourses describes these changes and transformations in the metaphorical terminology of the changing states of heat, light and water. He viewed man's internal condition as in a state of constant flux, and his efforts at spiritual guidance were toward that internal reordering through which one might receive the permanent spiritual transformation which can only come from God. Sufis refer to this permanent transformation as being "opened" by God, an "opening" which renders one receptive to higher spiritual substances.

In all this process the *murshid* acts as a guide. Strictly speaking, according to Tijani doctrine, spiritual guides or even the *shuyūkh* of the order could not of their own will bestow spiritual favour or grace (*baraka*) upon their followers. The *murshid* was able to direct others in their spiritual efforts because he had himself passed through this process. In addition, because he had been "opened" by God, spiritual forces or substances could be transmitted through him, but these could not be received by another individual unless the recipient had prepared himself spiritually for them. (This is the relationship of *tarqiya*, mentioned above.) Or so said the Tijani books. Popular West African belief, among Tijanis and Muslims in general, did not conform with this strict interpretation; most people believed that holy men possessed supernatural powers and that their blessings could be had for the asking. The vast majority of marabouts and *muqaddamūn* also embraced this popular belief and not a few offered their spiritual power for sale in the form of charms and fetishes.

These considerations bring us to a discussion of the relationships between Sufism as a personal search for the spiritual transformation which has been described here and Sufism as a popular manifestation of religious belief and practice. The vast majority of Tijanis would never undertake what Umar described as the *jihād al-nafs*; they would perform the prayers and recitations required of all members of the order, but probably for the most part not with the kind of concentrated attention demanded by the *shuyūkh*. Not even the gentle spiritual proddings of Cerno Bokar found a wide audience of determined spiritual acolytes. But Shaykh al-Tijani had promised exceptional benefits for all the members of his order, not just those who engaged in the rigours of spiritual self-discipline. He claimed to be superior to all the *awliyā'* and that consequently all members of his order, as well as their relations and descendants, would enter paradise "without reckoning or punishment."[51] The first of these statements angered many Sufis, including the leaders of the West African *Qadiriyya*; the second was considered by many scholars to be heretical since the subjection of all persons to the Last Judgment is one of the fundamental dogmas of Islam.[52] We cannot here enter into a discussion of the learned debates which centered on these doctrinal issues, although they greatly affected the early years of Tijani expansion. The point to be emphasized here is that the Tijaniyya addressed not just a scholarly and spiritual élite, but the Muslim population at large. The Prophet had ordered al-Tijani to transmit his *wird* "to every Muslim who requested it, no matter what his condition, great or small, free man or woman, obedient or disobedient."[53] In such circumstances, beliefs and practices which were widespread among the general population were bound to become mixed with Tijani practice, and the stricter doctrine was bound to become subject to looser and looser interpretation.

Our purpose here is to place Cerno Bokar in this wider context of Tijani belief and practice from the perspective of several aspects of Tijani doctrine which were particularly prone to distortion, such as the role of the *shaykh* and the *walī*, the performance of miracles, and the concept of intercession. There seems no reason to doubt that Cerno Bokar accepted all the tenets of Tijani doctrine, including Shaykh al-Tijani's more extreme claims; however, the interpretation and emphasis he placed upon the various elements of the doctrine were his own. Let us begin with the concept of *shaykh* or *walī*. Al-Hajj Umar stated that a *walī* is "one who knows nothing, becomes the companion to no one, and neither serves nor loves anyone except God." And the *shaykh* is "the perfected *walī* whose position among his people can be likened to the position of the Prophet among his community; pledging allegiance to him is like pledging allegiance to the Prophet, because he is a representative of the Prophet."[54] Every *shaykh*, then, is a *walī*; the *awliyā'* form a mystical élite, they are the leaders of the spiritual hierarchy. From the point of view of spiritual search, one could do no better than to find and submit to a *shaykh*. Who, then, were the *shuyūkh* and *awliyā'* of the Tijaniyya order and how could they be recognised? Of course, the founder himself, Ahmad al-Tijani, was a *walī*; he knew this because the Prophet had appeared to him while awake, not in a dream, and instructed him on his mission. Al-Hajj Umar devotes an entire chapter of the *Rimāḥ* to supporting the contention that a *walī* sees the Prophet while awake.[55] It will be recalled that Umar himself had been appointed by Muhammad al-Ghālī as a *khalīfa*, or successor, to Shaykh al-Tijani for all of West Africa. Umar considered the *khalīfa* to be "the representative of the *shaykh* in an absolute sense" and therefore the spiritual superior to the *muqaddamūn*.[56] The authority for this appointment had come from al-Tijani himself, in a vision; confirmation of the appointment came in subsequent visions of both the Prophet and al-Tijani who appeared both to Umar and to various prominent persons close to him in order to indicate his special status in the order.[57] In his descriptions of these visions, Umar refers to himself several times as a *shaykh*; we must therefore conclude that he also considered himself to be a *walī*.

Tijanis, like other Sufis, believed that visions were related to divine revelations. Although the Prophetic cycle had ended, some manifestations of God's revelations were still available to the most upright Muslims in the form of visions. Umar quotes al-Tirmidhī to the effect that "visions (*ru'yā*) are from God, whereas the dream (*ḥulm*) is from Satan."[58] The visions in which the Prophet appears are known to be sound, because "Satan cannot take the form of the Prophet."[59] Nor can Satan resemble the *shaykh*, because "the *shaykh* follows the Prophet." Therefore visions are very important to Tijanis for aiding them in their spiritual search and in indicating to them their spiritual guides. As we shall see below, Cerno Bokar was guided toward Shaykh Hamallah by a vision.[60]

Although one can prepare oneself to receive visions through a series of prayers called *istikhāra*, the vision itself is believed to come from a higher spiritual source. The conceptual pattern here is therefore similar to that discussed above with reference to the spiritual transformations of the Sufi search. Man receives visions through divine favour; he can only prepare himself to receive them, but he cannot directly induce them. Much the same can be said for miracles (*karāmāt*). Miracles are extraordinary events which manifest themselves through a *walī*, not due to his personal powers, but because he is close to God. In the *Rimāḥ* al-Hajj Umar follows the more orthodox Sufi line in warning against seeking miracles, and he quotes the rather vivid *ḥadīth* that "miracles are the menstruation of men."[61] Miracles were considered a test or a trial, because they tended to be a diversion away from spiritual efforts. Most of these doctrinal subtleties were lost, of course, on the majority of Tijanis and other Muslims. The occurrence of miracles was accepted as fact by all Tijanis; and these miracles were manifested through holy men and were believed to be signs of their closeness to God. It should come as no surprise that "miracle mongering" was widespread among those who wished to prove the powers of their particular *shaykh*.

Another concept which occupies a prominent position in Tijani doctrine is that of intercession. Strictly, intercession (*shafā'a*) refers to the Tijani doctrine that the Prophet Muhammad will intercede for all Tijanis at the Last Judgment and that they will therefore enter directly into Paradise. However, we wish here to discuss another concept which is occasionally referred to in popular belief as intercession.[62] This is the idea of the intermediary role of a *shaykh* in the transmission of spiritual grace. Al-Tijani claimed that the Prophet told him: "I am your intermediary (*wāsiṭa*) and the one who will aid your [spiritual] actualization, so abandon everything which you have received from the other Sufi ways."[63] Al-Tijani in turn became the intermediary for those who followed him, and the later *shuyūkh* of the order were seen to have inherited a similar spiritual capacity. The popular Tijani belief in many areas was that one's *shaykh* had the capacity to intervene on an individual's behalf with the higher spiritual powers. The difference between the popular belief and the actual doctrine is subtle but important. The doctrine views the intermediary as a vehicle for the transmission of spiritual forces; the individual receives or transmits these forces but he has no personal influence over them. An example of this concept can be seen in the following comment on the *dhikr* quoted from the *Rimāḥ*:

> Whenever one begins the *dhikr*, the image of his *shaykh* should be present in his heart, and he should seek his aid. The heart of the *shaykh* is turned toward the heart of his own *shaykh*, and so on to the level of the Prophet. And the heart of the Prophet Muhammad is constantly turned towards the Divine Presence. Thus, when one pronounces the *dhikr*, he should envisage his *shaykh* and seek the aid of his saintliness. Then aid will flow forth from the Divine Presence to the Prophet; then it will flow from the heart of the Prophet to the hearts of all the *shuyūkh* of all ranks until it reaches his *shaykh*, and then from the heart of his *shaykh* into his own heart.[64]

This spiritual chain of transmission is effective only insofar as each individual link has been properly prepared to perform his function. Similarly, at the very end of the chain, a supplicant cannot expect to receive the benefits of the *baraka* (spiritual grace) transmitted by his *shaykh* unless he is spiritually prepared. The popular practice was rather different to this; supplications were made profligately to holy men, both living and dead, in the belief that such requests would be granted. And not a few religious figures encouraged these beliefs.

Cerno Bokar embraced Tijani doctrine in its strictest sense. He never claimed to be a *shaykh* or a *walī*, although some people may have considered him so. He was given to visions, and he attempted to interpret them for himself and for his disciples. But we have no record of his having had a vision of the Prophet Muhammad. And although some of his disciples claimed he had been "illuminated" and "opened by God"[65] he himself remained unpretentious and humble in this regard, as his discourses reflect. When asked to discuss the various forms of "mystical light," he opened his remarks with the rejoinder, "I am not, as you believe, a man who has seen all these lights."[66] He seemed to strive to avoid the kind of veneration which might subvert his efforts to aid those around him in their personal religious and spiritual search. He addressed his disciples as "brother" and he refused himself to be called by any elevated titles. In response to the suggestion that he was possessed of special powers, he was rather direct: "Do not believe that we dispense miraculous means for curing ill souls. We aid our brothers by submitting to them holy verses for their reflection."[67] On one occasion a woman asked Cerno for a blessing which would render her "pleasant, affable and patient." He sent her home and admonished her that she possessed the capacity to achieve these qualities through her own efforts. In so doing, he told her: "The blessings which will come to you will be far superior to those which you could obtain from me; they will be from God and the Prophet."[68]

The claims by his disciples about Cerno Bokar's spiritual accomplishments, and his own disclaimers, say much about the dynamics of Sufi relationships. As Hampaté Bâ said, "a student can do nothing else but love his master, because he *is* his master. For him, he has accomplished everything. Otherwise, he would not have chosen him as a master; he is his model."[69] Becoming a Sufi disciple in the more profound sense of the term implied a personal desire to change one's state of being; part of the process of this transformation was to imitate the behaviour of one's spiritual guide. Even those persons in the order who were not inclined toward the more profound aspects of spiritual development looked to their spiritual guides for special spiritual benefits. It is therefore not surprising that people's personal hopes were reflected in how they saw their own spiritual superiors. By contrast, the guide himself, if he were honest, was required to temper the imagination of his disciples. This is why the descriptions of Cerno Bokar by his own followers usually tell us more about them than about him; and they also help us to see the kinds of concerns which brought people together in spiritual search.

I knew Cerno Bokar Saalif from the time of my adolescence, by his wisdom and his incomparable behaviour. As I grew older I continued to retain a great esteem for him. When I was of the age to marry I came into direct contact with him, in order to convert to religion, in order to understand my *dīn*, and subsequently to adopt the Tijaniyya order. . . . It was in 1933; I remember this date because it was the same year that I took the *wird*, it was the same year that my son Tijani was born, and it was the same year that I completely abandoned the cigarette. . . . That is why I remember it so well. Because each time that I ran into Cerno, I was smoking, and I was obliged to throw the cigarette behind me in order to greet him and shake his hand. But when I took the *wird* the time had come to abandon the cigarette, and I gave it up completely. . . . Cerno was never angry. Whatever the situation, he was never able to see two people in discord and not immediately try to reconcile them, man and wife, relatives, and even if it was a question of veritable enemies. He always tried to re-establish order. He followed precisely what the Qur'an said. . . . For me, personally, I never found anyone like him, until I was transferred to Timbuktu where I found Shaykh Tijani who was also a real man, a fervent Muslim.[70]

I know very little about Cerno Bokar because I did not study with him. It was my search for a *shaykh* which brought us together. I studied with Alfa Ali Sek; Cerno was also his *shaykh*, because he was closer to Shaykh Umar and because he was also master of the *wird*. . . . Cerno Bokar had no desire except the religion of God; that is what he searched for. He decided in his heart to work for what would bring him close to God. He became one who searched for truth, he became a friend of religion. He was very good; he gave sermons in order to show how religion should be practiced; there was no one like him.[71]

In all my life, among all the men I have met, I would place no one above Cerno. For me he is *insān al-kāmil* [the perfected man], but that does not mean that he *is* in fact *insān al-kāmil*, . . . because he would himself deny it. And I cannot know him better than he knows himself. The proof of it is how much he always asked his students to pray for him. . . . He did this many times in my presence; the more lowly the person's status the more Cerno requested his prayers. For example, an old woman might come, completely simple, in order to request his prayers. After Cerno had prayed for her he would say to her: "But you, too, you must pray for me." Many people were astonished by that. . . . That was a sort of consciousness of his state and of what man should be. It is a way of struggling against pride, and against the belief that one is better than others. As for me, I think that nothing is more dangerous in mysticism than to believe that one is superior to others.[72]

## NOTES

1. Discourse 36.
2. *Ibid.*
3. JM, I, 23, in a passage based on the writings of Ibn 'Arabī. For a discussion of the these ideas, see Henry Corbin, *Creative Imagination in the Sufism of Ibn 'Arabī* (Princeton, N.J., 1969), 114–6. The reader should note that portions of the *Jawāhir al-Ma'ānī* were apparently plagiarized from a biograpy of a late seventeenth century Sufi, Aḥmad b. 'Abdallāh Ma'n al-Andalūsī. I have not checked this biography in order to know how extensively 'Alī Ḥarāzim relied on this work, but this fact does not seem significant to our purposes here. Our concern is the *Jawāhir al-Ma'ānī* as a Sufi source book, not as an accurate account of Ahmad al-Tijani's life. See Abun-Nasr, *The Tijaniyya*, 24–5.
4. TB, 86; VE, 166–7.
5. JM, I, 12, quoting al-Sha'rānī.
6. See, for example, Abun-Nasr, *The Tijaniyya*.
7. The most extreme example of this is J.S. Trimingham, *A History of Islam in West Africa* (London, 1965); see also Oloruntimehin, *Segu Empire*.
8. TB, 84; VE, 158–9.
9. *Rimāḥ*, II, 209–36.
10. Amadou Hampaté Bâ claims Cerno was first given the *wird* by Amadu b. al-Hajj Umar; interview of 2 May 1978.
11. Interview of 1 July 1980.
12. Interviews with Amadou Hampaté Bâ of 2 May 1978 and 1 July 1980.
13. P. Marty, *Soudan*, II, 142ff.
14. Interview with Amadou Hampaté Bâ, 2 May 1978.
15. Interview with Amadou Hampaté Bâ, 1 July 1980.
16. Interviews with Amadou Hampaté Bâ, 2 May 1978 and 1 July 1980.
17. ANM, Fonds Récent, 4–E–18, Mission de Capitaine André, 1923.
18. This conclusion is drawn from references to his relationship with Cerno Bokar in ANM, Fonds Ancien, 1–D–49, Monographies du Cercle de Mopti, and Fonds Récent, 4–E–14, Enquête sur l'Islam.
19. Marty, *Soudan*, II, 215–7.
20. ANM, Fonds Récent, 4–E–18, Affaires Musulmanes, Mission de Capt. André, 1923.
21. Interview with Sory Hamadun Bala of 30 September 1977; they were Jibrīl of Amba, Bubakar of Kenje, Hamadun Bory of Karakinde, a Pullo, and Yaqūb, a Sarakolle from Tugan. Amadou Hampaté Bâ also claims to have been appointed a *muqaddam* by Cerno, interview of 8 July 1981.
22. *Rimāḥ*, I, 94, quoting al-Zarrūq. Baba Thimbely commented on this passage in an interview, 1 October 1977.
23. Baba Thimbely considered Cerno to be a *shaykh al-tarbiya*, interview of 21 January 1978.
24. Interview with Dauda Maiga, 30 September 1977.
25. Interview with Baba Thimbely, 29 September 1977; Amadou Hampaté Bâ gave a very similar account in an interview, 3 May 1978. Cerno Bokar was aided in his screening and selection of disciples by a leading scholar of

Bandiagara and a close friend, Alfa Ali Sek. It was he who determined if the person knew the fundamentals of Islamic practice, and he who explained the conditions for membership in the order, which had been stated by Shaykh al-Tijani himself. Without a letter of support from Alfa Ali, Cerno accepted no one into the order. Interviews with Baba Thimbely, 29 September 1977 and with Amadou Hampaté Bâ, 3 May 1978.

26. Baba Thimbely interview of 29 September 1977 and Dauda Maiga interview of 30 September 1977. The earliest archival reference to Seedu Nuuru being in Bandiagara is 22 March 1928: ANM, Fonds Récent, 1–E–31, Rapports politiques et rapports de Tournées.
27. JM, I, 122.
28. Marty, *Soudan*, II, 140.
29. For a general discussion of this subject, see Trimingham, *Sufi Orders*, and Schimmel, *Mystical Dimensions*.
30. *Rimāḥ*, I, 132–3; for a very different definition of *tarbiya*, which suggests the wide range of interpretation on such doctrinal matters present in West Africa, see the testimony of a Hausa informant in M. Hiskett, "The 'Community of Grace'," 120–1.
31. *Rimāḥ*, II, 211.
32. *Ibid*., II, 212, quoting from *Sirāj al mulūk* of al-Ṭurtūshī.
33. *Ibid*., II, 216, quoting from *Bahjat al-nufūs*.
34. *Ibid*., II, 213–4, quoting from *Sullam al-riḍwān li-dhawq ḥalāwat al-īmān*.
35. Discourse 9.
36. For a discussion of these and other attributes, consult Schimmel, *Mystical Dimensions*.
37. For an example of such a systematic discussion, see Abū Ḥāmid Muhammad al-Ghazālī, *The Alchemy of Happiness*, translated from the Turkish by Henry A. Homes (Albany, 1873).
38. Discourse 1.
39. Discourse 5.
40. Discourses 52 and 53.
41. *Rimāḥ*, II, 4.
42. *Rimāḥ*, II, 216, quoting *Bahjat al-nufūs*.
43. *Alchemy of Happiness*, 18ff.
44. TB, 84; VE, 158–9.
45. Discourse 49.
46. *Rimāḥ*, I, 133.
47. *Ibid*.
48. See above, p. 80.
49. *Rimāḥ*, II, 4.
50. *Ibid*.
51. For a list and discussion of these benefits, see *Rimāḥ*, II, 40–50.
52. For a general discussion of these issues, see Abun-Nasr, *The Tijaniyya*, 163–85.
53. JM, I, 122.
54. Taken from the headings of chapters 17 and 18 in the *Rimāḥ*, I, 113 and 117.
55. *Rimāḥ*, I, 198–211.

56. *Ibid.*, I, 184.
57. *Ibid.*, I, 184ff.
58. *Rimāḥ*, I, 192.
59. *Ibid.*
60. For a further discussion of this point, see Abun-Nasr, *The Tijaniyya*, 165–6.
61. *Rimāḥ*, I, 131. For a general discussion of miracles, see Schimmel, *Mystical Dimensions*, 199–213.
62. See J.R. Paden, *Religion and Political Culture in Kano*, 67.
63. JM, I, 51.
64. *Rimāḥ*, II, 2–4, quoting from Shaykh Jibrīl al-Khirmābādhī.
65. Interviews with Sori Hamadun Bala of 30 September 1977 and with Koola Sidi of 20 March 1978.
66. Discourse 55.
67. TB, 78; VE, 140.
68. Discourse 15.
69. Amadou Hampaté Bâ, interview of 12 May 1978.
70. Dauda Maiga, interview of 29 September 1977.
71. Baba Thimbely, interview of 29 September 1977.
72. Amadou Hampaté Bâ, interview of 12 May 1978.

# 6
# CRISIS

The two previous chapters have explored Cerno Bokar's Islamic world: his religious training and his teaching. This world was centered on his own compound, as a school or Sufi-*zāwiya*, and upon the mosque; its goals were spiritual and its attitudes toward ordinary life somewhat disdainful. The over riding concern for people in the *zāwiya* was eternal life after death; the pleasures and material rewards of ordinary life were seen as Satanic temptations to divert mankind from its real need to move closer to God, which could be accomplished only by religious devotion. This kind of world exists best in isolation and anonymity, because if it begins to exert strong and popular appeal it can become a severe threat to established authority. The tragic crisis which marked the final years of Cerno Bokar's life resulted from the fact that he could not to his own satisfaction fulfil his religious search within the confines of near anonymity demanded by French colonial authority. In 1937 he submitted to the spiritual leadership of Shaykh Hamallah of Nioro. He did this in complete accordance with Tijani doctrine as he understood it; al-Hajj Umar had strongly emphasized the need to attach oneself to a *shaykh*. Cerno had submitted to Hamallah only after lengthy fasts and prayers for guidance; he experienced indicative visions and he even personally travelled to Nioro in difficult circumstances to meet the man before he made his decision.

But this submission to Hamallah, no matter how religious in its motivation, thrust Cerno Bokar into a maelstrom of political turmoil. For Cerno Bokar, Hamallah may have been a Tijani *shaykh*; to many other Tijanis he was the proselytizer of a heterodox and unacceptable doctrine; to the French he was a threat to colonial security. Hamallah was anything but anonymous! In 1937 he had only recently returned to Nioro from ten years' exile for alleged anti-French activities; for the previous twenty years he had been viewed with suspicion and growing animosity by many leading Tijanis, especially the Umarians and certain members of the Taal family who saw his expanding following as a threat to their own spiritual authority. In selecting Hamallah as a *shaykh*, then, Cerno Bokar touched upon some raw nerves. The reactions reflected the severe tensions which gripped the Soudan of the 1930s on all levels of the social and political hierarchy: French policy toward Islam and especially toward Hamallah, rivalries within the Taal family, political disputes among the leadership of Bandiagara and the general unsettling effects of social and economic change.

## *Cerno Bokar's submission to Shaykh Hamallah*

In 1937 Cerno Bokar submitted to the spiritual authority of Shaykh Hamallah; in other words, he renewed his Tijani *wird* with him thus becoming an advocate of the "eleven beads." This event shocked the entire West African Tijani community, both "elevens" and twelves," and greatly disturbed the French; a prominent and respected member of the Taal family had become a Hamallist. Certain Umarian leaders feared that this act would strengthen the Hamallist forces, and consequently undermine their own position. Those French who were convinced of the subversive nature of Hamallism feared some sort of political explosion in the Bandiagara region, and the overwhelming influence of the proponents of these views ensured that Cerno Bokar's act would be engulfed in political turmoil. All the available evidence, however, suggests that Cerno Bokar himself harboured no political aims in submitting to Shaykh Hamallah; for him, it was a purely religious act. Of course, Cerno could not have been so ingenuous as to be unaware of the political implications of his submission; the oral accounts of this episode are replete with warnings given to him, even by Hamallah himself, that his submission might result in reprisals. But our argument here is that Cerno Bokar took his decision for motives as purely religious as one is likely to find or be able to document in historical research.

This assertion rests upon several themes in the evidence. First is the absolute necessity, as asserted in the *Rimāḥ*, for Tijanis to find and to submit to a spiritual *shaykh* or *walī*. Second is Cerno Bokar's insistence, under the most difficult of circumstances, that he travel personally to Nioro to meet Hamallah before making any public pronouncements about the man or his teachings. Considerable pressure to comment on Hamallah must have been brought to bear upon him long before 1937, when he went to Nioro. Finally, although his submission to Hamallah became public knowledge in Nioro during his visit, and although Cerno Bokar re-initiated some of his former followers into the "eleven" after his return from Nioro, he never publicly proselytized the "eleven" and was content to practice it in the privacy of his own home. No conceivable social, economic or political gain could have accrued to him as a result of his adherence to the "eleven;" indeed, his persistance in practicing it in the face of enormous pressure resulted in attacks upon him which left his ordinary life in ruins and probably led to the illness which caused his death.

In Cerno Bokar's view, his submission to Hamallah as his spiritual superior was in strict accordance with Tijani doctrine. Both the *Jawāhir al-ma'ānī* and the *Rimāḥ* provide extensive discussions about the necessity for the Sufi seeker to attach himself to a *shaykh*, because only thus could he possibly attain his goal.[1] These discussions also suggest that every age is provided with specially elevated individuals through whom spiritual benefits are transmitted to mankind from God and the prophets.[2] Of course, even having understood and accepted this doctrine, one is left with the daunting task of identifying a *shaykh*. We saw that the appearance of Hamallah as a *shaykh* was intimately connected with the problem of the succession of spiritual leadership in West Africa after the death of al-Hajj Umar, and that acceptance of him was affected not only by religious considerations, but also by social and political pressures. Cerno Bokar's own decision with regard to Hamallah could not have been free from all these same pressures, but in the end, we would argue, he submitted to Hamallah because of his personal conclusion that he was indeed a *shaykh*. Other esoteric considerations may have affected his decision, such as his understanding of the numerological significance of the numbers eleven and twelve, but the central theme of his acceptance was his evaluation of Hamallah as a "man of God."

Unfortunately, Cerno Bokar left no personal account of his relationship with Hamallah, so that our understanding of how he came to his decision must rely on external evidence. Hampaté Bâ's account of this process places Cerno Bokar's submission into the same framework as al-Akhdar's original discovery of Hamallah. According to him, in about 1927 Cerno Bokar received a letter from Alfa Hashimi b. Amadu (nephew of al-Hajj Umar, then resident in Saudi Arabia) describing the various characteristics by which one would be able to recognize the expected *khalīfa* or *qutb* who would spiritually rejuvenate the West African Tijaniyya. He also proposed to Cerno certain spiritual exercises which would aid him in avoiding error in this identification, including a fast of three years' duration.[3] In the course of these exercises (*circa* 1933, according to the reckoning given by Hampaté Bâ)[4] Cerno had a vision in his sleep which confirmed for him the spiritual authority of Shaykh Hamallah. The major shortcoming of this version of events is its failure adequately to assess the chronological development of Cerno Bokar's interest and concern *vis-à-vis* Hamallah himself. If a letter arrived in 1927 from Alfa Hashimi about the expected *khalīfa*, it could not have been written or read without specific reference to Hamallah, who by this time had been exiled to Mauritania and made the centre of deepening religious and political dispute. In addition, one must give some credence to the 1922 report, alluded to above, that Cerno and other leading Umarians had at least tacitly accepted Hamallah as a legitimate *muqaddam*. It seems possible that by the early 1930s, when Cerno experienced the visions which convinced him of Hamallah's status, the pressures would have become intense for some kind of public statement on the issue. To accept Hamallah as *muqaddam* was one thing; to accept the claims that he was *khalīfa* was quite another.

There was also a personal factor operating upon Cerno during this period in the form of a Hamallist who became his close friend in Bandiagara, a Moor named Muhammad al-Amīn ould Rashīd. The case of ould Rashīd not only illustrates the way in which the influence of religious orders spread through personal contacts; it also offers a glimpse into the vast social and economic network which supported Shaykh Hamallah. Ould Rashīd was a young merchant who came to Bandiagara sometime in the early 1930s to trade in cattle.[5] His activities were financed by another Moorish merchant who operated in Upper Volta, the Gold Coast and the Ivory Coast in this period, and who managed to slip some of his earnings to Shaykh Hamallah who was then in Adzopé.[6] As a Moor, he was able to operate on the Ivory Coast during this period only incognito; he was allegedly very black in complexion. Ould Rashīd was also a relatively well-trained scholar, and a respected chanter of the Qur'an; perhaps these interests formed the original basis of his acquaintance with Cerno Bokar. But ultimately the two men became close friends; they spent a considerable amount of time together and Cerno even helped ould Rashīd find a wife in Bandiagara when he decided to marry. Of course, the oral accounts are not unanimous on the details of their relationship. Some say that ould Rashīd was a Hamallist *muqaddam*; others that he kept secret from all Bandiagara, including Cerno, his Hamallist connections until 1936 when Hamallah returned to Nioro, at which time he revealed his affiliation to Cerno. But all agree that it was ould Rashīd who provided Cerno with his most detailed and his only first-hand reports on Hamallah, his personality and his spiritual attainments.

The visions which convinced Cerno of Hamallah's status therefore occurred amid increasing pressures for an opinion on this man's claims, in the context of a lengthy search for religious guidance on the issue, including an extended fast, and probably under the direct influence of his friend ould Rashīd. The first vision occurred as a result of performing an *istikhāra*, a request to God, in the form of a prayer accompanied by fasting, for insight into a given problem.[7] Shaken by this vision, Cerno performed a second *istikhāra* several days later as a result of which al-Hajj Umar appeared to him in his sleep to reassure him that the first vision was valid.[8] We reproduce here in full Hampaté Bâ's account of Cerno's vision, which is presented in his books as if Cerno were recounting it to Shaykh Hamallah:

> I saw eleven men who were walking in a forest at twilight, and among them I recognized Sharīf Muhammad al-Mukhtar [Tijani *muqaddam* in Nioro and former teacher of Hamallah who opposed his succession to al-Akhdar]. They were all covered with mud and suffering from an atrocious itching which had turned them into madmen. They were staggering in the sand, tearing their clothes and scratching themselves until they bled. I joined them and also

contracted their malady. We reached the top of a hill and we saw below a vast plain in which a pond extended as far as we could see. The water of this pond was white like milk. One of us said that now we could wash and drink. We quickened our pace, but a winged man emerged from the water, extended his arms and said to us: "It is forbidden to enter this water."

"But we have a *sharīf* among us. Let us drink."

"I know this better than yourselves, but still you may not enter the pond until its owner arrives."

Suddenly a strong wind arose and a shimmering cloud appeared on the horizon. A chant was coming from this cloud; we recognized the formula of the *dhikr*, the first part of the *shahāda*. Frozen with fear, we watched as this strange cloud came closer to us. It moved across the sky like a galloping horse. When it reached its zenith it disintegrated. It was composed of a crowd of winged men and the movement of their wings caused the shimmering which had struck us. The men entered the pond and disappeared. In one motion, the twelve of us moved forward to follow them; but the guardian stopped us with a gesture. Another gust of wind brought us a second cloud of winged men who repeated the same actions as the first. Then a third. Each cloud was more sparkling than the last and the voices which chanted the sacred formula became, with each renewal of the cloud, more harmonious. Behind the third cloud a mounted rider appeared. He was veiled and held a rosary in his hand. At the head of the horse, al-Hajj Umar held the bridal. . . .His name was inscribed in letters of fire on his chest. The horse reared in the wind, but al-Hajj Umar clung to the bridle. A gust of wind blew up the horse's mane which caused the cloth to slip from the face of the rider. I swear before God that the face which I saw was yours [i.e. Hamallah's]. The rider said to the guardian, "What do these people want?"

"They want to drink."

He dismounted and advanced toward the pond. At that point a wind of such violence arose that compared to it the previous gusts were like light breezes. The twelve were dispersed in the dust. The man who had your face took some of the milky water into the hollow of his hands and sprinkled me with it. My thirst and itching ceased. I heard a voice above the noise of the wind: "You will drink and you will wash, but later, not today."[9]

The explicit nature of the symbolism of this vision leaves little room for doubt about its meaning. Hamallah's role is legitimized through the agency of al-Hajj Umar himself, who is leading the *shaykh*'s horse no less. Even Muhammad al-Mukhtar, Hamallah's detractor in Nioro, is recognized among the "twelve" sufferers, whose travail can be relieved only by the milky white water which is Hamallah's to dispense. Although we have no means of confirming the specific contents of this vision, there is no reason to doubt that Cerno Bokar would have sought guidance through performing *istikhāra*, and that he would have placed great store upon his own visions. We also know from his discourses that visions were not unusual for him. But no matter how convincing this vision may have been to him, Cerno still made no public pronouncement about Shaykh Hamallah; apparently he refused to make a final decision until after he had met the man personally. The opportunity for such a meeting occurred in 1937 when Cerno's elder brother, Amadu, *imām* of one of the Bamako mosques, died. Cerno travelled to Bamako to offer his condolences to the family, and while there arranged, without official permission, to travel to Nioro by lorry. He made this trip against the advice of friends and family, who warned that Hamallah was still under heavy French surveillance, but Cerno was insistent, and he made the trip alone.[10]

How long Cerno had nursed a desire to see Hamallah is unknown, but June 1937 was certainly the first opportunity he had to make the trip. Hamallah had returned to Nioro only in the early part of 1936 from the Ivory Coast. Cerno spent two weeks in Nioro, often meeting Hamallah. In the end he renewed his initiation with him, thereby accepting him as his spiritual superior. Hamallah also re-appointed him *muqaddam*, but with the restriction that he could not appoint any new *muqaddamūn* into the "eleven beads," although he could re-initiate those he had already appointed. Hampaté Bâ is vague about the authorizations given to Cerno Bokar at this time,[11] although this seems an important issue. A letter from Hamallah to Cerno, written late in 1937, suggests that Cerno was seeking a broader set of authorizations. Hamallah wrote to him, "As for what you asked me concerning the matter of appointment as *muqaddam* (*taqdīm*), I am seeking the authorization from God Almighty, which I will send you if I obtain it. Be patient."[12] This exchange, if we have interpreted it correctly, seems rather conclusive proof of the centrality of religious issues in the entire affair for both Hamallah and Cerno Bokar. In his submission to Hamallah, Cerno had accepted a limited spiritual role; Hamallah would not modify it without some divine signal that this was appropriate. The signal would undoubtedly have been a vision of some sort.

## *The suppression*

Ironically, yet understandably, the last three years of Cerno Bokar's life, from 1937 to 1940, are more richly documented than any others. It has not been possible to consult all the relevant documentation, because Hamallist files in Mali are still not available for public scrutiny. Nonetheless, references in scattered reports, plus material from the Dakar archives, provide a fairly full view of French attitudes and activities relevant to Cerno Bokar during this period. Although these data, despite their relative abundance, do not allow us to present a definitive description of the course of events, they certainly offer an unusually clear view of the complex political interactions both between the French administrators and their subjects, and among the Africans themselves. From 1937 the French viewed Cerno with suspicion and even feared that he might bring unrest to the Bandiagara region as a Hamallist. The African agents who fed the French with much of their information were able to encourage this view. One of them had Cerno announcing on his return to Bamako from Nioro that "the time of the French has passed, and the time of *Sharīf* Hamallah has arrived."[13] Cerno's Tijani disciples, on the other hand, insisted that his motives in becoming a Hamallist were religious and that he never uttered a word in condemnation of the French. Most of them eventually followed him in his adoption of the "eleven beads," and some stood by him even when it had become highly dangerous to do so. Some of the leading Umarian Tijanis, especially Seedu Nuuru Taal, saw Cerno Bokar's adherence to Hamallah as a personal affront to the family and wanted him disciplined; others, notably Muntaga Taal in Segu and Tijani Agibu (chief of Bandiagara to 1938), ranged from neutrality on the issue to supporting Cerno in his religious decision.

Naturally, the interpretations of Cerno's own role during these tragic years vary according to the source. The only references to his active proselytization of the Hamalliyya or to agitation on his part are in French reports. Oral sources, drawn solely from his supporters, depict him as a withdrawn man of religion, the passive victim of political forces. Whether Cerno did in fact publicly proclaim his adherence to Hamallah must remain an open question, which we will examine in due course. Now let us try to trace the development of events from the time of his submission to Hamallah in June 1937 until his death in 1940. In so doing we will try to highlight the differing factions and their respective interests and points of view.

Cerno Bokar returned to Bandiagara by the same route by which he had departed, with stops in Bamako, Segu and Mopti. As mentioned above, the French were convinced that he had been proselytizing for the Hamalliyya, especially among his own family, since his departure from Nioro. A confrontation between him and Muntaga Taal certainly occurred in Segu.[14] But the role of Muntaga in this entire affair was ambivalent; we shall return to him below. It was in Mopti that Cerno Bokar had his first official encounter with the French, who had decided he should not return to Bandiagara unless he renounced the "eleven beads." All accounts agree on the nature of this first meeting. The *commandant de cercle* insisted that Cerno Bokar should abandon the Hamalliyya; Cerno steadfastly refused. An excerpt from the French report claims:

> In the course of interrogations on 17 July, Bokar Salif confirmed that he had become a convinced partisan of Shaykh Hamallah and that he had taken the rosary of eleven beads. But he refused to furnish any precise details to explain his conversion and would only say that he was free to choose his religion and that no threat or action could cause him to revoke his decision.[15]

A rather more colourful oral account from one of Cerno's former students corroborates the French report. It is presented in the form of a dialogue:
*Commandant*: Either you leave the eleven, or I will send you to Kidal [the infamous French prison in the Sahara desert northeast of Timbuktu].
*Cerno*: Take me to Kidal.
*Commandant*: Hunh?!
*Cerno*: Yes.
*Commandant*: I should take you to Kidal?
*Cerno*: Take me to Kidal.
*Commandant*: You had better think about that, first.
*Cerno*: Even if you ask me one hundred times, I will say that I will not abandon the eleven until I die. Take me to Kidal. Take me wherever you like.[16]

The *commandant* dismissed Cerno, presumably so that he himself could consider what to do. At this stage, according to the oral accounts, the *commandant*'s own chief interpreter, one Umar Sy, actively intervened in the affair in order to work out a solution acceptable to all parties. Although differing in detail, these accounts agree on the broad outlines of events. Nor do the French reports contradict the oral claims, although of course they make no mention of Umar Sy. Umar Sy advised his *commandant* that the French could only do harm to their own interests by disciplining Cerno Bokar. He advised that they should summon Tijani Agibu, the chief of Bandiagara and a relative of Cerno, to intervene and regularize the affair. This was done; Tijani came to Mopti with at least two other marabouts, one of them Alfa Ali Sek, a close friend of Cerno. Tijani was not interested in challenging Cerno Bokar's religious convictions; but he was concerned to maintain peaceful relations in Bandiagara. An agreement was reached among the gathered marabouts that the next day they would go before the *commandant* and claim that the entire matter was resolved. Cerno Bokar agreed not to speak or to contradict what was said; he was willing to do this because Tijani Agibu was prepared to turn a blind eye to his continued adherence to the "eleven" so long as he did not publicly proselytize. Some accounts attribute this entire plan to Umar Sy; but by whatever way it was concluded, it worked. The French were given the impression that Cerno had renounced Hamallah, although the oral accounts claim they were only told that there would be no trouble if Cerno was allowed to return to Bandiagara. The *commandant* in Mopti duly reported:

> Tijani [Agibu] Taal did what was necessary; Cerno Bokar Saalif Taal has solemnly declared before the Muslim notables of Mopti and Bandiagara that he has renounced his relationship to Shaykh Hamallah, and that he recognized his error and was re-adopting the rosary of "twelve beads."[17]

One thing is absolutely certain. No matter what the French or anyone else were led to believe, Cerno Bokar did not sever his relationship with Shaykh Hamallah, to whom he wrote after his return to Bandiagara, the reply to which we have already discussed. The tone of Hamallah's reply in no way suggests any break in relationship between the two men.[18]

Cerno Bokar upheld his end of the bargain with Tijani Agibu and allowed everyone in Bandiagara, including some of his own disciples, to believe that he had renounced Hamallah. Undoubtedly some people close to him knew the truth of the matter, and had received the "eleven" from him, but they were enjoined to secrecy. This is evidenced by the testimony of Baba Thimbely, then a relatively young scholar and disciple of Cerno Bokar in the Tijaniyya. He did not realize that Cerno had retained the "eleven" until mid-1938, and on learning that this was so, he asked to be given it. Cerno Bokar agreed, but directed him to keep his new affiliation secret: "You must hide yourself. You will be with those of the 'twelve,' and you must resemble them. You will simply omit one recitation [of the *jawharat al-kamāl*]. No one will know the difference."[19] Thus Cerno's religious affiliation was kept quiet; perhaps it was an open secret, but Tijani Agibu was true to his word to the French. There was no trouble in Bandiagara over the "eleven beads."

However, in May 1938 Tijani died. He was succeeded by his younger brother Mukhtar who was manoeuvred into exposing Cerno Bokar's loyalty to Hamallah, resulting in a ruthless purge of Hamallists in Bandiagara. Mukhtar was appointed through the direct intervention of Seedu Nuuru Taal in Dakar, although not without local opposition. The French considered him a "mediocre" candidate for the office but were not much concerned since his responsibility was "limited to the town of Bandiagara . . . and to two insignificant villages."[20] In fact, Mukhtar was a man of no political experience or aptitude, and French opinion of him declined from "mediocre" in 1938 to "very bad" by 1948. Ironically, although he had apparently been personally devoted to Cerno Bokar before his appointment as chief, he was easily manipulated into believing that his own reputation and position would be damaged if Cerno were allowed to continue practising the "eleven."

Hampaté Bâ attributes the origins of the moves against Cerno Bokar to one Agibu Usman, who not only opposed Mukhtar's appointment but also carried a grudge against Seedu Nuuru. His alleged motive was to render Mukhtar unpopular by persuading him to attack Cerno Bokar.[21] But this seems a rather obtuse method of discrediting Mukhtar, and it also would have served the interests of Seedu Nuuru, who made no attempt to hide his dislike for the Hamallists. One cannot of course completely reject the possibility that Agibu Usman acted in this way, but other factors also seem to have been at play. In about June 1938, Seedu Nuuru visited Bandiagara to offer his condolences to the family of the deceased Tijani Agibu. During this visit he openly stated his opinion that he did not consider Shaykh Hamallah to be a "great man." He also allegedly let some persons know of his concern that if action were not taken against Cerno Bokar then he feared that trouble would erupt in the entire area, with more and more people beginning to follow him.[22] These statements are attributed to Seedu Nuuru by only one informant, Baba Thimbely, who also claimed that it was only through Seedu Nuuru's public comments that he came to realize that Cerno Bokar had retained the "eleven." Perhaps, then, it was that Agibu Usman calculated that he could discredit Mukhtar by taking up Seedu Nuuru's lead in moving against Cerno:

Whatever the intrigues behind the scenes, it seems fairly clear that the first public disclosure of Cerno's continued recitation of the "eleven" came from persons who concealed themselves in his compound with the sole purpose of exposing his activities.[23] And it was Agibu Usman himself, on behalf of Mukhtar, who first confronted Cerno Bokar on the issue of the "eleven." Knowledge of these facts is essential to an understanding of how events developed, because the French in Mopti and Bandiagara, on learning that Cerno was reciting the "eleven," immediately jumped to the conclusion that he was preparing a campaign to spread Hamallism. No doubt Mukhtar encouraged them to interpret events in this way. Their first reports, at the end of October 1938, claimed that Cerno was "preparing" to agitate in favour of the Hamalliyya.[24] A week later, after an interview with the *commandant de cercle*, Cerno was reported to be resolute in his intention to continue his religious practices. Confronted with his promise the year before to leave the "eleven," he is reported to have replied, "The word one gives to a chief is not the same as that which one possesses in one's heart."[25] The French also claimed that Cerno and his followers had begun to recite their prayers publicly: "gathered in a circle, they recite their litanies for hours while Cerno, also praying, continually walks around them."[26] They added that Cerno had also begun to appoint *muqaddamūn* for the further spread of the "eleven." No local evidence exists to support the claim that he had appointed new *muqaddamūn* in the Hamalliyya, but he does seem to have taken the veil of secrecy from his affiliation. Perhaps he did this because Mukhtar had failed to uphold the agreement concluded by his predecessor, Tijani, to tolerate his practice of the "eleven" so long as it was kept secret. The evidence leaves no doubt that it was Mukhtar who first broke this agreement.

Local French authorities were anxious to nip this affair in the bud. They advised that Cerno's school should be closed, his students returned to their home villages, and he himself "isolated." They were particularly concerned about those of his followers who worked in the French administration, of whom only three were named,[27] and about his influence among the Dogon, who boasted a long history of resistance to colonial authority. But Bamako was never able to convince the Governor General in Dakar that Cerno Bokar should be officially punished or disciplined. They feared that any French action might only enhance his prestige and that of the Hamalliyya.[28] The best that Dakar could produce was a warning to Cerno that if his activities exceeded religious bounds, he might suffer disciplinary action.[29]

This warning was transmitted in January 1939; it could have had little impact on Cerno, because what the French could not effect officially, Mukhtar had already accomplished for them in his position as chief of Bandiagara. Toward the end of November 1938, Cerno Bokar and his followers were publicly banned from using the Bandiagara mosque. Cerno's school was closed, he was in effect placed under house arrest since he could not walk through the town in safety, and he was placed under such close surveillance that only the most courageous of his friends dared to continue to visit him. In addition, pressure was brought to bear on susceptible families, especially the Taal, to force women married to Hamallists to leave their husbands. Dauda Maiga lost all his four wives in a matter of days.[30] All these events are reported both in oral accounts and in French reports,[31] but none of them resulted from official French action. For their part, the French transferred out of Bandiagara any of Cerno's followers who were in their employ (like Dauda Maiga) and increased their surveillance of the movement.

The severity of these actions may well have exceeded the original expectations of any of their perpetrators. Perhaps no one had anticipated the kind of defiance they actually encountered, first from Cerno Bokar and later from some of his more fiery followers. Cerno Bokar had no intention of compromising on an issue he considered to be his own personal affair. Nor could those who had chosen to follow him into the "eleven," especially those who stood by him after the October disclosures, be expected to back down. A situation laden with emotion was transformed into a dangerous confrontation in which all the forces of family anger, religious self-righteousness, and political power were ranged against Cerno Bokar and his small band of followers. In the face of all this, Cerno retreated to his own compound, virtually never to emerge from it again; he lived the remaining months of his life almost completely secluded from the community. The motives for this retreat are nowhere explained. Fear could have been a factor; some evidence suggests that at the height of the affair he might have been attacked if he were seen in public. He may also have been despondent over the fact that his fellow men and his relatives could act in such a way, although his discourses suggest that he had never laboured under an over-optimistic view of human nature. Perhaps he was unwilling or not sufficiently interested to carry his beliefs into the public domain, especially in the charged political atmosphere which had been created. Certainly his life betrays not the least interest in politics. For eighteen months he had been content to pursue his Hamallist recitations in the privacy of his own home. Perhaps he withdrew with the intention of continuing that policy, resting content in the conviction that his religion was a matter of concern only to himself and to his God. Such a withdrawal could also be interpreted as a kind of defiance; he had been publicly humiliated, but he continued to practice the "eleven," and no one could force him to desist from it.

Cerno's withdrawal may not have been politically motivated, but it was not without political impact. Some of his followers continued to defy their adversaries. And it is probable that physcial violence did not erupt only because the French managed to defuse the situation by expelling some Hamallists from Bandiagara and by imprisoning others. Two of the more active agitators were Dauda Maiga and Koola Sidi, a cousin of Cerno Bokar and a long-time disciple. Unlike Cerno, who had retreated in the face of pressure, these two men were defiant. Relatively young and of tempestuous temperament, they not only took a stand for what they considered their religious integrity, but they were angered by the political machinations which had created the crisis. Their backgrounds were very different. Dauda Maiga was of servile background, French educated with only the briefest introduction to Qur'anic studies. Koola Sidi was descended from the local Futanke aristocracy and a well-trained religious scholar. Dauda, an employee of the French school system, tended to look to French administrative authority for the redress of his grievances; he referred every incident to the *commandant de cercle*, and there were quite a number: expulsion from the mosque, public abuse of his mother in the Bandiagara market, and the forced dissolution of his four marriages.[32] He even wrote an article in the monthly journal, *Le Soudan*, in which he defended the Hamallists. The French simply transferred him out of Bandiagara. Koola Sidi posed a rather different kind of problem to the administration. He was allegedly "recruiting and instructing" new Hamallists from a widespread area, who passed through Bandiagara, or who had specifically come there for religious instruction. Many of these were Mossi. Ejected from the mosque, he intended to build another exclusively for Hamallists, and even though Cerno Bokar had withdrawn from public view, Koola Sidi continued to conduct public processions and prayer meetings. The French finally imprisoned him for a time, which seems effectively to have put a halt to his activities.

This policy of suppression was not without its critics, even among staunch Umarian Tijanis. Muntaga Taal of Segu provides one of the more interesting cases in this regard. He was not happy with Cerno Bokar's submission to Shaykh Hamallah, and presumably told him so; but at the same time, he was prepared not only to tolerate Cerno's personal decision,[33] but also to support him at the height of the crisis. At some point after Cerno's expulsion from the mosque, Muntaga visited Bandiagara. He refused to pray in the mosque, and on Friday even went to Mopti so as to avoid the necessity of praying that day in the Bandiagara mosque.[34]

But neither tacit support from Muntaga nor express criticism from other quarters in West Africa could change the situation in Bandiagara. Cerno Bokar had been isolated and the local Hamallist organization crushed.

## *Cerno Bokar's death*

Cerno died in February 1940 after a prolonged illness which in its final stages must have been particularly painful.[35] If death brought Cerno release from the tribulations of the last months of his life, the rituals attending his funeral were not allowed to proceed in peace. Mukhtar quickly intervened to bar Cerno's former students and disciples from having any part in the burial. Some, who had begun to prepare the corpse for interment, were chased from the house; Alfa Ali Sek, a friend of Cerno but also a supporter of Mukhtar, was allowed to perform these functions.[36] Nor were Cerno's people allowed to accompany the body to the cemetary,[37] although one witness described the funeral in miraculous terms: "In the bush [surrounding the cemetary] there were many people, though one could not tell if they were human or not. . . . All the bush had become as people to attend his corpse."[38]

After Cerno was laid to rest, a formal interdiction was proclaimed against visiting his grave. Most of those who dared to defy this ban did so only at night. Dauda Maiga was, as usual, unbowed by these prohibitions. After learning of Cerno's death, he took the first opportunity to come to Bandiagara to pay his respects. He found most of his friends too afraid to accompany him to the cemetery; only one person went with him, and when they discovered no headstone had been placed to mark the grave, Dauda explains what he did:

> Nothing had been placed on the grave. Amadou [Hampaté Bâ?] had promised to send a headstone in cement, but it had not yet arrived and while waiting for it one could find good stones here which could be engraved. So I told Yusuf, the son of Ancamba Nandigi, to find us a good stone at Dukombo [a village near Bandiagara]. Only they were afraid to bring it. "You are afraid?" I asked. "Then leave Dukombo at dusk, around 6 or 6.30. You bring it to me after dusk." He brought the stone . . . and I summoned the blacksmith Hammaci to

engrave it. . . . When it was completed we formed a small delegation to go and set it up.

When I was about to leave to return to my post, my comrades said to me, "That's not the end of it. You are going to leave, but we are certain they are going to pressure us and start asking questions. I answered, "It is simple. If they ask you who placed the stone, just say 'Dauda,' that's all." And in fact no one asked. Because in those days I was really hot-tempered. I didn't let anything pass, not anything.[39]

The French reports make no mention of the emotion and tension which surrounded Cerno's death. They were apparently unaware of the alleged "miracles" which attended his funeral, and of the extraordinary efforts and courage required of his devotees who wished to pay their last respects. Their primary concern was the fate of the Hamallist "sect" in Bandiagara. Their observation in the 1940 Annual Political Report for the Soudan was succinct:

In the subdivision of Bandiagara (Mopti *cercle*), the death of Cerno Saalif Taal has deprived the Hamallist clan of its chief in the region. He does not seem to have been replaced; none of his disciples has become the titled representative of the sect, which in this country seems to be dormant.[40]

The official French opinion of Cerno Bokar might well be summed up in a notation entered into his dossier after he was released from Mopti in 1937 and allowed to return to Bandiagara: "to be placed under close surveillance because of the weakness of his character (his successive conversions prove it)."[41]

These few comments serve only to emphasize the tragic nature of Cerno Bokar's death. Cerno was not an ambitious man, and had he not been the great-nephew of al-Hajj Umar he would undoubtedly have been even less well known than he was. Even as a Taal, he could count only a very small number of truly devoted disciples who were so firmly convinced of the soundness and sincerity of his example that they were prepared to follow wherever he led. Not that he had any desire to lead; the discourses which follow reveal something of his humility in his repeated comments to those around him about his own limitations. These disclaimers were only necessary, of course, because some people insisted upon attributing to him spiritual achievements which he refused to admit. Given the nature of Muslim society and belief described in this book, such attributions are not surprising. Nor is it surprising that after his submission to Shaykh Hamallah some Umarian Tijanis viewed him as a religious deviant and some French administrators saw him as a political threat. But none of this predictability reduces the ultimate tragedy of Cerno Bokar's life which was that the political forces which destroyed him were incapable of comprehending what he was actually trying to teach, and uninterested in doing so. The tragedy was therefore more than personal; it penetrated deep into the West African society of which Cerno was a member. It was not only the French who failed to understand what Cerno Bokar was about; very few Africans could see beyond the political conflict to the man himself. His stature as a religious leader in Bandiagara, founded upon a lifetime of study and reflection, seems to have vanished almost overnight.

The idiom of West African Islam practiced by Cerno Bokar may seem strange and superstitious to many readers, preoccupied as it was with "secrets," visions, esoteric manipulations with numbers, and so forth. But an appropriate judgment of Cerno Bokar as a man should not rest so much on any evaluation of the validity of the beliefs of his society, but upon a consideration of his own personal confrontation with these beliefs. Cerno Bokar took seriously the doctrines of his faith and sought honestly to put them into practice. His contemplative inclinations were intimately related to the sincerity of his religious belief; in order to strive toward his self-imposed goals, he had constantly to reassess both his goals and where he was in relation to them. This was his essential message, and this was the simple yet extraordinarily demanding task which he set before his disciples. Only his own words can communicate the immediacy with which Cerno Bokar was able to express this appeal to religious search; we therefore turn now to his discourses.

## NOTES

1. See especially chapters 13–19 in the *Rimāḥ*.
2. *Rimāḥ*, I, 96.
3. TB, 41–2; VE, 52.
4. VE, 94.
5. One account asserts that ould Rashīd first came to Bandiagara in order to try to buy young girls to sell as "servants" (Sori Hammadun Bala, interview of 30 September 1977). This account is interesting because it connects the availability of children for sale to the necessity of finding money to pay taxes during "the years of the difficult tax." No other references to these years of heavy taxation or to any related sale or pawning of children have been found.
6. See Traoré, *Contribution*, 184–5. This merchant's name is variously given as Sidi Muhammad (Sori Hammadun Bala, interview of 30 September 1977) and Sidat ould Babana (Amadou Hampaté Bâ, interview of 2 May 1978).
7. For a description of *istikhāra*, See R. Dozy, *Supplément aux Dictionnaires Arabes*, 2e édition (Paris, 1927), I, 415.
8. TB, 56; VE, 94.
9. TB, 54ff; VE, 92, ff.
10. VE, 86–7.
11. TB, 59; VE, 97.

12. Undated letter from Hamallah to Cerno Bokar from the library of Baba Thimbely, Bandiagara.
13. ANM, letter from Koulouba to Governor-General, 30 July 1937.
14. See VE, 100–2; also Amadou Hampaté Bâ, interview of 2 May 1978.
15. ANM, letter from Mopti to Koulouba, 21 July 1937.
16. Sori Hammadun Bala, interview of 30 September 1977.
17. ANM, letter from Mopti to Koulouba, 21 July 1937; for oral accounts see TB, 61 and VE, 102–7; also interviews with Sori Hammadun Bala (30 September 1977), Baba Thimbely (29 September 1977), Dauda Maiga (29 September 1977) and Amadou Hampaté Bâ (2 May 1978).
18. Cited above, note 12.
19. Baba Thimbely, interview of 1 October 1977.
20. ANM, Fonds Récent, 2–E–11, Fiches de renseignement de Chefs de canton, Bandiagara.
21. VE, 108ff.
22. Baba Thimbely, interview of 1 October 1977.
23. ANM, letter from Mopti to Koulouba, 22 February 1939. This information comes from oral depositions recorded in Bandiagara on 6 November 1938.
24. ANM, telegram from Mopti to Koulouba, 31 October 1937.
25. ANM, letter from Koulouba to Governor-General, 16 November 1938.
26. *Ibid.*
27. Including Dauda Maiga, one of my informants.
28. ANM, letter from the Governor-General to Koulouba, 3 January 1939.
29. ANS, 2–G–39/8, Soudan, Rapport Politique Annuel, 1939.
30. Dauda Maiga, interview of 29 September 1977; in this interview Dauda recalled losing his wives only later, on a visit to Bandiagara after having been transferred to Niafunke. Other evidence suggests the marriages were dissolved in late 1938 and early 1939; available evidence did not allow the resolution of the discrepancy in these dates.
31. ANM, letter from Mopti to Koulouba, 6 February 1939.
32. Dauda Maiga, interview of 29 September 1977.
33. Two reports allege this: Baba Thimbely, interview of 29 September 1977, and ANM, letter from Mopti to Koulouba, 6 February 1939.
34. Baba Thimbely, interview of 29 September 1977.
35. TB, 65ff; VE, 114ff.
36. Baba Thimbely, interview of 29 September 1977.
37. TB, 70; VE, 121.
38. As told to Baba Thimbely, interview of 29 September 1977.
39. Dauda Maiga, interview of 29 September 1977.
40. ANS, 2–G–40/10, Soudan, Rapport Politique Annuel, 1940.
41. ANM, Fiche de renseignement, 20 July 1937.

# Part III
# THE SPIRITUAL DISCOURSES

"The greatest knowledge is to know that one does not know."

"Search in truth, and continue to search, for he who searches will find."

"In order that one's heart should be filled with the remembrance of the Lord, one must look upon Him each day as a new discovery."

Cerno Bokar, 1933

The discourses published here are an unusual collection of historical documents. They preserve a body of oral religious teaching in a state close to its original vitality and freshness, which provides an intimate glimpse into the workings of the mind of a West African mystic. What we see here is not a systematic presentation of religious concepts nor an ordered series of directives to disciples, as might be presented in a scholarly book. Rather we are placed in direct communication with what "search" meant to Cerno Bokar in a form which, although not free from inconsistency or even from occasional contradiction, is all the more impressive for the spirit of humble and ceaseless questioning which it portrays. Many of these discourses are answers to questions posed to Cerno Bokar, but they contain nothing of the dogmatic heaviness which often pervades religious writings. Quite the contrary; they reveal a kind of respect mixed with wonder which might be experienced in the face of a new discovery.

Perhaps the ultimate goal of all Cerno's study, teaching and searching was, to use his own words, "to recognize the existence of God and His Oneness" (Discourse 1). As we have seen, in Cerno Bokar's view, this goal required a fundamental knowledge of Islamic dogma, including a study of *tawḥīd*, as well as a sincere commitment to the practice of Islamic rituals, such as prayer and fasting. But Cerno also asserted that "in order that one's heart should be filled with the remembrance of the Lord, one must look upon Him each day as a new discovery" (D. 11). Search is therefore pursued through renewal; each day one seeks to encounter God with all the naive excitement with which one greets a new discovery. The discourses include a number of examples of Cerno's own sense of discovery, none more moving perhaps than an incident concerning his dog (D. 49). While walking to his fields in the oppressive heat which immediately precedes the start of the rains, Cerno was struck by the fidelity of his dog which continued to follow him despite its obvious exhaustion.

This faithfulness touched me deeply. I did not know how to appreciate the act of this animal, ready to follow me to the death without any necessity for himself, and without being constrained to do it by anything whatever. He was loyal because of the fact that he considered me his master. He proved his attachment to me by risking his life with the sole aim of following me and being at my side.
"Lord," I cried out in an outburst of feeling, "Cure my troubled soul. Render my fidelity similar to that of this being whom I disparagingly call 'dog.' Give me, like him, the strength to be able to scorn my life when it is a question of accomplishing Your will. And give me the strength to follow the road on which You place me without asking 'Where am I going?' "

The fidelity of his dog reminds Cerno of the weakness of his own fidelity to God. He consequently requests that God renew his strength and his resolve to follow the 'road of religion." A similar note of humility is sounded throughout the commentaries here published. It is as if Cerno Bokar is constantly questioning his relationship to God, and constantly questioning himself. Indeed, one might even say that for him the quest — his personal search for truth — consisted of an attitude of persistent questioning.

It is this same persistent questioning which he tried to impart to his disciples. Amadou Hampaté Bâ relates a delightful story which in more than one way reflects Cerno Bokar's skill at bringing questions before his students and disciples:

One day Cerno was speaking about *ḥuḍūr ar-rūḥ*, the presence of the divine light within, or its action upon, a material question. He explained all this very well, and each time that he asked the students if they understood, they responded, "We have understood." But as for me, I said I had not understood anything. There was a cousin of mine in the group who said to me, "Really, you were born stupid and you will die stupid! What Cerno has just said is clear." I replied that in any case I did not say it wasn't clear, I said I had not understood.
Cerno said to my cousin, "Alfa, you have understood?" He replied, "But Cerno, it is clear." At which Cerno got up from his place and told Alfa to sit in it and to explain to everyone what had been said. Complete silence! Cerno asked, "What's this, Alfa? You have understood?" My cousin replied, "I thought I understood." "Well, it looks as if Amadou is not as stupid as you!"
Then Cerno said, "I see that we have not understood." And he asked for a mirror to be brought to him, which he placed in the sun. He continued: "Let us consider that the light of the sun represents the divine light. Look over there at the dark corner of the vestibule. What is there?"
"Nothing," someone replied.
"Be careful of being hasty," Cerno said. "When Satan placed his first son in the world he named him Haste. You must never act hastily and thereby make a judgment about something which you have not investigated. It is dark over there, and your eyes have not penetrated the darkness. How do you know there

is nothing? You should say 'I don't know.' Because the greatest knowledge is to know that one does not know. *Anndude anndaa yo woni anndal manngal.*"

Then Cerno continued: "When we are in ignorance, it is the light of God which descends into us in order to clarify what we don't know, in order to dissipate the darkness in which the thing we don't understand is enveloped. It is the darkness which hinders us from understanding it. If the light of God comes, it will dissipate the darkness and we will understand the thing we did not understand. We are considering that the sun is the light of God, and that the corner is the thing we don't understand." Then Cerno adjusted the mirror so that the sun's rays were reflected into the corner of the vestibule, and it was illuminated as if with a torch. "There," he said, "what is in there? What do you see?" One person said he saw an ant, another a stalk of straw, and yet another a stone. "A moment ago," Cerno said, "you claimed there was nothing there, and now we see all of nature there in symbiosis: you have the animal, the vegetable and the mineral. The clarification of the divine light acts exactly like that. But the mirror is the heart. You see that the mirror is clean; the heart must also be pure so that it can receive the divine light and reflect the light in order to clarify what you wish to know."[1]

"The greatest knowledge is to know one does not know." This statement contains the essential message of the story, and epitomizes the force of Cerno Bokar's spiritual search. Everything and everyone constantly placed in question. The discourses include several examples, similar to that in this story, of a person caught up short and thrown back on himself, in question. Sotoura seeks a benediction to soothe her short temper; she is sent away to nurture her own capacities for love and indulgence (D. 15). Someone has been influenced by the reputation of Cerno's teaching and asks to become his disciple; he is told that no man ever "accords exactly with his reputation." He must decide for himself (D. 47). And even those specific questions which are posed directly to Cerno are often not directly answered; or else the response is designed to lead to yet more questions. One is advised to meditate on certain verses from the Qur'an; or one is given a response which may be filled with metaphorical power but which requires considerable pondering before its meaning can be grasped. One might take as an example here Cerno's numerous comments on faith. According to Islamic theology, faith comprises certain specific beliefs: in God, the Last Judgment, the angels, the revealed books, the prophets and the divine decree. But if one reads carefully all that Cerno Bokar says in his discourses on the subject it is clear that for him faith is also a material substance shared by all men but which differs in quality according to its state. These changes in the "state" of faith are described by metaphorical reference to light, water and heat.

A Sufism which is expressed in the metaphorical language of parables, or which seeks to pose ever more profound questions rather than provide easy answers, may seem a long way from the Sufism of "eleven beads/twelve beads." And yet we must remember that Cerno Bokar, although he professed his own interpretations of Tijani doctrines, fully accepted them in their strictest sense. The Sufism of Cerno Bokar consists of a mélange of all that we have attempted to describe in previous chapters about the Tijaniyya and the *kabbe* as well as of the thoughts contained in these discourses. Many readers may find the content of the discourses more appealing as an expression of mystical search than the doctrines of the Tijaniyya, but for Cerno Bokar all these were part of a greater whole. What we might perceive as contradictions were not so for him. How, one might ask, can the spirit of incessant questioning revealed in the discourses be compatible with the kind of claims made by Ahmad al-Tijani for the Sufi way which he founded? Cerno Bokar would undoubtedly answer that this is because there are many "truths" with respect to man, although there is only one Truth with respect to God. Depending on the nature of the man in question, there are different religions, different forms of faith, and different expressions of Sufism. They all "true" only in the sense that they can lead to the "Truth."

## *A critique of the Discourses*

This collection of discourses was discovered in the library of the Centre de Hautes Études sur l'Afrique et l'Asie Modernes (CHEAM) in Paris (formerly the Centre de Hautes Études d'Administration Musulmane) under the title "The Parables of Cerno Bokar." They were recorded by Amadou Hampaté Bâ in 1933 when he spent approximately six months in intensive study with Cerno Bokar and was then himself initiated into the "secrets" of Sufism. This period of special study was noted in interviews with several persons who were in Bandiagara at the time,[2] and Hampaté Bâ has also given a brief description of how he collected this material.[3] Because at the time he was unable to write in Fulfulde, he wrote down Cerno Bokar's comments in a direct French translation. These texts were later rendered into a smoother French version, which appears in the CHEAM document. Most of the quotations from Cerno Bokar which appear in *Tierno Bokar, le Sage de Bandiagara* and *Vie et Enseignement de Tierno Bokar* are based on the CHEAM document, of which they constitute about half the total number of "parables."

These published versions of the texts often differ in relatively minor detail from those of the CHEAM document, presumably because they were modified in order to achieve a more precise or clear language. This entire process of recording in direct French translation with subsequent modifications is, of course, unfortunate. Although we are deeply indebted to Hampaté Bâ for any texts at all which survive, and these certainly retain a high degree of freshness of presentation and reveal with great honesty both the content and process of Cerno's thinking, the absence of the original Fulfulde texts presents many problems. From a purely technical point of view, one would like to know the original Fulfulde words used by Cerno for certain terms, such as *âme* (soul) or *esprit* (spirit or mind). And Hampaté Bâ himself has commented on the difficulties of rendering Fulfulde into literary French.[5] In addition, questions must inevitably arise as to the accuracy of these texts which have been preserved and transmitted in a way which allows for no possibility of confirming their precise content. None of the persons interviewed in Bandiagara felt competent to comment on this aspect of Cerno's teaching, but excessive weight should not be placed on negative evidence of this kind; they had not enjoyed such intimate relations with Cerno Bokar as did Hampaté Bâ,[6] and of course only he felt called upon to record Cerno's words. Hampaté Bâ claims that these texts are faithful transcriptions of Cerno's words to which he has added nothing (taking into account the conditions of collecting them, as explained above). On the other hand, he candidly confessed to me that these ideas have become so much a part of him that at times he becomes confused between what were Cerno's thoughts and what are his own. It must be emphasized that the problem here being discussed only presents itself to the historian who seeks to reconstruct the content of Cerno Bokar's thought and teaching. Amadou Hampaté Bâ has devoted much of his life to the transmission of Cerno's teachings as he understands them; for him the precise re-statement of Cerno's words is less important than the communication of the essential spirit of the teaching. This said, Hampaté Bâ's published versions of the texts are extremely faithful to those in the CHEAM document. A few words and phrases have been modified to improve clarity of expression, but the basic ideas expounded in the texts remain untouched.

The internal evidence of the texts also presents some problems. One must seriously doubt that Cerno Bokar would have spoken about a conductor in an electrical circuit (D. 36), especially when he seems only to have learned of the existence of radio from Hampaté Bâ in 1933 (D. 6). Nor does it seem likely that he would have described the formation of fog in scientific language (D. 37). On the other hand, a note of authenticity is struck by the existence in the collection of an incomplete text (D. 48), to which is added the comment: "The master was interrupted by a visitor, and we never heard the rest of the story, alas." Indeed, the overwhelming weight of the internal evidence suggests that these texts are the products of a West African Muslim and Sufi of the early twentieth century, although as discussed above we have no means of verifying conclusively that they are Cerno Bokar's exact words. In no way does their content contradict the doctrines of Islam or of the Tijaniyya order; indeed, they show a deep understanding of them. They reflect the concerns of a person primarily occupied with the elaboration of his own personal religious understanding as well as the understanding of others. Finally, all the metaphors, examples and commentaries on social and political life mentioned in the texts are drawn from West Africa, and often even more specifically from the Niger river valley. Even if the sum of all this evidence cannot prove that these texts present Cerno Bokar's ideas in a completely unmodified form, it is still difficult not to conclude they are the product of the traditional West African Muslim culture of this century.

We have called the texts "discourses" rather than parables, because this seems to be the best English word to describe their character and content. A few might be considered parables in the strict sense, but many more tend to be comments, observations or answers to questions; and all represent Cerno Bokar's efforts to instruct and enlighten students, disciples and others around him. Most of the English translations presented here are published for the first time; they represent about two thirds of the total number of discourses in the CHEAM document. Where appropriate, references are given to published French versions, although these occasionally differ from the CHEAM texts because of subsequent revisions for publication or because some have been published only in part or even in divided form. We have not noted these details. The only notes added to the texts themselves are those which might be useful in explaining unusual or unfamiliar terminology. We have, however, attempted a brief introductory analysis of some of the major themes and ideas contained in the discourses.

## *The content of the Discourses*

Cerno Bokar's discourses might be seen as reflecting the life and concerns of his *zāwiya*, isolated from the turmoil of the outside world; here only the faintest echoes of French colonial authority or of African political and religious disputes are heard. Recorded in 1933, they are from the period preceding Cerno's submission to Shaykh Hamallah, although by then Hamallah and Hamallism were both exerting great pressure on religious and political life; we find no mention of such specific issues here, or of many other less elevated matters which must have exercised the minds of teachers and students. The discourses represent a "higher teaching" designed to nurture man's spirit in a movement away from "this world" and towards "God and His Truth." Of course, the content of this collection represents that which Hampaté Bâ has selected to record from a much larger range of material. And although what appears here certainly does not exhaust the range of subjects which might have been discussed within the *zāwiya*, even on religious questions, we should accept the likelihood that the style of discussion and presentation is typical of Cerno Bokar as a spiritual guide and teacher, and that the subjects expounded here were among those of greatest personal concern to him. The discourses elaborate some of the themes which were introduced in earlier chapters of this book: the nature of man as a seeker of religious understanding, the nature of the soul (*nafs*) and the nature of religion itself. We also gain great insight into Cerno Bokar as a visionary and as an interpreter not only of his personal visions but of the world around him. The most vivid image which emerges from these discourses is of a man who speaks and understands the language of metaphor, and herein lies the essence of his religious teaching both in terms of substance and of style.

*The language of metaphor.* We have already touched upon this subject in our discussion of Cerno Bokar's religious studies. Three important aspects of analogical reasoning might be re-stated here, since they bear directly on Cerno Bokar's thought as expressed in the discourses. First, analogical reasoning is one of the primary methods employed by Sufis to comprehend the divine, hidden Reality underlying all manifested existence, including the Qur'an. Secondly, this form of reasoning found wide-spread expression in the science of numerology (including the science of letters, *'ilm al-ḥurūf*), a study taking numerous forms, some of which were condemned by orthodox scholars. The science of numerology was considered to be secret knowledge in West Africa, and its precepts were transmitted only to specially qualified individuals by means of an "initiation;" these secrets were also exchanged among initiates. Because it was considered secret, only a few references to numerology appear in the discourses (D. 5, 32, 41), in one instance with a specific mention of the restricted availability of this knowledge (D. 32). But one must not conclude from this absence of comment any lack of interest in the subject on Cerno Bokar's part; indeed he was an initiate into this science and the esoteric interpretation of his *mā 'd-dīn* was based upon it.[7] Thirdly, analogical reasoning allowed for the exercise of unlimited creative imagination in the transmission of a religious tradition whose essential substance was considered inviolable. A teacher could employ metaphor and analogy in any form which he wished so long as he preserved intact the basic tenets of Islam.

To a certain extent, of course, the use of metaphor and analogy is the result both of cultural tradition and of personal style. Both traditional African and Islamic societies exploit extensively the didactic potential of parable, proverb and story, and therefore of metaphor and analogy. Cerno Bokar seems to have combined within himself not only this dual African and Islamic cultural heritage, but also a personal acuity of observation and a disarming degree of sincerity. Quite a number of his stories are about himself, interpretations of his visions or clear explications of the lessons he has drawn from personal experience. This candid openness deepens the impact of what he has to say; one is inevitably moved by the humility of this man who is willing to share his innermost thoughts, especially when those thoughts reveal that he felt he too still had much to learn and a long way to travel in his own personal search. One might argue that the sharing of personal experiences as a form of teaching was a matter of personal inclination or style, but the practice has many precedents in Islamic literature. The *ḥadīth* themselves are accounts of Muhammad's experiences and behaviour which became a basic source for the subsequent compilation of Islamic law; a good Muslim should emulate the behaviour of the Prophet. Sufi literature also contains many examples of didactic stories drawn from personal experience, the aim of which is not necessarily emulation but where the lesson to be learned is often very clear. Al-Hajj Umar, who was not much given to this kind of personal confession, nonetheless recounts many stories of this kind in the *Rimāḥ*. One example of these can be cited here; it touches on a subject we have discussed, the bestowing of secret knowledge, in this case the Great Name of God. The story is told by Yūsuf b. al-Ḥusain ar-Rāzī (d. A.D. 916)[8] that on learning that Dhū'n-Nūn possessed the Great Name of God, he travelled from Mecca to meet him. He stayed with the great Sufi master for over a year serving him and even instructing him in matters of theology. Then, longing to return to his people in Khurasan, he expressed this desire to Dhū'n-Nūn and asked to be given the Great Name. Dhū'n-Nūn did not reply to this request and spoke not a word to Yūsuf for six months. Then one day he summoned him:

> "Do you know a certain friend of mine who lives in Fustat and who visits us?" And he named the man.
>
> I replied, "Yes, certainly." So he gave me a bowl with a lid secured on it with a handkerchief, and he told me, "Deliver this to him in Fustat."
>
> I took the bowl from his hands and found it very light, as if there were nothing in it. When I reached Fustat I said to myself, "Dhū'n-Nūn is sending me to a man with the gift of a bowl with nothing in it; I must see what is in it." When I untied the handkerchief and opened the lid, a mouse leapt from the bowl and fled. I became angry; I though Dhū'n-Nūn was mocking me and at the same time my anxiety about [not accomplishing] what he had asked did not disappear. I returned to him filled with rage.
>
> But when he saw me he smiled because he knew what had happened, and he said, "O foolish one, I entrusted you with a mouse and you betrayed me, so how can I entrust you with the Great Name of God?"[9]

This story does not communicate such intimacy as Cerno Bokar's account of his dog, related above; on the other hand, it is much more sophisticated. At one level, its lesson is clear: a person cannot be given a secret if he cannot safeguard it. But there is also a much more subtle message: Dhū'n-Nūn had created the circumstances in which Yūsuf could see for himself why he should not be entrusted with the Great Name, and Yūsuf's suspicious behaviour was the inevitable result of his inner state. Sufis believe that a man's outward manifestations are dependent on his inner state of being in a manner analogous to the relationship which exists between created existence and divine Reality. The "inner" or "hidden" dimension determines the "outer" or "manifested."

Cerno Bokar was well acquainted with this genre of story; he encouraged people to attempt "to uncover the secret" which he claimed was buried in traditional stories of all sorts (D. 44). But he himself did not seek to transmit hidden messages; his personal metaphorical descriptions are expressed in direct and lucid language. He did suggest that one should meditate on verses of the Qur'an, or on events which occur in ordinary life, in order to explore their various hidden meanings. And his advice on this is explicit:

> Observe everything with the eyes of your profound intelligence and in the light of the law of analogy which connects the events and elements of the three kingdoms of nature one with another. Once you have discovered this secret mechanism, it will aid you in implanting within yourself the truth of divine matters which are situated beyond the letter of the Qur'an. Then you will know the significance of the verse: "[He] teacheth man that which he knew not" (D. 8).

He also said:

> God has no need of reason nor of human intelligence. He gave them to us for use in this life; therefore we are not to bring them untouched to the grave, that is, to live and die without meditating on and drawing spiritual profit from the events which happen to us and from the things which we ascertain (D. 49).

To Cerno Bokar analogy and metaphor were not simply a matter of style, although he often employed them as pedagogical aids; they form the very essence of what he wished to study. Indeed, one gains the impression from this collection of discourses that his ultimate aim was to sharpen the agility of the mind so that it could move instantaneously between various metaphorical planes. Numerous examples of his own ability to do this appear in the discourses. Someone questions the curious (to many Africans) European custom of growing flowers and he replies that flowers are a mystical path; he even cites a relevant Qur'anic verse on which to meditate.[10] The blinding flash at night of automobile headlights recalls to him the blinding flash of divine light which can "burst suddenly upon the vision of the initiate, flooding his breast and holding him fast, immobile and stupefied" (D. 14). The implications of this kind of teaching are profound, because if every ordinary event and object can remind one of its hidden or esoteric analog, then a person can use his ordinary life as a constant and ever-present vehicle for coming back into touch with his personal spiritual search. Cerno Bokar certainly succeded in doing this for himself. Absolutely nothing seems devoid of its spiritual analogy: the foliage of trees, the rainbow, the road leading to the European settlement, even the coquette cleaning her teeth!

*On the nature of man and religion.* Cerno Bokar's discourses present a provocative commentary on man and his religion. His views were not dogmatic, but were singularly tolerant and sensitive; the basic religious tenets which he emphasized in his teaching did not differ from those preached by other Muslims in that he placed primary importance on the recognition of "the existence of God and His oneness" (D. 1), which implied the necessity for all men to submit to God and His law. But his interpretations were often at variance with predominant Muslim thought of the time. He saw the world as divided between those who believed in one God, and those who did not, and he was much more concerned to encourage the unity of the believers than to condemn the unbelievers (D. 3). His discourses are laced with pleas for unity and co-operation among believers who, he felt, attested "to the same truth" whether they were Muslims, Jews or Christians (D. 3). This tolerant and at times almost ecumenical attitude was justified by the Muslim doctrine that all the forms of monotheism which preceded Islam were valid. The first of these was the religion of Abraham, of which Islam considers itself a direct descendant. Tolerance of this sort was not universal in West Africa, but nor was it unusual; it was based on the Qur'an itself, and we have seen that the *kabbe* also made explicit reference to the Pentateuch of Moses, the Psalms of David and the Gospels of Jesus, as well as to the Qur'an.

Cerno Bokar was well aware that his views on these matters differed from those of many Muslims around him. But what is most essential for us to grasp in seeking to understand his thought is that he attributed these differences, not to any social, political or intellectual influences to which he or others might have been exposed, but to the level one attains in the development of personal faith. The operative conceptual pattern here is hierarchical and it relates to all aspects of Cerno's thought. We can probe this concept somewhat more deeply in examining Cerno's attitude to the *jihād* of the sword, which he described as "the mutual killing to which the sons of Adam submit in the name of a God whom they pretend to love very much, but whom they adore poorly by destroying a part of His work."[11] This attitude, like that of religious tolerance, was not unusual in West Africa, despite the far-reaching series of *jihād*s which had swept across the region in the late eighteenth- and nineteenth-centuries. One could argue from the texts of the discourses themselves that Cerno Bokar had reached his conclusions through his own reasoning about the nature of man. Every human being, he asserts, has been endowed with "a particle of the spirit of God" (D. 1). So how can one be anything but tolerant toward the "vessels" which contain this particle; and how can men ever justify destroying one another in the name of God? Cerno even reinforces this position by quoting the Qur'an to the effect that "there is no compulsion in religion" (D. 1).

Although this kind of logical presentation of Cerno's thought is not without justification, he also says something quite different about how one comes to oppose the waging of *jihād*. Warfare in defence of religion, according to him, is characteristic of a certain group of people, "the common man, the masses, and teachers who are attached to the letter [of the law]" (D. 32). Among Muslims, these are the people who understand their religion as requiring nothing more than a strict and literal conformity to every aspect of the religious law. According to Cerno Bokar, the purpose of the religious law is to limit and contain the behaviour of man, "to deprive the faithful of the excessive liberty contained in the dissoluteness of irreligion" (D. 36). These constraining demands of the law are necessary for all Muslims; everyone must submit to the law. But Cerno Bokar did not believe that the practice of religion was defined solely by the precepts of the law, as do (according to him) most Muslims. Higher, more refined forms of religion exist, and movement between these different "levels" of religious life are determined by the nature and quality of an individual's faith. The faith of the majority of people is such that it can only relate to the specificity of the law and of ritual. This kind of religion is narrow, limiting and "intransigent" in belief, which is why its adherents often resort to war in defence of their beliefs. The second "level" of religious practice includes that minority "who have worked and successfully faced up to the trials . . . of the rigid law which admits no compromise" (D. 32). These people also conform to the law, but they can also see beyond it; their faith is more fluid and flexible, not in the sense that their religious practice differs from that of other Muslims or that they adhere to other doctrines, but in that they can "accept truths from wherever they come" (D. 32). They perceive that the essence of all monotheistic religions is the same and that all believers worship the same God, and they can accept the outward diversities of religious practice because they are aware that all of them lead to the same goal. Consequently, they are much less likely to resort to warfare on behalf of their religion. The third and highest "level" of faith is that possessed by a tiny élite who are capable of directly contemplating divine Truth; these are the saints of Islam.

These three levels of faith, and their corresponding forms of religious expression, conform to the Sufi doctrine, which Cerno Bokar taught in his *mā 'd-dīn*, that religious practice occurs on three levels, *sharī'a* (the law), *ṭarīqa* (the way), and *ḥaqīqa* (the Truth). Although we know from his teachings in the *mā 'd-dīn* that Cerno considered a certain amount of religious knowledge an essential pre-requisite for entry into the Sufi way, and although he stated explicitly that the constituent elements of the second "level" of faith "derive from understanding," his comments in the discourses depict faith as a quality (or a material substance) which can be modified not through reasoning but through religious practice, specifically through the recitation of prayers or *adhkār*. Cerno Bokar was not anti-intellectual — we have explored his belief that it was through the intellect that man becomes convinced of his need for religion — and the discourses provide many examples of how the intellect is employed to aid man's search by meditation on the Qur'an or in deciphering the esoteric lessons concealed in manifested existence. But it is only through recitations that faith is transformed, and a more refined quality of faith brings one a new capacity for understanding. This kind of thinking underlies Cerno's belief that not everyone is capable of understanding numerological analyses. Faith and understanding therefore progress together through the hierarchy of religious experience toward the perception and understanding of the "Truth."

In addition to variations in the quality or "level" of faith, Cerno Bokar also thought that men differ among themselves in the nature of their "carnal souls" [*nafs*]. The carnal soul includes all those functions which man shares with the animals as well as what Cerno called his "psychic states;" this concept of the soul might be very generally compared to the contemporary western concept of personality. Man approaches religion, as indeed he approaches all his activities, through the agency of his carnal soul. Cerno believed that all men are religious, because as descendants of Adam all had been endowed with "a particle of the spirit of God" (D. 1). But because of the wide variations in the nature of the carnal soul, all men were not receptive to the same kind of religious teaching or preaching, the effectiveness of which depended on a clear understanding on the part of the teacher or spiritual guide of the nature of the soul of the student or disciple. With proper teaching and guidance every person possessed the inherent capacity to progress through the Sufi way toward the "Truth" (D. 18). But most people did not embark on this level of religious search because they were unable to overcome the barriers constructed by their own "carnal souls." Cerno Bokar encouraged all people to pursue their religious search to the extremes of their personal capacities, but he knew that only very few persons would enter the Sufi way.

*The dynamics of spiritual search.* According to the scattered references that we find in the discourses, Cerno Bokar seems to have thought that man was comprised of one invariable element, a particle of the divine spirit, and at least two variable elements, his soul and his faith. Man is also endowed with intellect, a function which sometimes seems to be part of the soul, sometimes more akin to the divine spirit. Intellect first brings man to his religion and it further aids him in the development of his religious understanding as he learns to observe the world "in the light of the law of analogy." But there is also a higher intellect through which one can perceive ultimate Truth; this perception passes through what Ibn 'Arabī called "the eye of discernment" (See above, pp. 105–6). This function of intellect seems to be closely associated with the divine particle which God has placed in man, as Cerno Bokar described it. Spiritual search is therefore aimed at the activation of this higher intellect through the dual process of refining one's faith and overcoming the obstacles of one's carnal soul.

The divine particle which is man's heritage from God is enveloped within the carnal soul. As Cerno described it, "God caused a rain of passions to shower upon the original human principle which He planted in our father Adam; these are estimated to comprise nine-tenths of the states of the soul" (D. 41). The carnal soul plays host to all man's moral and religious disabilities; it is the seat of all his "faults," such as excessive egoism (D. 18), failure to control his emotions (D. 9), and desire for the material rewards of this world (D. 12, 27, 31, 33, 37, 61). The struggle to overcome these faults is likened to Abraham's preparation to sacrifice his son Isaac (D. 35), but like Isaac the soul is spared and in fact becomes the vehicle for spiritual transformation. If the disciple must struggle to bring spiritual discipline to his soul, his teacher or guide must seek to nurture and prepare it for ultimate transformation. The trials through which the soul passes depend upon its "psychic state" (D. 5). Some souls must be "soaked in love" and "opened to charity" (D. 33); others, which Cerno likened to sandy soil, respond quickly but with results which last only a short time (D. 56); and still others, like clayey soil, respond slowly to religious teaching, but with results which remain firmly rooted once they take hold (D. 60). Indeed, the optimum condition of the soul is like that of a properly loaded canoe on the River Niger: not so overladen that it will capsize, but reasonably ballasted so that it can effectively navigate through any "waves of temptation" (D. 40).

"Whatever the nature of the soul, the spoken recitation of the first formula of faith is recommended: 'There is no god but God.' It is the best mental devotion which one can perform in order to please God" (D. 5). Whereas to please God is the most important reason for repeated recitations of His name, the practice also produces other important results. Prayer and recitation introduce a kind of "mystical heat" into the soul which augments its "laudatory capacity" (D. 52) and "keeps alight the spiritual ember'' which is ignited within it (D. 53). This same heat also maintains and transforms man's faith. Cerno Bokar is not explicit concerning his understanding of the relationship between man's soul and his faith, although some of his comments imply that he saw the latter as a kind of life blood of the former. Faith is comparable to air, he said: ''Both are equally indispensable to human life, so much so that one cannot find a man who sincerely believes in nothing.''[12] But his favourite metaphor for faith was water which he said has ''neither colour, odour, taste nor form; it takes on the shape of the objects which contain it'' (D. 34). Faith is contained within the soul, and both container and contained can be transformed through the heat produced by the adoration of God and the recitation of His name. The soul can be crystallized into ''the state of a mystical diamond'' (D. 43), whereas faith can be sublimated into a vapour which rises toward God (D. 32).

Cerno Bokar was most eloquent in his descriptions of the various degrees of faith. The first is solid, ''subject to a rigorous determination . . . and intransigent and hard like the stone'' from which it takes its name. The second is liquid in nature; it ''undermines the faults of the soul'' and adopts a shape in the form of its recipient, penetrating each individual according to the ''accidents of his moral terrain.'' It is subtle and forms a ''body in perpetual motion.'' The third degree is like a vapour, void of all material weight, which rises ''like smoke into the heaven of holy souls'' (D. 32). Corresponding to these three levels of faith are three degrees of mystical light. The first is likened to the flame which man himself can ignite: it illuminates and heats only a limited space, and it can be easily extinguished. The second is the light of the sun which illuminates and heats everything on earth; it is constant, vivifying and immutable. The third emanates from God, ''it is a darkness more brilliant than all lights combined; it is the light of Truth'' (D. 55).

Cerno Bokar's spiritual search was contained within the second degree of faith; his goal was the ''light of Truth,'' but he never claimed to have glimpsed it. His ceaseless questioning and pondering conformed to the nature of his subtle and supple faith. His concern that one should be ''constantly occupied with reciting the name of the Lord'' (D. 5, 7) emerged from his conviction that the mystical heat generated by recitations maintained a higher degree of faith and aided in the purification of the soul. The more refined one's faith and soul, the more profound became one's understanding of the hidden realities underlying God's creation, and the closer one came to perceiving the light of Truth.

## NOTES

1. Amadou Hampaté Bâ, interview of 2 May 1978.
2. Interviews with Sori Hammadun Bala, Baba Thimbely and Koola Sidi.
3. VE, 127–8.
4. I discovered the CHEAM document in May 1978 when in Paris for an extensive set of interviews with Hampaté Bâ. He apparently did not know of the existence of this copy, having misplaced his own, and I therefore arranged for him to have a photocopy.
5. VE, 128.
6. Except for Koola Sidi, who was not particularly willing to be interviewed in the first place, plus the fact that he was extremely feeble. The subsequent interview was therefore very brief and did not touch on this subject.
7. See Ch. 4. Apparently Hampaté Bâ has become increasingly willing to discuss certain aspects of numerology; see especially, *Jésus vu par un Musulman* (Dakar-Abidjan, 1976), and "Jésus et Hasdu, Conte initiatique de la mystique peule, enseigné à la Zaouia da Bandiagara par Tierno Bokar Salif Tall," *Bulletin de l'IFAN*, XXXI, sér. B, no. 3 (1969), 754–86.
8. Schimmel, *Mystical Dimensions*, 171, calls Dhū'n-Nūn the "part-time master" of Yūsuf b. al-Ḥusain.
9. *Rimāḥ*, I, 197–8.
10. See TB, 35; VE, 43; Monod, "Homme," 153.
11. TB, 84; VE, 158–9.
12. TB, 82; VE, 148–9; Monod, "Homme," 156.

# THE SPIRITUAL DISCOURSES

1. Are the children of the same father, in spite of their physical differences, any less brothers and legitimate sons of their parents? It is from contemplating this truth that we come to pity those who refuse to recognize the spiritual ideas of believers from religions [different from their own], and who deny them a place in the brotherhood of the one God, the unique and unchanging Creator. For us, with all due respect to those attached to the letter [of the law], only one thing counts above all other: to recognize the existence of God and His Oneness.

Thus, brother in God who comes to the threshold of our *zāwiya*, abode of love and charity, do not provoke the follower of Moses. God has given witness that he said to his people:

> . . . Seek help in Allah and endure. Lo! the earth is Allah's. He giveth it for an inheritance to whom He will. And lo! the sequel is for those who keep their duty (to Him) (VII, 128).

Neither should you provoke the follower of Jesus. God has said, in speaking of the miraculous child of Mary, the Virgin-Mother:

> . . . and We gave Jesus, son of Mary, clear proofs (of Allah's Sovereignty) and We supported him with the holy Spirit (II, 253).

And as for the other humans? Certainly, let them enter and even greet them fraternally in order to honor in them their inheritance from Adam, of which God has said:

> And when I have fashioned him and breathed into him of My Spirit, then fall down before him prostrate,. . . (XXXVIII, 72).

This verse suggests that in each [human] descendant, due to his inheritance from Adam, there is a particle of the spirit of God. How could we dare to scorn a vessel which contains a particle of the spirit of God?

You, who come to us and whom we consider not as a student but as a brother, reflect and meditate on this verse from the Book of Guidance:

> There is no compulsion in religion. The right direction is henceforth distinct from error. And he who rejecteth false deities and believeth in Allah hath grasped a firm handhold which will never break. Allah is Hearer, Knower (II, 256).

(VE, 147–8)

2. Do you know a part of the earth which receives neither the light of the sun nor that of the moon, nor that of any one of the numerous stars and planets which ornament the sky, nor the rays of dawn, nor the reddening glow of the setting sun? It is only in this place that man might have the right to question the existence of God. In every other place where one perceives His wonders, the heart, the mind and the eyes with which we have been endowed must cause us to think upon the author of such beauty.

You who come to us and whom we consider not as a student but as a brother, reflect. Before entering the *zāwiya* where love and knowledge are sought, meditate on the lights of the verse and benefit from it:

> And of His signs is this: He created you of dust, and behold you human beings, ranging widely! (XXX, 20).

(TB, 78; VE, 140–1)

3. There are only two categories of people in this world: those who believe in God and who are distributed among the diverse forms of religion, and those who doubt the existence of God and who are similarly distributed among the diverse forms of the negation of the existence of God. These two groups are diametrically opposed. They form two camps in perpetual combat.

What is tragically ridiculous and not to the honor of the human spirit is that the believers in God war among themselves as if they did not say the same thing and attest to the same truth.

As for us, we embrace the doctrine which states that all who believe in the existence of God form one family united by a single idea. The mutual opposition of various believers emerges from certain [lower] human causes the origin of which is to be found in extreme racism, in the diversity of languages, and especially in the egoism which pushes each to seek to maintain an exclusiveness.

As for you, brother in God, who comes to the threshold of our *zāwiya* hoping to find here the tranquility which is lacking in your heart, before allowing any utterance to leave your mouth, meditate on these verses of the Qur'an:

> Turning unto Him [only]; and be careful of your duty unto Him, and establish worship, and be not of those who ascribe partners [unto Him];
>
> Of those who split up their religion and became schismatics, each sect exulting in its tenets (XXX, 31, 32).

(TB, 20)

4. The coquette, in order to please her partners, cleans her teeth morning and night. She perfumes her mouth by chewing the resins of plants or pleasant-smelling roots.

Adepts, do the same thing on the spiritual level: perfume your breath by means of the emanations which result from the frequent citation of the divine name in order to please God, the most faithful and marvellous of lovers.

If you hear me and wish to lighten the material burden of your soul, before entering our *zāwiya*, which is a centre for the praising of God, meditate on the following verses:

> So Glory be to Allah when ye enter the night and when ye enter the morning —
> Unto Him be praise in the heavens and the earth! — and at the sun's decline and in the noonday (XXX, 17–18).

5. There are several methods for washing laundry, each of which depends on the nature of the material — whether it is coarse or fine. A blanket of thick wool is stamped on with the feet or beaten with a cudgel. A *boubou* of fine European cloth is pressed between the hands.

It is the same with human souls. The trials through which they pass in order to attain the degree where the spirit is constantly occupied with reciting the name of the Lord are more or less violent in accordance with one's psychic state. But whatever the nature of the soul, the spoken recitation of the first formula of faith is recommended: "There is no god but God."

It is considered the best mental devotion which one can perform in order to please God, whose primordial attribute is Being-Oneness.

Adept who comes to me, your brother in God and not your Master, as it pleases you to proclaim it, meditate on the twelve elements of this formula of faith in its triple division.* This formula exalts the emanations of the Creative Entity; it establishes the differentiation of the essence, and plunges the soul into communion with the Source of all existences in God.

Being is One. The creative Entity is endowed with anteriority, with eternity, with plenitude and with originality. Differentiation establishes that life, wisdom, hearing, sight, will, speech and creation belong to the Being-Oneness. Meditate on the following verses:

> He is the First and the Last, and the Outward and the Inward; and He is Knower of all things (LVII, 3).

*The first portion of the *shahāda*, or Muslim formula of faith, *Lā ilah illā Allāh*, is composed of only three different Arabic letters; *lām*, *alif*, *hā'*, the entire phrase consisting of twelve letters:

The Beneficent
Hath made known the Qur'an.
He hath created man.
He hath taught him utterance
The sun and moon are made punctual.
The stars and the trees adore (LV, 1–6).
Vision comprehendeth Him not, but He comprehendeth (all vision).
He is the Subtile, the Aware (VI, 103).

6. Amkullel* has told us that the white men have discovered a way to diffuse written and verbal messages everywhere in the world at the same instant. I do not doubt his assertion, nor does it surprise me. I know that the human mind, drawing upon divine strength as it does, has not yet spoken its last word, nor produced its final work.

This discovery leads me to the following reflection: how can man in future dare to doubt the divine omnipresence when man himself has been able to create a device capable of sending messages everywhere at the same moment? Allah, may He be glorified, was correct about His human creation, against whom He said:

Read: And thy Lord is the Most Bounteous.
Who teacheth by the pen,
Teacheth man that which he knew not.
Nay, but verily man is rebellious
That he thinketh himself independent! (XCVI, 3–7).

7. The power of God is like a barrier which surrounds heaven and earth. Everything has its origin within it and everything eventually collides with the eternal walls of this shell and returns to its point of departure. Our actions, good or bad, once in movement evolve and eventually strike against this barrier. This collision augments their force and changes their direction; formerly moving from the center outwards, their movement is reversed. Thus the effects of our actions return to us like the wave which having struck the shore returns toward the center of the stream.

Brother in God, who wishes to become an adept in this *zāwiya* of true communion, since our actions return to us, pronounce the sacred name 'Allah' ceaselessly day and night. Pronounce it gently in your heart, inwardly in your spirit, as if your lungs were filled while blowing the steer's horn trumpet. This name, more than any other, evokes the

*Nickname given to Amadou Hampaté Bâ, meaning "little Kullel." Kullel was a well-known raconteur in the household of Hampaté Bâ's adoptive father. See D.24 and Hampaté Bâ, *L'Étrange Destin de Wangrin*, 7–8.

essence of divinity. It agitates and brings about the emanations from the "ether of [God's] attributes" in the form of waves of spiritual well-being. These will rise up and return toward your spirit, the center from which your invocation originated. Our happiness and our unhappiness depend on our own actions. God has said, and we must meditate on it:

> And whoso doeth good an atom's weight will see it then,
> And whoso doeth ill an atom's weight will see it then (CXIX, 7–8).

(VE, 172–3)

8. Since the arrival of the Europeans, who among us could doubt that a large road must inevitably lead to an agglomeration of white man's houses?

How is it then that we cannot convince ourselves that the religious way created by God and maintained by His prophets leads to the divine residence? Do not refuse to God what you accord to man created by Him.

Brother in God, at the threshold of the *zāwiya* of knowledge, observe everything with the eyes of your profound intelligence and in the light of the law of analogy which connects the events and elements of the three kingdoms of nature one with another.* Once you have discovered this secret mechanism, it will aid you in implanting within yourself the truth of divine matters which are situated beyond the letter of the Qur'an. Then you will know the significance of the verse:

> [He] Teacheth man that which he knew not (XCVI, 5).

9. When sheep become agitated, the shepherd is no longer able to guide them. Then one sees him doing everything to prevent them from scattering.

What is true for the temporal shepherd is also useful for the spiritual shepherd. Each of us is a shepherd for his passions. Certainly it is necessary to master them. They are just another kind of sheep. We must avoid the possibility that they will leap over our heads, overrun us and drag us into a moral abyss, a valley where neither the soul nor the spirit can survive.
(TB, 86; VE, 166)

10. God has not imposed on us [the duty] to change the course of a great stream of water leading to the sea. He has taken charge of that

*The animal, vegetable and mineral kingdoms.

Himself. He has charged us with the modification of the flow of our ideas in changing them from a bad to a good direction.

The fact that God has breathed into us a portion of His spirit gives us a means to orient ourselves. This gift from Him renders us somewhat responsible for the consequences of our orientation, good or bad. This truth is exemplified by the following verse, which we submit for the meditation of those of sound judgement:

> Allah tasketh not a soul beyond its scope. For it [is only] that which it hath earned, and against it [only] that which it hath deserved (II, 286).

(TB, 87)

11. In order that one's heart should be filled with the remembrance of the Lord, one must look upon Him each day as a new discovery.

12. A straw hut in which a group of young men is sleeping catches fire during the night. The group awakens with a start and each jumps up to get out. People come to their aid and find them naked, but no one dreams of laughing at their nakedness. On the contrary, everyone is in agreement in saying that nothing is lost since everyone has escaped alive.

In what way might this situation from earthly life aid in spiritual advancement?

What is the temporal world if not a burning hut where each individual should only be concerned with the safety of his soul, abandoning to the flames the trifles which we call riches, royalty, power and worldly pleasures?

13. A mother says to her child, an infant of five years, "Go to bed." The boy obeys. He lies down with his head toward the north and his feet toward the south. His mother says to him, "I don't want to see you lying like this; turn the other way."

The child obeys, but he curls up. His mother intervenes again, "I would like to see your body extended to full length and not curled up like a small shell."

The obedient child straightens himself and asks, in his small, innocent voice which seeks only to please, "Are you happy, mother?"

"Yes, my little father," replies the mother.

"Does my mother wish me to go to sleep?"

"Of course, my little father," she says.

The child closes his eyes and sleeps, after having said, "My mother, take care with the lamp, so that it doesn't go out, and watch over me so that the naughty mice don't come to nibble my toes.''

Brother in God, this story, rather than amusing you, should cause you to reflect. Be in the hands of God like this child in the hands of his mother. Seek nothing else but the desire to please God. Don't lose confidence in God. Accept the position He chooses for you; efface your own will and abandon yourself to His. When and how He wishes you to change, thus will you change without complaining. Ask Him to do with you as He pleases.

Ask Him, as evidence of His satisfaction, to keep watch over your sleep and over the interior light which illuminates you so that material temptations, which are also kinds of perfidious mice, do not slip among the shadows of laxity and gnaw on your two big toes: 'Love and Charity.'

14. One night an automobile suddenly directed its headlights toward me and I was blinded. I did not know where to direct my step and stood frozen in my tracks ready to be hit.

This state only lasted a few seconds. Nonetheless it permitted me to transport myself to the divine plane, to the station which precedes that of ''Life in God'' where the light bursts suddenly upon the vision of the initiate, flooding his breast and holding him fast, immobile and stupefied.

Thus I was reminded of the light of mystical reality. When it surprises the soul in the shadows of this world, the soul is blinded to the point of being unable to discern men, beasts, buildings or roads. Everything disappears from one's eyes, giving way to the light. The soul becomes incapable of distinguishing one thing from another, and thus attains the stage where one is no longer able to see structures, where one is no longer able to preoccupy oneself with judging anything or anybody.

15. The worthy Sotoura, a woman of the quarter, came one day seeking Cerno and said to him, ''I am very quick-tempered, the least thing affects me very deeply. I would like a blessing from you, a prayer which could render me pleasant, affable and patient.''

She had not completed relating her story when her son, a baby of three years who was waiting for her in the court yard entered, holding a board with which he struck a forceful blow on the head of the poor woman. She looked at the baby, smiling, ''Oh what a naughty boy who mistreats his mother . . .!''

''Why didn't you flare up at your son, you who are so quick-tempered and lament so for yourself?''

"My son is but an infant — he does not know what he is doing. One cannot get angry with a child of this age."

"My good Sotoura," Cerno said to her, "Go, return to your house. When someone irritates you, think of this board and say to yourself: 'In spite of his age, this person is acting like a child of three years.' Be indulgent; you can do it because you have just done so with your son. You will no longer be quick-tempered, and you will live in happiness, cured of your malady. The blessings which will come to you will be far superior to those which you could obtain from me; they will be those from God and the Prophet. The person who withstands and pardons an offence is like a great tree which the vultures have fouled while resting on its branches. The repugnant appearance lasts only for a part of the year. During each rainy season God sends a series of downpours which wash it from the top to the roots, and He dresses it in new foliage. The love which you have for your child, try to spread it among all of God's creatures. God views His creatures like a father his children. You will be placed on a higher rung of the ladder, where by means of love and charity, the soul sees and weighs up an offence only in order to pardon it better."

(TB, 37–8; VE, 46–7)

16. A hideous worm is located in a cavity in the tooth of a pig. If he remembers the Lord who created him and implants this memory within himself, then his contingent state, no matter how repulsive it might be, will not be able to separate him from the source of all existence which is in God. He will be better off than the luminous worm who, because he is in the earth beneath some holy place,* is complacent in himself because of the holiness of the place and thus forgets God.

The first obscure worm lives continually in God through his thought and spirit. The second spends his time congratulating himself and admiring his residence, which in spite of its sanctity is ephemeral due to its contingent state.

17. One night I was praying in a room which was lit by an oil lamp. Suddenly a wind entered the window and the light began to flicker. Instead of a clear light, the room was plunged alternately into semi-darkness and light. This change was so rapid that I could not even think "light" without seeing darkness, nor think "darkness" without seeing light. Under the effect of these regular and rapid combinations

***Bakka* in the original; I have been unable to discover the meaning of this word and have translated it contextually.

of light and darkness, my eyes were no longer able to discern anything. Due to my loss of concentration, my prayer became disrupted, first in my mind, then in my physical movements.

This state caused me to meditate on faith, that interior light which illuminates our soul. I said to myself, "Surely, one whose faith vacillates will find his soul plunged into the darkness of uncertainty. This darkness penetrates our soul and hinders the divine light from establishing itself and clearly illuminating the 'hut of flesh' which is our being. We must close our senses to dark things, which for the light of the spirit of the believer are a perfidious wind which penetrates through the open windows of our moral lapses, causing the light of faith within us to flicker."

From that time I have been able carefully to close the openings of my soul and of my heart, and especially the gateway of my spirit, to all exterior winds except those which breathe in me the name of God and [the words] "love" and "charity."

18. Faith and Truth, in that they are connected with God, are not the prerogatives of one individual, nor one race, nor even one country. One who believes that these virtues are the privilege of his family is as foolish as one who might say, "The sun shines only for my family; the rains fall and the streams flow only for my people." One who would like to keep for his own people all good and virtue will himself be impoverished and become an eternal invalid.

Why an eternal invalid? Because each day he will see appearing on the scene of life a person foreign to his family, and sometimes of less noble ancestry, who possesses the privilege he wishes to monopolise. To believe that all creatures are loved by God is a great step toward goodness and truth. To condemn irrevocably or dismiss a creature from the possibility of perfection or from the mercy of God is a giant stride toward the kind of thought which engenders the evil of egoism, a pitiable and incurable state of mind.

19. Some one told me that Salli Malal,* a contemporary of al-Hajj Umar, contradicted the Pullo proverb which says: "The advantages which God dispenses unexpectedly are not held in a closed hand."

Salli rejoined, "If these advantages were scattered as one says, the blind would have gathered them all up."

This retort could only apply to material advantages, and such like. As for spiritual benefits, the proverb is sound. Certainly God accords his

*See Henri Gaden, *Proverbes et maximes peuls et toucouleurs* (Paris, 1931), 91.

grace to everyone, without any consideration, neither physical, nor racial, nor continental.

20. Which is the human being who has nothing, will have nothing and will remain with nothing? He is the one who, knowing nothing, pretends to know everything. He will have nothing in the sense that his pride will prevent him from admitting his weakness and from requesting that he be instructed. And he who knows nothing, and who does nothing in order to know, will remain with nothing in the matter of knowledge.

21. Faith, like a capricious bird, escapes from time to time from its celestial nest. It flies down to earth, knocks on one door and another, alights on one roof and another. It finds refuge only in the heart of one who, before going to sleep, piously invokes the name of God. Faith enters the breast of such a man, who will awaken closer to God.

22. In truth, beauty of the body is only partly a favor, while beauty of the spirit is complete.

Whatever be the form of physical beauty, it erodes or fades with time. The handsome man of today will tomorrow be a withered old man, shrivelled with wrinkles like an ape.

Intelligence, one of the forms of spiritual beauty, produces fruits which once conveyed are perpetuated and transmitted from age to age with a vigor which can constantly augment their power.

The difference between these two is that material beauty appears on a screen which is subject to ageing, whereas spiritual beauty etches itself on an imperishable element which extends over a vast area. One is an allegory of the perishable, and the other the symbol of real existence: the eternal.

23. Brother in God, who comes to seek our advice, make your personal recitation of the name of God your amulet. Leave aside the man who wishes to play tricks with faith; at the end of the voyage of souls, there will be for him a disagreeable deception; for he will be frustrated of that which he believes he has gained.

To be sure, female trickery in this life can procure considerable material goods, but only one day of male trickery suffices to ruin the work of several years of the first.

The female ruse consists of commerce and of all means, honest or dishonest, employed to amass material advantage. The male ruse is war.

Faith is the one fortune against which these two ruses, even united, can do nothing. It is the virtue of faith that it preoccupies common men, pushing them to the point of disputing among themselves, while leaving the true believer indifferent and serene. Strength of faith permits one to remain detached both from the army of the poor, who lament over their impoverished family, and thus rebel, and from the wealthy whose affluence makes them arrogant and who are poisoned by their [concern for] high rank and their [search for] pleasure.

24. One day Bokar Paté and I found our friend Kullel, the jovial and well-known raconteur, not feeling well. He was trembling and groaning.

"What is the matter?" asked Bokar Paté. "Your condition suggests that you won't be recounting any stories this evening."

"I have a severe stomach upset."

Bokar Paté said to him, "One pays dearly for having partaken of so many different dishes at once."

Bokar Paté's observation on the material plane has its analogy on the spiritual level. Those who delude themselves with immoral enjoyments will one day be subject to an indigestion much more painful than that which gripped Kullel. Moral faults are like an array of various dishes, one seeming more delicious than the next, but with the added complication that the more one eats, the more one wants to eat.

One who stuffs his mind with unhealthy ideas constipates his faith and suffers from indigestion of God's religion. Instead of intensifying the interior flame which heats and maintains his faith, he will see it extinguished and transformed into a thick ash which will smother this sacred flame and obliterate its glow.

Would that love and charity for all were your preferred and regularly consumed dishes; then you would not cease to live in God and for God.

25. Man was created by the power of God. He is thus composed of a portion of divine matter which has melted and dissolved within him. The flesh which covers this divine matter is like a crust pierced with nine or eleven major openings and a multitude of minor ones.

Thus several blows of the 'hoe of preaching' will suffice to provoke a volcano of religious feelings.

26. Our planet is neither the largest nor the smallest of all those which

our Lord has created. Those who inhabit it are therefore unable to escape from this law:

We must believe ourselves neither superior nor inferior to all other beings.

The best creatures among us will be those who are imbued with love and charity and with the proper consideration for their fellow-men. These creatures will be upright and luminous like a sun which rises straight up into the heavens.
(Monod, "Homme," 155)

27. As soon as the object of our physical activities exceeds [the three basic necessities] of drawing our nourishment from our mother earth and [seeking] the indispensible materials for the construction of our shelter and the manufacture of our clothing, then we are infected with a virus of trickery. This state predisposes us to disguised thievery, which in turn stimulates us toward shameless pillage, which in turn leads us to an unconscious condition in which one will even kill provided this will lead to fortune.

But, Brother in God! Ask yourself what one gains in winning only material fortune. The pure mind motivated by sound reason will tell you that what one gains can never be securely maintained. Material fortune is like the assorted débris which the winds of chance have just blown from one place and deposited temporarily in another. Only a moment later a gust will carry it once again to yet another distant, unknown place.

28. Who is better acquainted with butter* than He who created the animal and vegetable which produce it? When you are to be anointed, brother in God, request that it be God Himself who gives you the required substance. When it is God who gives the material for anointing His servant, the holy odor will persist forever. When this odor is given off into the air, it will attract the favors of superior forces charged with vigilance and protection. In conventional human language these forces are called aid, providence and mercy.

29. To neglect as much as possible the religious education of children, to smile at their lack of preference for study and pious exercises, and at the last moment to confide them to a grasping and poorly instructed

*Butter of traditional West African manufacture is not congealed, but viscous like vegetable oil.

teacher, all this will cripple their souls and make them inept in their movement toward God. At the very moment when they seem out of danger, the great wind of perdition will suddenly rise against them, swelling their breasts and dragging them into the vast lake of profligate life where, receiving no mercy, they will sink while fishing for forbidden fish.

30. An old man, in the company of a strong young man, is crossing a slippery plain.* The young man is full of vigor. Each time he slips he allows himself to slide along, stopping himself just before he would fall. He manages to right himself each time and laughs at his athletic prowess. The old man is full of prudence. When he slips, trembling all over, he invokes the name of God in order not to fall. He succeeds nonetheless in righting himself after several awkward movements.

The young man says to him: "Here, old man, use me for support and you won't fall. I am young and vigorous."

The old man replies: "I won't forsake the name of God which I invoke. He will serve me as support."

Two steps further on the young man slips, fails to stop himself and falls sprawling at full length crying out, "Oh, my ribs!" Whereas the old man who has slipped at the same time succeeds in keeping himself upright and regaining his balance. The old man says to the younger, who is sprawled on the ground, "My good fellow, what would have become of us if I had held on to you for support?"

"We would have fallen on one another like ripe fruit from a tree," replies the young man.

The old man adds: "My boy, one must never rely solely on one's own strength. It may let you down."

Aspirant who comes to us, fear God and divert yourself from all belief in your self sufficiency. Don't scorn the correction that God gave to the pretentious young man in causing his vigor to fail him when at the same time He allowed the old man to overcome his weakness.

31. When certain misfortunes strike the world, some people can see, although helpless against them, the appearance of maleficent attitudes. These can stifle both the divine law and [ancient] customs which were instituted by a wisdom of which we are ignorant or which we fail to appreciate because of our inadequate knowledge.

Nowadays honest men who remain devoted to the ideals of good and moral action are seen by the libertines and the ignorant as people

*The clayey soil of Masina becomes very slippery when wet.

lacking any ability. They are sometimes accused of being stupid; some only see them as imbeciles, to whom one must pass some money in order to discharge their duty, and to exact from them some malleable yellow gold when they have to redeem a debt which they have often contracted without really knowing how.

Oh brother in God, who comes to us to seek the way which leads toward good, this is the time of the reign of Satan. He chases the name of God from our memories and the idea of pity from our thoughts. Nowadays all mouths conjugate the verb "to want to earn" in the first person, present indicative. "To earn" has become an imperative duty; the manner of doing this is only a means. One is little concerned to know if it is legal or not. The overseer of the market plunders the merchandise; the criminal avoids prison by financial means. He who gives a lot, even if he steals a lot, will be considered as most pious by religious leaders, and as the best of subjects by the officials and servants of the temporal chiefs. This a time when the poor, honest man lives and dies unknown. He will be lucky if he is not dishonoured by everyone, even by his own family.

This is a time when the aspirant should pray as follows: "Oh God, I am seized with embarrassment because of my sins and those of my contemporaries. Insure that Your holy name spreads the light and fills the human hearts with Your divine force. Only this can divert us from the road of evil and perdition."

32. "Cerno, how many kinds of faith are there?"

O, my brother, I do not know precisely how many. One cannot count up the kinds of faith as one can count domestic animals, nor can one measure it like the distance between Bandiagara and Mopti, or between Mopti and Sofara. Nor can faith be weighed like the millet of Bankass or the fruit in the market of Dourou. For me faith is, in part, the sum total of trust that we have in God, and in part our fidelity toward our Creator. Faith experiences both moments of elevation and moments of decline. It varies according to people and their circumstances.

I can only give a general outline of faith, which I would do as follows: There is *ṣulb* or solid faith; there is *sā'il* or liquid faith, and finally there is *ghāzī* or gaseous faith, the most subtle of all the forms. Numerologically, faith can be written as 1342 of which the root is 1 + 3 + 4 + 2 = 10. In considering the constituent elements of 1342, one notes that it is formed by the first four numbers: 1,2,3,4. The secret of faith is to be found in these numbers, in other words, in unity, the binary, the triad and the quarternary. A numerological explanation is not within the grasp of everyone, so we will explain it in another way.*

*The number 1342 is obtained by totalling the numerical value of the letters in the words *ṣulb* (92), *sā'il* (332) and *ghāzī* (918).

The first degree of faith, *ṣulb*, is solid faith. It is suitable for the common man — the masses — and for the teachers who are attached to the letter [of the law]. This faith is channelled by prescriptions imposed by a law drawn from revealed texts, be they Jewish, Christian or Islamic. At this level faith has a precise form. It is subject to a rigorous determination which admits no foreign element. It is intransigent and hard like the stone from which I draw its name. There is also another, more mystical, reason: the numerical value of *ṣulb* is 92. Faith at the degree of *ṣulb* is heavy and immobile like a mountain. At times it prescribes armed warfare if this is necessary to gain respect and to assure its position.

*Sā'il* faith is that of men who have worked and successfully faced up to the trials of *ṣulb*, of the rigid law that admits no compromise. They have triumphed over their faults and have set out on the way which leads to truth. The constituent elements of this faith derive from understanding. It values truths from wherever they come, considering neither their origin nor the date of their existence. It gathers and assembles them in order to make from them a body in perpetual movement. The parts of this body do not arrange themselves in one particular form. They effect a flow which is constantly forward, like the flow of the molecules of water which emerge from the mountain hollows and trickle across varied terrains, flowing together and increasing in size to streams which finally, as rivers, are thrown into the ocean of Divine Truth. This faith, due to its subtle, liquid nature, is strong and undermines the faults of the soul, erodes the rocks of intolerance and spreads out, taking on a shape which is not fixed as in the case of *ṣulb* faith but borrows the form of its recipient. This faith penetrates individuals according to the accidents of their moral terrain, never changing its essence and never retreating whatever detour might be necessary to avoid temptation, an obstacle which Satan places on its road.

*Sā'il* faith manifests itself as gigantic mystical waterfalls, falling from the mountain into the ravine of active life. It contracts into a sinuous thread in order to traverse the steep pass which Satan has placed on its route. It expands into a great flood, playing across a country worn flat by the adoration of God and made favourable to its full extension. *Sā'il* faith disciplines the adept and makes of him a man of God capable of hearing, listening to and appreciating the voices of those who speak of God. This faith is vivifying. It is of the middle degree. It can solidify like hailstones when it must move to the range of souls of the degree of *ṣulb*. Similarly, it can become more subtle and rise as vapour toward *ghāzī* faith in the heaven of absolute truth. This faith is that of men who walk in the straight way which leads to the city of peace where man and animal live in common and in mutual respect, where the elements of the three kingdoms live in brotherhood, and the adepts of this faith stand against war. This faith is the ante-chamber of truth.

*Ghāzī* faith is the third and final form. It is decidedly more subtle, and it is the attribute of a specially chosen élite. Its constituent elements are so pure that, void of all material weight which would hold them to the earth, they rise like smoke into the heaven of holy souls, expanding to fill them. The faith of the sphere of truth emerges entirely from this last form. Those who reach this faith adore God in truth in the light without colour. On this sublime plane *ṣulb* faith, which has emerged from revelation, and *sā'il* faith, which has emerged in turn from this uncompromising way, both disappear to make a place for one sole thing, the Divine Truth which flourishes in the fields of Love and Truth.
(TB, 76–8; VE, 137–9)

33. Cerno, what do you say of those who have given themselves over solely to temporal matters?

One must pray for the safekeeping of these souls. Souls which confine themselves to material things alone will in the end find themselves vitiated by the noxious germs of materialist desire. At a given moment they enter a state of moral combustion. This state impoverishes them in relation to the love of God and enriches them with the cinders of desire. In order that these souls may not be pushed down this path toward death, one must not smother the voice in them which speaks of faith. One must soak such a soul in the vitalising element of love. For this one must open the soul to charity, so that one's thoughts can be aerated with the meditation and recitation of the name of God.
(TB, 87)

34. Cerno, is it true that faith can change?

My habit of observing and reflecting on changes of states permits me to say that the interior religious heat of man maintains his faith. The factors which cause this heat to vary are often external. If this heat augments its power under the effect of the enthusiasm of conviction, it heats the liquid *sā'il* and renders it more subtle, which is to say that it transforms it into *ghāzī* faith. On the contrary, if the said heat diminishes in power, the faith cools. It congeals, becomes hard and later sinks.

As for the true essence of faith, we do not agree with those who believe it is subject to diminution. Certainly it does not vary [in essence], but its temperature can fall or it can rise so high that it will sublimate. In the latter case, it is transformed into a spiritual vapour. In our eyes, water, the element which God has used to give and maintain the lives of all beings, symbolises faith better than any other element. This is the major reason why our Lord Muhammad frequently appealed to the symbolism of water when teaching hidden mysteries. Water has neither colour, odor, taste nor form. It takes on the shape of those objects which contain it. The same is true of faith.

35. He who has truly seen the Revealer has seen Him fully in the heaven of great visions. He has seen, and his heart, beating with charity, is not that of the evil one who refuses to communicate the mysteries to those who are worthy of them.

Enamored of God! Come to us; chase away Satan by stoning him, as Abraham did long ago. Make ready your soul so that like Isaac it can be offered in sacrifice. Heed the reply we give to those who, thirsting for God, ask us, "What is the element which most appropriately symbolises faith?" Among the four "mothers" — earth, fire, air and water — none is better than the last for symbolising religion. Religion is for the soul what water is for nature.

(*a*) Water has been given by God a dissolving power. Religion is remarkable for the properties of destruction it exercises over ideas and custom which are anterior to it.

(*b*) Water in a state of complete purity is rarely found in nature, and no religion remains in the state of its original purity. Many social factors intervene to alter it.

(*c*) Even water which is drawn at its source contains matter which is dissolved in it, having penetrated through the strata of the earth. Religion, even in its original state, retains some vestiges of earlier local traditions.

(*d*) To obtain pure water, one must filter it. To purify one's religion, one must subject it to the effervescent action of the dogmatic science of initiation.

(*e*) Just as water is indispensable to the germination of the life of all beings, so religion is essential to the development and expansion of the spirit.

(*f*) Water dissolves nutrient materials from the soil and permits their absorption by plants. Religion dispenses a teaching which gives the soul the spiritual food which strengthens it.

(*g*) Water ensures material hygiene; religion ensures moral hygiene.

36. The *sharī'a* (the law) and mysticism, an initiatic teaching, are two different matters, but they complement one another and cannot proceed without each other.

The essential goal of the *sharī'a* is to deprive the faithful of the excessive liberty contained in the dissoluteness of irreligion. The *sharī'a* thus obliges the faithful to ameliorate his conduct so as to prevent his falling into the unregulated life of the humid lowlands which are unfit for spiritual cultivation. Without a *sharī'a*, which punishes those exterior moral faults which wound one's sense of modesty and propriety, some will-less men would fall neglected and at the mercy of whatever fanatic wanders the streets where depraved morals are born and where the seed and roots of morality are rotting. The articles of the *sharī'a* are thus like "moral drains" whereby the misconduct which hearts imbibe must flow away.

If one compares the *sharī'a* to a network of drains, mysticism might be thought of as an irrigation system. In effect, the role of mysticism consists in imparting to the human spirit the knowledge of God, which is a sort of subtle water, the lack of which renders the spirit similar to dry and burning soil. Mysticism is the consequence of two things:

(*a*) a revelation given by God to a man of His choice, the prophet who teaches and propagates it;

(*b*) a lived experience in which the intuition might be activated as a result of a lengthy meditative observation by an individual predestined for the divine light.

The first form is an emanation obtained from the source and gathered into well-guarded and venerated books. In each form of religion these books are like reservoirs in which one gathers rainwater. These books, like the reservoirs of material water, must be guarded well in the interest of the very life of the community. The second form, or the other aspect of mysticism, is comparable to the water which, by his ingenuity, man has gathered by means of dams and canals.

In effect each theologian can draw from the holy books, these well-guarded reservoirs, the elements of a spiritual teaching, and then they can prepare the necessary diversions [as canals] which are best adapted to the mentality and evolution of his contemporaries in order to direct them as necessary in accordance with their development. This last aspect of mysticism suggests an auxiliary conductor between two points in a closed circuit.

Before giving out your teaching, brother in God who wishes to work for the propagation of the idea of God against the disorder of "to-live-however-you-like," take the measure of the people you intend to teach. If they are "flat" with regard to spiritual ideas you can employ the system which we call "inundation." Whatever be the subtlety of your teaching, the people will be penetrated slowly or quickly according to the difference of their natures, and you are sure to bring them to the enviable degree of complete submersion. This state prepares the way for *ghāzī* faith, which tends to occupy the greatest space possible in rising upwards and always going higher to the center of all intelligence.

But when you feel your people are spiritually "slight," instead of the "inundation" method of teaching, practice what we call the "trickling" method, because in this case their spirit will be similar to a sloping terrain. Divide them up as if digging mystical terraces, each on a different level from the others, by means of which you divert your lessons. You will change the symbols of your teaching without changing its essence when passing from a superior terrace to one immediately below.

Rest assured that in this way your word will penetrate your students without obliging them to make a steep ascent on which even the most sincere might stumble.

(TB, 74–5; VE, 130–2)

37. The desire of man to acquire divine things is like water exposed to the sun. It evaporates and spreads into the atmosphere of love. It descends to earth again only in the form of vivifying rains. Whereas the desire of man to acquire terrestrial things is like a fog formed in the lower atmosphere. It can never move from its saturation point, the place where the idea of God becomes cool, and where mystical visibility remains always bad. Where does one observe this fog of the [carnal] soul and spirit? On the banks of unregulated and Godless lives which run in pernicious rivers and stagnate in filthy ponds, in cabarets, etc.

38. Cerno, how do you explain that people who do not live in the same place can conceive the same idea?

Men, both good and bad, communicate among themselves by the same means. Those who have the idea of God as their foundation perceive, in spite of time and distance, identical ideas of the same grandeur. Those who think evil do the same regardless of time and space.

39. The religious teaching of a prophet, or of a person enamored of God, is comparable to pure water. One may drink it without any danger to one's moral health. Such a teaching will be superior and intelligible. Like pure water, it will contain nothing of a flavour that could vitiate one's taste for the good. This teaching matures the spirit and purifies the heart because it contains no impurities which might obscure the soul and harden the heart. We cannot recommend strongly enough that one should learn the theology of the revealed religions. They are for everyone, like drinkable water. But we also counsel that they should be assimilated slowly, and that one should guard against accepting "murky"

theologies, for they can infest the soul with a kind of moral Guinea worm.

It is commonly recommended that you do not drink cold water when you are perspiring. We suggest, for our part, that when your soul is in a state of mystical warmth you do not read just anything. Just as it is necessary for our physical health not to drink muddy water which is swarming with all kinds of little creatures, for our spiritual health too it is necessary to avoid introducing just any teaching into our minds. (TB, 83)

40. If one fills a canoe to the brim with sand and launches it upon the Niger, what will happen?

It will sink, of course.

Why?

Because the water will give way under the weight of the sand, and the canoe will lose one of its essential virtues, buoyancy. The force which keeps the canoe afloat will be made less powerful than that which pushes it downward. The unavoidable result of these two forces no longer neutralising one another and thus establishing an equilibrium will be the sinking of the canoe.

That which is a visible fact for the canoe is also useful for our soul, this great canoe which God through His power has launched on the Niger River of our existence. The soul must traverse this river and in so doing run many risks. He who fills his soul to the brim with the sand of material desire will make it heavier than the spiritual stream upon which it must navigate. In this case, his effort, instead of being exercised from the material toward the spiritual — or, in other words, from the lower toward the higher under the influence of worship — will be effected in the contrary direction: from the spiritual into the obscurities of the material. This downward pressure will upset the canoe of the soul which will capsize in the course of its mystical crossing.

If the overloaded canoe of the soul cannot float and must capsize, I counsel you not to launch your canoe on the mystical Niger without loading it to a reasonable degree with material things; due to excessive lightness it would be at the mercy of the waves of temptation and would capsize in midstream. Reason is aided by dogma to prescribe judiciously how to load one's canoe in the precise manner necessary so as to be able to cut through the waves and clear one's way.

41. Cerno, why is it that certain men, despite their shameless public conduct, do not fall under the occult law conforming to verses 7 and 8 of *Sūra* 99 (And whoso doeth good an atom's weight will see it then; And whoso doeth ill an atom's weight will see it then)?

My friend and brother in God, do not doubt a letter of the Holy Book, all the more so two verses composed of twenty-two letters each. The fact that these two verses are formed by twenty-two letters is a profound sign to indicate the secret of the order of harmony they symbolise. Know that God Eternal is not limited; consequently He has no need to hurry like we do.

The divine law is well-tempered, although inflexible. God caused a rain of passions to shower upon the original human principle which He planted in our father Adam; these are estimated to comprise nine-tenths of the states of the [carnal] soul. The Lord, in not punishing us immediately after each misdeed, is taking into account our weakness resulting from these passions which have been injected into us. In order that a man shall be publicly punished and put to shame, his hidden bad actions which escape the reproaches of his fellow-men must attain, analogously speaking, a weight greater than that of his good actions, both visible and hidden, together with that of his visible bad actions. When a man is in this state, one says that the hidden bad actions are heavier than the sum of the hidden and visible good and the visible bad. Then he will capsize, and the exterior world becomes a witness to his sinking, or, in other words, his public shame.

42. Cerno, what is your opinion of a defense attorney?

What is his professional activity?

He pleads for justice in return for a salary.

A *muḥāmin*!* Here, in truth, we have a person with one foot in paradise and the other in hell. Heaped up before him he sees the truth and lies, the law and blasphemy. How he comes out of this situation depends on his retracting one foot to join it with the other. As for me, I see this profession from several angles. On the whole it seems rather useless. If it is not useless, it casts a terrible slur, first on the integrity of the judges in applying the law, and second on the steadfastness of the law itself. If the judge is truly upright and the law is steadfast in its application with respect to everyone, the intercession of the lawyer loses its purpose. The parties should be able to go before a magistrate who will do his duty equitably and strictly, without failure or prejudice. He should render such a judgment as is in the interest of public morality, which a steadfast law is charged with protecting. Such a situation makes the lawyer's role unnecessary.

If, on the other hand, the judge has a soul which is rotten, I believe it is more expedient to buy the judge, who will settle the matter, rather

*Arabic for lawyer. Cerno Bokar's view of the dispensation of justice is an Islamic one.

than to pay a lawyer who can only seek to influence the judge in favour of his own client. A Pullo proverb says: "Rather than pay someone to argue a case, better to retain the one who pronounces sentence." This second situation makes the lawyer no less useless.

Cerno, were not the prophets all lawyers, analogously speaking?

O my friend, may God open your intelligence! It is a tempting comparison, which is not without good sense, but there is a great difference which makes it collapse under examination: the salary.

Here is verse 20 of *Sūra* XXVIII:

> A man came running from the furthest part of the city; he said: "O my people, follow the apostles. Follow those who demand no salary from you and who are guided in the right path."*

The phrase "who demand no salary from you," placed in the mouth of a man by God on behalf of the apostles, is explicit. If the prophets intercede like lawyers, they do not do it in consideration of a salary. Another lesson which we can draw from this example is that to resemble something is not the same as being identical to it. Symbolism follows an immutable law which one must not pervert.

43. The soul of a human being, of whatever race, is transformed into the state of mystical diamond from the time that worship crystallizes his spirit. His colour or birth plays no part whatever with regard to the production of the light of faith: no matter what the social conditions or the weight of birth of a person who has reached this degree, no external element will be strong enough to disintegrate or corrupt it. To the adepts who have reached this degree, one has only one recommendation to make: that they should beware of their own dust, that is, of admiring that which comes from them. Admiration of oneself is among the most powerful mystical faults which can pervert the soul of the worshipper, even if he has arrived at the spiritual level called the "diamond," where the lights of the hidden name appear in colourless rays.

*This Qur'anic reference is very confused. The original text of the discourse gives the reference of *Sūra* XXX, verses 19–20. But the passage seems to refer to *Sūra* XXVIII, verse 20, which is as follows: "And a man came from the uttermost part of the city, running. He said: 'O Moses! Lo! the chiefs take counsel against thee to slay thee; therefore escape. Lo! I am of those who give thee good advice.' "

This passage of the Qur'an continues with Moses actually being hired for a set period of time by a family, although he does not originally demand a wage for his services. In another passage (*Sūra* XVIII, verse 65) Moses is in the company of Khidr, to whom he suggests he could have demanded money in return for repairing a wall. (For Khidr, see Schimmel, 105–6)

44. Cerno, what do you think of traditions?

Respect them. They constitute a goodly sum of the spiritual element arising from the decomposition of the spirit of those who have gone before us and who happily have not broken with God as we have done. One must meditate on the traditions, whether they be shorter or longer stories, whether they be more or less important or didactic, and so on. One must seek to uncover the secret which is enveloped within them. One must dig deeply in them as do the seekers for gold in the mines of Bouré. Each story, each vignette, is a gallery, and in their impressive entirety they form a mine of information which the ancients have bequeathed to the moderns by region, race, family and often by an individual. Of course, to work profitably in this mine, to move about there in every direction, one must have a lamp — or, in plain language, a key or a master.

(TB, 91; VE, 184)

45. When the flames of ambition burn in the heart and cause the waters there to boil to the point that they dry up, then man is perverted from his noble nature and he turns only toward that which will procure him what he desires without consideration for the legitimacy of the means, nor the moral consequences of his acquisition.

46. Language is a fruit of which the skin is called chatter, the flesh eloquence, and the seed good sense. Those whose profession it is to flatter the masses* know the uses of all these parts, and they employ them in a marvellous fashion.

47. Cerno, I have heard people speak well of you and of the efficacy of your teaching. I wish to choose you as my master.

O brother in God. Flattered though I am, before anything else I am a human being, subject to physical and moral contingencies. I have some advice to give you which is worth months of fruitful study. A man never conforms exactly to his reputation. Admirers falsify it by exaggerating his real merits, while antagonists disparage them whenever possible. To avoid acting according to one of these preconceptions, it would be good for you, and perhaps for me too, if you would listen to me for days, examine me for weeks and stay near me for months before deciding to choose me as your mentor and your brother.

(TB, 39; VE, 48)

*The reference here is to the griots or praise singer-musicians.

48. One day I had a vision of two young women. They had the same name but were completely different from one another.

"Who are you?" I said to them.

"We are Deference," they replied.

"Why do you have the same name although you differ from one another?"

The one who seemed more endowed with good sense said to me, "I am the Deference born of respect, while my companion is Deference born of fear. We inhabit the same royal palace . . ."*

49. One day I was going to the fields, accompanied by my faithful dog, guardian of our farms and sworn enemy of those monkeys who devastate them. It was the time of the great heat of April. My dog and I were so hot that it was only with great pain that we were able to breathe properly. I had no doubt that in the end one of us, perhaps myself, would faint. Thanks to God, we came upon a thicket of clustered branches, with a thick covering of green leaves. My dog, whimpering slightly, raced toward the shadow. But when he reached it, he did not stay there, but returned to me, his tongue hanging out, his lips sagging, his pointed, white teeth bared. His sides throbbed rapidly making me realise how exhausted he was. I moved toward the shade, and the dog became happier. But I decided to continue on my way. He whined plaintively, but nonetheless followed me, his head more bowed, his tail curled between his legs. He was visibly in despair, but decided to follow me whatever the consequences.

This faithfulness touched me deeply. I did not know how to appreciate the act of this animal, ready to follow me to the death without any need of his own, and without being constrained to do it by anything whatever. He was loyal just because he considered me his master. He proved his attachment to me by risking his life with the sole aim of following me and being at my side.

"Lord," I cried in an outburst of feeling, "cure my troubled soul. Make my fidelity similar to that of this being whom I disparagingly call 'dog'. Give me, like him, the strength to be able to scorn my life when it is a question of accomplishing Your will. And give me the strength to follow the road on which You place me without asking where I am going. I am not the creator of this dog, and yet he obeys me blindly and follows me docilely at the cost of a thousand pains which weigh heavily on his life. It is You, Lord, who has endowed him with this virtue. Give,

*The following note appeared after this discourse: "The master was interrupted by a visitor and, alas, we never heard the rest of the story."

Lord, to all those who ask You, and to me in particular, the virtue of love and the courage of charity."

I retraced my steps and sat down in the shade. My companion, now very happy, lay down in front of me so that his eyes were turned toward mine as if to have a serious conversation with me. He extended his two front paws, raised his head up, and while lying there, kept watch on me so as not to miss any of my movements. A few minutes later we had no more trace of fatigue.

God has no need of reason nor of human intelligence. He gave them to us for use in this life. We are not therefore to bring them untouched to the grave, that is, to live and die without meditating on and drawing spiritual profit from the events which happen to us and from the things which we ascertain. I began to meditate. Where am I? I am under a tree with thick foliage. The words "thick foliage" caused my mind to reflect on verses 13 to 16 of *Sūra* LXXVIII:

> And [We] have appointed a dazzling lamp,
> And have sent down from the rainy clouds abundant water,
> Thereby to produce grain and plant,
> And gardens of thick foliage.

The two last words forcefully hold my attention. They constitute the subject of my meditation.

Since I have been under this thickly foliated tree I have begun to feel relaxed and restored. When I was in the sun, I was beginning to lose my sensibility and my capacity for movement and to lapse into a state of faintness, death's younger brother. I can say as much about it as about my companion.

Why these two states? They are the result of two phenomena. Far from the tree — that is, in the sun — there is an atmosphere which boils with heat and compresses the chests of both humans and animals. Under the tree there is a temperate atmosphere which restores our physical organs to their normal functions. Additional data or reflection are not required to enable us to realise the existence of two elements. In the sun there is an element which can kill men or animals by acting against their organs or respiration. In the shade of the plant there is a vivifying element which destroys the unbreatheable element spread by the solar heat.

In Fulfulde the first element is called *olowere* and the second *yarara*. *Olowere* derives from the overheating of breatheable air by the sun's rays. This phenomenon is identical to what occurs when food is overheated and cannot be consumed without danger. Similarly, air which is overheated by the sun cannot normally be breathed without burning the passages of the respiratory organs. *Yarara* in this case is inherent in the green leaves of the foliage. Why green? Because (according to my experience) the tree covered with dead leaves does not provide the same wellbeing. From all this, I draw the conclusion that green plants contain a vivifying property with the power to transform an atmosphere that has been overheated by the sun into breatheable and comforting air. Therefore, in a green plant there is a principle necessary for the maintenance of the life of men and animals.

This principle which emanates from green plants awoke in me another idea, this time on the immaterial plane: paradise, as it is metaphysically described in the Qur'an. In my opinion, the green of paradise is a spiritualisation of the green plants of the material world. This comparison caused a brilliant flame of comprehension to spring up in my mind, which allows me to say that paradise, as it is described, is a symbolic garden of eternal verdure. This eternal verdure attenuates the rays of divine light which are too strong to be supported by our vision. In this garden, which is forever green, the elect can look on the Essential Light and assimilate the emanations of the source of eternal life while listening to the voice of their Lord with ears purified from all materialism. They thus enter into the state of beatitude described in verses 10 and 11 of *Sūra* LXXXVIII: "In a high Garden / Where they hear no idle speech."

Brother in God, while awaiting the opportunity to enter the celestial garden of tomorrow, respect the present great garden which constitutes the vegetable kingdom. Refrain from uselessly destroying the least plant, for it is an allegory which God causes to emerge from the earth for our instruction, our nourishment and our comfort.
(VE, 162–5)

50. In a vision I saw two cultivators, sowing and working side by side in two different fields. They were right next to one another at the edge of the fields without either one paying any attention to his comrade.

What were these two sowers? Two symbolic preparers, one broadcasting his seed on the material field, the other confiding the seed of divine truth by the handful to the spiritual field. The seed which they plant, although watered by the same rain, the word, will produce shoots which bear different fruit. The shoots in the field of the first sower will bear the "seeds of partiality," that is of discord and hatred among those who eat it. The shoots in the other field will bear the "seeds of sympathy and abnegation," bringing altruism and unity to those who eat them.

A luminous being intercedes each time between the two cultivators. It is Sound Reason, eldest daughter of Providence, who watches over the border in order that Error, the youngest daughter of Gloom, does not cause the two sowers to plant in one another's fields. If that occurred, the order of things would be upset, and the affairs of God and of the devil would be so confused that the world would enter into chaos.

51. The physical beauty of women is a trick which Satan constantly employs in order to disguise the trap he sets daily against man. It is one of the great miracles when man is attracted to it but does not get caught.

52. Every believer is able to ascertain for himself that there are times when his worship is very alert and others when it is less so, even with the best will in the world. This is because there is a mystical heat which comes from God through the multiple citation of His name and penetrates the adept, heating his soul, which, like an iron being heated in a forge, has its laudatory capacity mystically augmented. To fail to mention the divine name cools the heat which warms the soul; and the soul then loses its capacity, just like the iron, when cooled, is reduced in volume.

Mystical cooling and heating are thus produced in us through the number of times and the manner in which we repeat the divine name and His attributes. Happy is he who in the course of the day can recite the name Allah 34,500 times at the most or 960 times at the least.
(VE, 173–4).

53. The light which springs forth from the name Allah when one mentions it augments the power of the mystical spark which God puts in every soul as it comes into the world. To repeat constantly the name Allah or the formula attesting to the unity of the Divinity is a sure way to introduce into ourselves the breath of air which will maintain the mystical heat without which the spiritual ember ignited in us will smother and be transformed into black coal, that is into a bitter material containing enough acid, morally speaking, to poison our entire spiritual organism.
(VE, 174)

54. According to some well-informed persons, God, in creating us, placed in the centre of our hearts a black point. Only Jesus and his mother were not charged with this weighty burden, but the point remains in the rest of us, who are less favoured than them. But God in His mercy has turned it into charcoal, that is into a material capable of becoming red hot. And it is left to us to make it red hot through prayer, love and charity.

55. Cerno, how many kinds of mystical light are there?

O, my friend, I am not such as you believe me to be — a man who has seen all these lights. I will nonetheless speak to you of three symbolic lights, two material and one spiritual. Their sources are distinct from one another.

The first, and least elevated, is that which we draw from material when we ignite it. This light is individual; it can heat and illuminate only a strictly limited space or body. This light corresponds symbolically to the faith of the mass of individuals who have not climbed very far up the mystical ladder. At this degree the adepts are not able to move beyond the imitation of the letter. The gloom of superstition surrounds them, the cold of incomprehension causes them to shiver. Frightened and paralysed by so many contingencies, they continue to crouch in a little corner of the tradition where they move as little as possible. This light is that which animates the religious persons who are at the degree of law and faith called *ṣulb*.

The second light is that of the sun. It is above the first in the sense that it is more general and its power is more extensive. It illuminates and heats everything which exists on earth. This light symbolises the faith of middle degree on the mystical path. This second mystical light, like the material sun, dissipates all shadows from the time it comes into contact with them. This dissipation of shadows, no matter how dense and durable, is not its only characteristic, but it is a vivifying source for all creatures and has no consideration except to exercise this role. This light symbolises the light of adepts at the mystical degree of faith called *sā'il*. They know that the way is one, like the unity of the sun is one for our universe.

Like the material sun which illuminates and heats all beings, the adepts who have achieved the middle degree of light proceed and treat as brothers all those who live under the sun and receive its light. They do not scorn the first light, because it plays an indispensible preparatory role. But they are no longer like little insects who dance around a flame and sometimes inadvertently get burned. The difference between these two lights is that the first, like the light which it symbolises, can — according to circumstances — be extinguished and relit. It can be transported from one place to another, and it can change its form and power. Whereas the second light, like that of the sun, remains fixed and immutable in perpetuity. It will always come from the same source and will remain consistent throughout the centuries.

The third light is that of the center of all existence — namely God. Who would dare to describe it? It is a darkness more brilliant than all lights combined. It is the light of truth. Those who have the good fortune to reach the degree of this light lose their identity and become like a drop of water which has fallen into the Niger, or into a sea of

infinitely vast extent and depth. At this degree Jesus became the spirit of God, Moses his interlocutor, Abraham his friend, and finally Muhammad the Seal of His Messengers.*
(TB, 75–6; VE, 135–7)

56. The four elements — earth, water, air and fire — also symbolise the human condition. When God created human souls, he distributed them among these materials, and He beamed the rays of divine truth upon them. All souls dominated by matter stopped the pure light due to their opacity; this light could only play upon their surfaces. Souls whose nature was like water, because of their transparency, were easily traversed by this light of truth, whereas souls whose nature was like fire and air became two variable lights, themselves capable of emitting rays which illumine the way leading from the shadows toward the light.

57. When the rays of faith — this light which comes to us from God — penetrates the dark interior of our human nature, the laudatory soul awakens.† But not all souls awaken in the same manner from the sleep of irreligion. Some are like those men who in the morning, instead of quickly opening their eyes and spontaneously getting up, toss and turn on their beds. They do not get up until late, and even then against their inclination. Whereas others are like the dog, cat and other wild animals which at the least sensation wake up and in one bound are on their feet.

Faith is one of the great favours which God, in His kindness, dispenses to human beings. This gift can come to us in two different ways: through the mediation of a master's teaching or directly, penetrating us like the rays of the sun when one partly opens the door on a sunny day. This latter kind of faith is radiant, but it might be poorly appreciated by others because it is personal. Whereas the first kind is like a light which we see in a reflective surface, such as water or a mirror. The difference between these two states of faith is considerable, although the essence of faith itself remains the same.

58. Initiation places a fundamental importance on one's name. The individual's given name, or the name by which he is customarily known, can be used according to the science of mystical analogy to situate him in relation to the four elements: water, air, earth, fire. Each

*These prophetic attributes are all derived from the Qur'an. For a fuller discussion of them, see Muhyi'd-dīn Ibn 'Arabī, *The Wisdom of the Prophets*, 1975.

†Whether Cerno Bokar was here making a reference to a specific transformation of the soul is not clear. Sufis designated several different stages through which the soul progressed in its mystical path. See Trimingham, *The Sufi Orders*, 153.

of these four elements is composed of other subtler elements, four for earth and two for each of the three other elements.

59. Cerno, what does the sand teach us?

Sand symbolises a soul which quickly learns to worship but lacks the elements suitable for long-lasting faith. A "sandy" soul can produce a beautiful faith, even decorated with multi-coloured flowers, but it lasts only a short time.

60. There are souls which are analogous to clayey soil. These souls, when in contact with the rains of preaching, become compact. When the preaching stops for a time, they harden and finally rebel against religious discipline. Before beginning a religious enterprise, one must know the nature of those with whom one is concerned. With a group or an individual whose soul is "clayey," a "tuberous" form of teaching is required, that is to say, one which is discreet but tenacious and which penetrates to the interior of the soul.

61. The human spirit has the nature of metals which are more or less oxydisable. There are men who have a precious spirit, like gold or silver. These are the elect who can be exposed to the air of material temptations without suffering its oxydising action. Their senses are obedient to them instead of dragging them along. Those who have a spirit of the nature of iron must guard against exposing themselves to the air of material pleasures and especially against burying themselves under the humid soil of debauchery and intemperance. In these kinds of places an organic agent will develop which gives birth to the moral rust which will attack their defenseless spirit. It is not given to everyone to comprehend the mechanism by which the invisible rust of profligate materialism leads to the moral destruction of the soul, but everyone can observe and understand the effect of material rust, this deep red "disease" which attacks iron and progressively destroys it, silently and unremittingly.

One must combat the rust of the soul. It attacks faith, corrupts morality, perverts the spirit of nations and throws them into the atrocious conflicts which makes them more savage than the carnivores of the forest. This rust distorts men to the extent that they celebrate and rejoice over having caused many deaths. They go to the extent of affixing insignia on the chests of those who have been the most impetuous in the work of destruction so that no one can be unaware of their macabre exploits.

APPENDIX I

# THE MĀ 'D-DĪN

The *mā 'd-dīn* is the second lesson of the oral catechism which Cerno Bokar composed and taught in Bandiagara. The full text of the catechism can be consulted in VE, 195–239 and TB, 96–120. It is presented in the form of a story in which a Dogon convert named Ancamba requests a Muslim teacher, Sisse, to instruct him in Islam.

The first lesson of the catechism is called "The Primordial Pact," in which Sisse demonstrates that God has endowed man with reason so that he can employ it in his quest for salvation. It is reason, Sisse explains, which differentiates man from the animals, which among men differentiates the believer from the unbeliever, which among believers differentiates the learned from the ignorant, and which among learned believers differentiates the just from the evil. This lesson ends with Sisse's injunction to Ancamba to "undertake the conquest of religious knowledge," which at the least requires that one should learn the first and the last ten *suwar* of the Qur'an, study the concepts of theology which constitute "the esoteric meaning of the *shahāda*" which is "indispensable and largely sufficient," learn the prescriptions of ritual purification, and be initiated into Sufism. The second lesson is the *mā 'd-dīn*, reproduced here, and the third lesson is called the "Synthesis of the Esoteric Teaching" or the "Internal Law," which is a discussion of the general principles of Sufism and of the specific injunctions of the Tijaniyya order.

Each lesson of the catechism was accompanied by a mnemonic pattern of lines and dots which was traced in the sand to aid the student in remembering the texts. A modified version of the pattern used in teaching the *mā 'd-dīn* appears on p. 95; the letters and numbers have been added to assist the reader in following the progression of the teaching in conjunction with the pattern. The following text has been translated from VE, 209–218; it takes up the conversation between Sisse and Ancamba.

## *Second Lesson*. WHAT IS RELIGION? (*Mā 'd-dīn*)

Sisse smoothed the sand, impressed a point into it and said, "Interrogate me." Ancamba posed questions and Sisse responded:

9. What is religion? Religion is a way (a road).
8. How many ways have there been? There have been seventy-three.
7. What is their condition? The first seventy-two are ways of error.
6. Only the seventy-third is the path of rectitude,
5. the unique attaining to God.

4. From our father Adam until our Lord Muhammad, all have followed the same path:
3. It is called ISLAM.
2. It is the path of deliverance.
1. It is the way of salvation, the Hanifiyya Way.

Upon what is this path constructed? It is constructed upon three pillars, which are:
A. *Islām* (submission to God),
B. *Īmān* (faith), and
C. *Iḥsān* (faultless conduct).

Of what does *Islām* consist? *Islām* requires five obligatory actions. What are they? They are:
*A*1. The articulation of the double formula of faith, without which no act is valid: "I bear witness that there is no god but God, unique and without partner; and I bear witness that Muhammad is His servant and His messenger."
*A*2. The performance of the five daily prayers.
*A*3. The payment of *zakāt* (the annual tithe intended for the poor).
*A*4. The fast during the month of Ramadan.
*A*5. The pilgrimage to the sacred House, to Mecca.
*A*6. As for the pilgrimage, it is required only of those able to accomplish it.

These are the fundamental dogmas of the degree, *Islām*.

Of what does *Īmān* consist? *Īmān* consists of belief in six principles:
*B*1. God,
*B*2. the Last Judgment,
*B*3. the angels,
*B*4. the revealed Books [including those which preceded the Qur'an],
*B*5. the prophets of God,
*B*6. the decree of God.
*B*7. Whether this decree brings something pleasing
*B*8. or distressing,
*B*9. pleasing, such as having a good son,
*B*10. or distressing, such as union with a bad spouse,
*B*11. one must believe in both cases that everything comes to us from God.

Of what does *Iḥsān* consist? *Iḥsān* commands:
*C*1. Adore God
*C*2. as if you see Him,
*C*3. because if you do not see Him,
*C*4. He sees you.

Ancamba continued: "I have asked you about the ways. You told me there are seventy-three. You chose one of them and affirmed that it is the only true one leading directly to God. You told me that this path was constructed upon three pillars: *Islām*, *Imān*, and *Iḥsān*. I learned that each of these pillars is composed of acts and principles. Thus *Islām* includes five, *Imān* six and *Iḥsān* four. Be patient, Sisse, for I am a novice. It is very important for me to question you so that I can clarify my knowledge."

Sisse, always obliging, said to him, "Interrogate me as you wish. I will hide from you nothing of what I know."

"What," said Ancamba, "is the esoteric teaching of the double formula of the profession of faith, the *shahāda*?"

Sisse first placed his finger on the point for *Islām* (A1) and then moved it to make a new point (A7) in order to explain:

A7. The Creator has performed two well-known miracles for you.

A8. He gave you life.

A9. He developed it in you.

Man is obliged to bear witness to this. Each of these divine manifestations has its appointed time.

A10. God models man in his mother's womb and through the effect of His power sustains life there for the prescribed term.

A11. Then He causes the infant to see the light of day through birth. And He aids the infant through His actions until the completion of his growing up.

A12. At an age which He chooses, He endows him with a mind (Reason) and imposes duties upon him.

A13. The first act, before any other duty, is the articulation of the formula of the profession of faith (*shahāda*).

The scholars have affirmed that whoever is unaware of the esoteric teaching of the *shahāda* will in no way enjoy the privileges attached to *Islām*. What is the hidden teaching of the *shahāda*? It is knowledge *in* God. What can one know in God? What one can know in God is not tangible. One can know three states of God:

A14. that which is necessary for Him,

A15. that which is impossible for Him,

A16. that which is contingent for Him.

What is necessary for God? Twenty-five attributes are necessary for God:

D1. existence,

D2. anteriority,

D3. permanence,

D4. difference (from created things),

D5. self-sufficiency,

D6. unity,

D7. power,

D8. will,

D9. knowledge,

D10. life,
D11. hearing,
D12. vision,
D13. speech,
D14. to be powerful,
D15. to exercise will,
D16. to be omniscient,
D17. to be living,
D18. to be hearing,
D19. to be seeing,
D20. to be speaking,
D21. to be without self-interest,
D22. to be without obligation to act,
D23. to be not susceptible to force,
D24. to be not bound by habit,
D25. that He brought the world into being.

What is impossible for God? Twenty-five attributes are impossible with respect to God:

E1. non-existence,
E2. beginning,
E3. termination,
E4. similarity (to created things),
E5. need (of something other than Himself),
E6. existence of an equal to Him,
E7. impotence,
E8. (to act through) constraint,
E9. ignorance,
E10. death,
E11. deafness,
E12. blindness,
E13. muteness,
E14. that He be impotent,
E15. that He be constrained,
E16. that He be ignorant,
E17. that He die,
E18. that He be deaf,
E19. that He be blind,
E20. that He be mute,
E21. that He be self-interested,
E22. that He be obliged to act,
E23. that He be susceptible to force,
E24. that He be bound by habit,
E25. that the world is anterior (so that He did not bring it into being).

What is contingent for God? The contingent for God constitutes a kind of middle way between the necessary and the impossible attributes. The contingent can either exist (like the necessary) or not exist (like the impossible). For example, the decision, for God, to create or to leave something in the nothingness is contingent.

The twenty-five necessary attributes plus the twenty-five impossible attributes comprise the fifty articles of the hidden teaching of the first part of the *shahāda*: "I bear witness that there is no god but God, unique and without partner."

What, therefore, is the esoteric teaching of the second part — "I bear witness that Muhammad is the servant and the messenger of God"?

It is the knowledge of the prophets.

How can one know the prophets?

The prophets are recognised by three states:

A17. by that which is necessary for them,
A18. by that which is impossible for them,
A19. and by that which is contingent for them.

What is necessary for the prophets and what is impossible for them? Necessary for the prophets are:

F1. fidelity,
F2. truthfulness,
F3. making known (the message of God).

As a result, what is impossible for them are

G1. deception,
G2. lying,
G3. concealing (the message of God).

What is contingent for the prophets?

F4. Prophets are subject to human contingencies.
G4. It is therefore impossible for them to be above human contingencies.

Of what does the faith of the prophets consist? It consists of their belief in:

F5. the previous prophets,
F6. the angels,
F7. the revealed Books,
F8. the Last Judgment.

It is therefore impossible for the prophets to deny:

G5. the previous prophets,
G6. the angels,
G7. the revealed Books,
G8. the Last Judgment.

The total of that which is necessary, impossible and contingent for the prophets, added to their articles of faith, constitutes the sixteen articles of the esoteric teaching of the second formula of the profession of faith: "I bear witness that Muhammad is the servant and messenger of God."

We have related the assertion of the scholars, "Whoever does not possess knowledge of the hidden teaching of the double formula of the profession of faith, articulates it without effect." And whoever articulates it without effect is not a believer, and the unbeliever is not on the way toward salvation.

We are thus happy to note — and we thank God for it — that the teaching of the *shahāda* consists of fifty articles for the first formula and sixteen for the second, a total of sixty-six [the numerical equivalent of the word Allah].

May God, who has enabled us to know these sixty-six points, cause us to utter the *shahāda* at the moment of our death, as the last act of our life, Amen.

APPENDIX II

# THE LITANY OF TIJANI PRAYERS

The Tijani litany consists of three sets of prayers which are recited at specified times in addition to the five daily prayers required of all Muslims. They are the *wird*, the *waẓīfa*, and the *ḥaḍra*. This terminology can be somewhat confusing. Hampaté Bâ says (in VE, 231) that all these prayers together constitute the Tijani *wird*, although al-Hajj Umar refers to them collectively as the *adhkār* and employs the term *wird* to designate only the first set of prayers (called by Hampaté Bâ, the *lāzim*). Umar specifically states that it was the first set of prayers which the Prophet Muhammad ordered Shaykh al-Tijani to transmit to all Muslims who requested them. Abun-Nasr also employs this usage. This interpretation suggests that entry into the Tijaniyya order was effected by receiving an authorization to recite the *wird* (the first set of prayers listed below) and that authorizations to recite the other prayers were granted later. This procedure seems to have been the intention of Shaykh al-Tijani, and would conform to the progressive or "initiatic" nature of membership in the order which is suggested in much of the literature.

The following information is from *Rimāḥ*, I, 229–30, although the translations of the texts of the prayers are from Abun-Nasr, *The Tijaniyya*, 50–7. This information can also be found in VE, 231–6.

The *wird* includes three recitations to be recited twice daily, in the morning before the dawn prayer, and in the afternoon.

1. 100 times the formula "I beg forgiveness from God."
2. 100 times the *ṣalāt al-fātiḥ*: "O God, bless our master Muhammad, who opened what had been closed, and who is the seal of what had gone before; he who makes the Truth victorious by the Truth, the guide to Thy straight path; and bless his household as is the due of his immense position and grandeur."
3. 100 times "There is no god but God," called the *hailala*.

The *Waẓīfa* includes four recitations recited at least once daily before the morning prayer, but a second time in the evening if one wishes.

1. 30 times the formula, "I ask forgiveness from God, the Great, of whom there is no other god but Him, the Living and the Self-subsisting."
2. 50 times the *ṣalāt al-fātiḥ* (as above).
3. 100 times "There is no god but God."
4. 11 or 12 times the *jawharat al-kamāl*: "O God, send benediction upon and salute the source of divine mercy, a true ruby which encompasses the centre of comprehensions and meanings, the son of Adam, the possessor of divine Truth; the most luminous lightning in the

profitable rain-clouds which fill all the intervening seas and receptacles; Thy bright light with which Thou has filled Thy universe and which surrounds the places of existence.

O God, bless and salute the source of Truth from which are manifested the tabernacles of realities; the source of knowledge, the most upright; Thy complete and most straight path.

O God, bless and salute the advent of the Truth by the Truth; the greatest treasure, Thy mysterious Light. May God bless the Prophet and his household, a prayer which brings us to knowledge of him.''

The *ḥaḍra* is a group recitation held each Friday afternoon during which the *hailala* or simply the name Allah is recited. The number of recitations is not specified.

APPENDIX III

# CONDITIONS OF MEMBERSHIP IN THE TIJANIYYA ORDER

The following conditions are explained in *Rimāḥ*, I, 211–28, from which these passages are translated (see also VE, 233–9). Only the first twenty-one conditions are obligatory for all members; the last two are encouraged for those who can achieve them.

1. The *shaykh* who transmits the *adhkār* should be authorized to do so by proper initiation (*talqīn*) from the founder or by someone who has been properly authorized to do so.
2. Those who seek initiation must free themselves from the *wird* of any other *shaykh* which may have been required of them and abandon such a *wird* and never return to it.
3. One must not visit any saints living or dead (implying that the disciple is bound to the one *shaykh* who has initiated him).
4. One must seek to observe the five daily prayers in a group and to fulfill the requirements of the *sharī'a*.
5. One must ceaselessly love the *shaykh* until his death, and one must love the successor (*khalīfa*) to the *shaykh* and all that which was close to the *shaykh*, such as his chosen followers and his directives, in the same way that one loved the *shaykh*.
6. One must not think that he is secure from the ruses of God (see Schimmel, *Mystical Dimensions*, 127–8).
7. One must not express any insult, hatred or animosity toward the *shaykh*.
8. One should persevere with the *wird* until death.
9. One must maintain a firm belief [in the *ṭarīqa*].
10. One must remain free from all blameworthy acts.
11. A disciple should be properly authorized to recite the *dhikr* through a genuine initiation (*talqīn*) by someone who has received a genuine authorization from the founder or from another authorized person.
12. One must gather in a group for [the recitation of] the *waẓīfa* and for the recitation (*dhikr*) of the *hailala* on Friday afternoon.
13. One must not recite the *jawharat al-kamāl* without performing the ritual ablution with water.
14. One must refrain from any activities which might result in the rupture of good relations between himself and his fellow-men, and especially between himself and his brothers in the *ṭarīqa*.
15. One must not be negligent of the *wird*, such as delaying it from its proper time, except for good cause.

16. One must not presume to bestow the *wird* without a genuine authorization to do so.
17. One must respect everyone who has been affiliated with the *shaykh*, especially the eminent members of the *ṭarīqa*.
18. [For the recitation of the *dhikr*] one must be concerned for the cleanliness of one's clothing and one's person;
19. one must be concerned for the cleanliness of the place where one is sitting;
20. one must sit and face the *qibla* unless one is travelling, one is very close to the *ka'ba*, or one is in a group;
21. and one must refrain from speaking [words other than the *dhikr*] unless absolutely necessary.
22. If one is able, one should envision the image of the founder before him from the beginning of the *dhikr* until its end, and one should seek assistance from him. And what is preferable to that, and more beneficial, more exalted and more accomplished, is to envision the Prophet.
23. One should call to mind the meanings of the formulations of the *dhikr* if one is able to understand them.

APPENDIX IV

# A NOTE ON ETHNICITY

The matter of ethnicity is extremely complex, and in recent years a welcome debate on the precision of its definition has begun to emerge in the West African literature. Ethnicity is primarily a question of identity, and identity is in fact a multi-dimensional process; it varies with who is doing the identifying and in what context. A Pullo, for example, has no need to identify himself as a Pullo when he is among other Fulbe; he would identify himself by family, lineage, clan or perhaps village. But if he travelled from Masina to Bamako, he would be seen as a Pullo; and in Paris, among other Africans, he would be a Malian, although to most Europeans he would be an African. This example suggests that one's identity becomes more abstract the further one moves from home; and the same is true of ethnicity. In this book we usually speak of ethnic groups as if they were clearly defined, homogeneous entities; the "Fulbe," the "Dogon," etc. And of course, this level of abstraction is usually appropriate to the topics under discussion. But it is also necessary to point out, especially to readers who are less familiar with the region here under study, that these general designations can be misleading.

The Fulbe, in the narrowest sense of the term, are semi-nomadic cattle keepers; but when one speaks of the "Fulbe of Masina" one denotes a much larger socio-economic and political agglomeration of farmers and craftsmen as well. These non-pastoralists constitute the subordinate classes of a larger Pullo society into which they have been integrated and acculturated. They speak Fulfulde and, depending on the context, they consider themselves Fulbe, even if they know their "true" ethnic origins to be something else. Of course, many of these are the descendants of slaves, but many also descend from free people who voluntarily settled in this region, intermarried and became "Fulbe." This example suggests the dangers inherent in employing ethnic designations carelessly; the pastoralist Fulbe do not consider these subordinate classes in Masina to be "true" Fulbe, and if one defines them in strict genealogical and socio-economic terms, they are not. But if one includes the characteristics of language, culture, and polity in the definition, as most outsiders do, they certainly qualify as Fulbe.

The movement and mixing of peoples was extensive in West Africa, as the result of war, migration, commercial activity and even, if on a much smaller scale, the search for Islamic scholarly training. Cerno Bokar had close relationships, both as a student and as a teacher, with persons from almost every one of the ethnic groups listed in this appendix. Not all societies were as aggressively integrative as the Fulbe;

the Dogon do not seem to have brought many outsiders into their society, although we know so little of Dogon history that one can in no way be certain of this impression. The Marka merchants, however, not only amassed great numbers of slaves, but they also seem to have accepted the inclusion of freemen into their commercial enterprises, who intermarried, adopted the Marka language, and in this case Islam, and who became "Marka."

The concern of contemporary scholars to explore the dynamics of "shifting ethnicity" has sounded a note of warning about the unqualified use of ethnic terminology. But while these kinds of studies deepen our understanding of African society and history, we must also remember that indigenous African ideas about ethnicity have always been present and significant. These were concerned with ethnicity not as a subject of study, but as a method of identification, that is, of distinguishing oneself from others, and secondarily of distinguishing among the various groups of others. African ethnic designations of other groups therefore tend to be coloured by highly stereotypical and sometimes denigrating overtones. And many of the designations adopted in European usage were not those by which Africans called themselves, but those given them by outsiders. It was not until twenty years after the French established their official presence among the Dogon that they actually began to refer to them as Dogon; before that they employed the Fulfulde word "Habe" which is a derisory generic term for non-Fulbe. Stereotypical attitudes, of course, are not limited to Africans but are universal. And not all Africans endorsed them; Cerno Bokar was highly critical of such prejudices. The French were not immune to them; they were quite prepared to label all Futanke as "treacherous" or all Muslims as "fanatical." The manipulation of stereotypes is not a major concern of this book, but it plays an important role in some of the events portrayed. Hamallah was opposed by some people because he was a Moor, and he challenged the religious leadership of many Futanke, a charge which gained a sympathetic response in some quarters even though the Tijani leadership in West Africa was very mixed ethnically. French antagonism to Hamallah was enhanced by the claim that he was a fanatically anti-French Muslim, even though no evidence could ever be documented to this effect. These phenomena were not manifestations of "tribalism," nor are they exclusive to Africa. They reflect the manipulation of stereotypes and they are universal.

The descriptions presented here make no claim to being definitive, although they have been informed by the many concerns discussed above. They are more historical than anthropological in that they attempt to define different groups both as they were seen by their contemporaries in the early twentieth century, as well as with some regard for recent scholarship. This approach has been adopted, not in order to perpetuate stereotypes, but to aid the reader in understanding the weight which ethnic terminology carried for the contemporaries of Cerno Bokar.

*Bambara.* The Bambara, known generally to themselves as Bamana, constitute the majority of the population of Mali. Their language is of the Mande family, and they are primarily agriculturalists. Much of al-Hajj Umar's *jihād* was fought against Bambara populations, and his conquests of both Kaarta and Segu resulted in the demise of Bambara kingdoms. Although the Bambara represent only a small minority of the Masina population, and Cerno Bokar seems to have had little contact with them in Bandiagara, his mother may have left Segu because of the general fear after the French conquest that the Bambara were to be returned to political authority there.

*Dogon.* The Dogon are a Mande speaking people who live along the Bandiagara cliffs as well as on the plateau above and the plain below. The Fulbe called them Habe, a derogatory term for all non-Fulbe, and this name was used by the French until about 1914 when colonial administrators began to gain adequate access to the Dogon and to acquire reliable knowledge about them.[1] An extensive anthropological literature exists for the Dogon, but unfortunately very little has been written on their history. They were organized in relatively small political units, and considerable variation exists among them in social and religious practice and even in dialect. Consequently one should be wary of any generalizations put forward about "the Dogon." Having said that, we will generalize by adding that the Dogon of the Bandiagara plateau, where they constituted about 45 per cent of the population in 1914, tended to side with the Futanke in their struggles against the Fulbe in the nineteenth century. They also maintained a lengthy resistance against the French. In the twentieth century when some Dogon began to adopt Islam, they often did so through the agency of Futanke religious teachers. Cerno Bokar enjoyed considerable influence among certain Dogon communities.

*French.* The French are included as an ethnic group because they share all the generic qualities of other groups listed here: common language, culture, religion and socio-economic structure. Most important, they were seen by all Africans as a separate, clearly identifiable group. The French were the most recent conquerors and rulers of the middle Niger River valley, following in the footsteps of the Futanke, the Fulbe and the Bambara of Segu. French rule was more extensive and more effective than that of its predecessors, although it was administered by a very small number of people. The vast majority of Africans never had any direct contact with Europeans, so that stereotypes about them were plentiful.

*Fulbe* (singular, Pullo). The Fulbe are found throughout Sudanic Africa from Senegal and Guinée in the west to the modern Republic of the Sudan in the east. In Masina the Fulbe are divided into a complex social and economic system of classes or castes. The semi-nomadic pastoralists consider themselves the "true" Fulbe, who uphold the traditional values of their culture, and who maintain rather strict endogamous rules of marriage. But these pastoralists are in close relationships with the so-called "settled" Fulbe whose ranks include not only farmers and craftsmen, but warrior classes and even certain groups of Muslim clerics. The origins of these various Fulbe classes are shrouded in myth. Certainly many of the farmers and craftsmen are descendants of former slaves or free immigrants who submitted to Fulbe hegemony. But the origins of the "warriors" or the *jawaambe* (a class of free men who acted as the clients and associates of Fulbe rulers[2]) or even of the Muslim clerical classes, still demand fuller exploration by scholars.[3] In the early nineteenth century Masina had been united into a tightly controlled Muslim state as the result of a *jihād* led by a Pullo cleric, Shaykh Amadu Lobbo. Hamdullahi, the captial of the new state, became an important centre of Islamic scholarship, and the people of Masina were subject to an intense campaign of Islamization. But by the 1860s the ideals of the founders of the new Masina were in decay, and the armies of al-Hajj Umar conquered Hamdullahi on the pretext that they had supported the non-Muslim state of Segu against the *jihād*. In 1914, the Fulbe constituted about 30 per cent of the population of the Bandiagara plateau.

*Futanke.* Literally, "the people of Futa" (known also as Futankoobe in Fulfulde and as Tukolor in the French literature). Strictly, the Futanke were by origin Fulbe; they spoke varying dialects of Fulfulde and resided primarily in the regions of Futa Toro, Futa Jallon and Futa Bundu. They tended, however, not to be pastoralists but members of the settled classes and castes of Pullo society. Recruits from the three Futas formed the core of al-Hajj Umar's early religious community and fighting force. As the *jihād* was extended, an increasing number of persons from various ethnic backgrounds were absorbed into Umar's army and community, and in Masina the term Futanke came to refer to all those who fought for the *jihād* and governed the conquered territories of the nascent Umarian state. At the end of the nineteenth century many Futanke emigrated eastwards in an attempt to escape Christian domination, and in the twentieth century they constituted only a tiny minority of the population of the French Sudan (less than 1 per cent of the population of the Bandiagara plateau). Nonetheless, even after their political eclipse by the French, their religious influence was extensive, both as scholars and as leaders of the Tijaniyya Sufi order. Cerno Bokar was a Futanke.

*Hausa.* The Hausa are the major ethnic group in what is now the far north of Nigeria. Cerno Bokar's maternal grandfather al-Hajj Seedu Hann, who was either Pullo or Futanke, had joined al-Hajj Umar in Hausaland; it is possible that his wife, Inna, Cerno's grandmother, was Hausa. Aissata, Cerno's mother, sought and received support among the community of Hausa merchants in Bandiagara when she moved there in 1893.

*Juula.* See *Marka*.

*Kunta.* The Kunta are an Arab group residing in the central Sahara. One of their number, Sīdī al-Mukhtār al-Kuntī (*d.* 1811) was responsible for the extensive spread of the Qadiriyya Sufi order in West Africa in the eighteenth century. As a *shaykh* he gained a certain political as well as religious influence, especially among the inhabitants of the south-central Sahara and the Sahel. His descendants attempted to retain this influence; by the mid-nineteenth century the most prominent Kunta leader was Aḥmad al-Bakkāy who was then resident in Timbuktu. He sought first to contain the rising power of the Fulbe of Hamdullahi, and later that of al-Hajj Umar. Al-Bakkāy and the Kunta were the major opponents to al-Hajj Umar's proselytization of the Tijaniyya in West Africa.

*Marka.* Marka is the Bambara term for the Soninke merchants (also called Juula) who have been plying trade in the western Sudan for many centuries. They speak a Mande language, are Muslim, and have been responsible for the early spread of Islam in much of West Africa.

*Moors.* The Moors are the Arabic speaking inhabitants of southern Mauritania. Their social organization is reminiscent of the Fulbe in that it is composed of putatively dominant warrior groups as well as subordinate castes of craftsmen and Muslim clerics. Many Moors were also involved in long distance trade. Shaykh Hamallah's father was a Moor.

*Mossi.* The Mossi are the most prominent ethnic group of Upper Volta, and major Mossi settlements existed not far from Bandiagara. Some Mossi were resident in Bandiagara and many others came there to trade or to pursue religious studies.

*Pullo*. See *Fulbe*, of which it is the singular.

*Soninke*. See *Marka*.

*Somono*. The Somono are a Mande speaking fishing group who live along the Niger River in the region of Segu. They had been influenced by Islam; one of Cerno Bokar's early teachers was a Somono.

*Wolof*. The Wolof are one of the major ethnic groups of Senegal. Wolof were present in the French Sudan primarily as merchants.

## NOTES

1 Fawtier, "Le Cercle dc Bandiagara," *Bulletin du Comité de l'Afrique Française, Renseignements coloniaux*, 1914, 70–1, makes the first reference to them as Dogon which I have found in the literature. All population estimates which occur in this Appendix for the Bandiagara plateau are taken from this article.

2 See VE, 108.

3 See the introduction to Willis, ed., *Studies in West African Islamic History*.

# SOURCES

## *Archival sources*

Archives Nationales du Mali, Bamako (ANM)

*Fonds Ancien*, séries:

1D-Monographies-Études-Coutumiers

2D-Organisation Administrative

1E-Affaires politiques;

Rapports politiques

Renseignements politiques, cercles.

2E-Politique indigène

Notes et Fiches de Renseignements sur les chefs et notables, cercles.

4E-Politique musulmane

Correspondance, cercles (politique musulmane)

Rapports sur l'Islam et les confréries musulmanes, cercles

Renseignements sur les marabouts et les personnages religieux, cercles

Police musulmane, cercles.

1G-Enseignement

Écoles coraniques-Rapports

Statistique des écoles coraniques-cercles.

*Fonds Récent*, séries:

B-Correspondance générale

D-Administration générale

1E-Affaires politiques

2E-Politiques indigènes

4E-Politique musulmane

1G-Enseignement

Écoles coraniques

Archives Nationales du Sénégal, Dakar (ANS)

1G-Études générales: Missions, Notices et Monographies, 1818–1921.

2G-Rapports périodiques, 1895–1940.

15G-Affaires politiques, administratives et musulmanes, Soudan, 1821–1920

Correspondances indigènes, 1840–1900

Généralités, 1880–1920

19G-Affaires musulmanes, AOF, 1900–1920

Institut Fondamental d'Afrique Noire, Dakar (IFAN)

Fonds FIGARET, Cahier 6, Retour de Nioro du Tierno Bokari Salifou, par Amadou Hampaté Bâ (in Fulfulde and French).

## *Oral material, recorded on tape*

"*Kabbe tawīdi*," recitation in Fulfulde recorded in Tera *cercle*, Niger, by Boubou Hama; a copy of the tape is held in CELTHO, Niamey, Niger.

Amadou Hampaté Bâ: 2, 3, 4, 5, 6 and 12 May 1978 in Paris; 1 July 1980 in Bamako; 7 and 8 July 1981 in Paris.

## *Interviews*

*Copies of the following interviews are deposited in the Institut des Sciences Humaines, Bamako, Mali*:

Baba Thimbely (initiated into the Tijaniyya by Cerno Bokar; reinitiated by him into the Hamalliyya): 29 September and 1 October 1977; 21 January 1978, in Bandiagara.

Dauda Maiga (initiated into the Tijaniyya by Cerno Bokar; probably reinitiated by him into the Hamalliyya): 29 and 30 September 1977 in Bandiagara.

Sori Hamadun Bala (a former student in Cerno Bokar's school): 30 September 1977 in Bandiagara; 10 October 1977 in Mopti.

## *Unpublished material*

Aḥmad Bābā al-Tinbuktī. *Al-La'ālī al-sundusiyya fī 'l-faḍā'il al-Sanūsiyya*. Bibliothèque Générale et Archives, Rabat, Morocco. D984, fols. 107b–132a.

Bâ, Amadou Hampaté. "Les Paraboles de Tierno Bokar." CHEAM 50354.

Baṭrān, 'Abd al-'Azīz 'Abdallah, "Sīdī al-Mukhtār al-Kuntī and the recrudescence of Islam in the Western Sahara and the Middle Niger." Ph.D. thesis, University of Birmingham, 1971.

Brown, W.A. "The Caliphate of Hamdullahi, ca. 1818–1864." Ph.D. thesis, University of Wisconsin, 1969.

Jah, Omar. "Sufism and Nineteenth Century Jihād Movements in West Africa: a case study of al-Hājj 'Umar al-Fūtī's Philosophy of Jihād and its Sufi Bases." Ph.D. thesis, McGill University, 1973.

Muḥammad al-Wālī b. Sulaimān. *Al-Manhaj al-farīd fī ma'rifat 'ilm al-tawḥīd*. BN, Arabe 5541, fols. 130–51, and Arabe 5650, fols. 111–30.

Quesnot, Fernand. "L'Évolution du Tidjanisme sénégalais depuis 1922," CHEAM 2865 (1958).

Rocaboy, Ct. "L'Hamallisme," CHEAM 1153.

Traoré, Alioune. "Contribution à l'étude de l'Islam. Le Mouvement tijanien de Cheikh Hamahoullah." Thèse de 3° cycle, Université de Dakar, 1975.

Willis, J.R. "Al-Ḥājj 'Umar b. Sa'īd al-Fūtī al-Tūrī (*c.* 1794–1864) and the Doctrinal Basis of his Islamic Reformist Movement in the Western Sudan." Ph.D. thesis, University of London, 1970.

Zebadia, Abdelkader. "The Career and Correspondence of Aḥmad al-Bakkāy of Timbuktu." Ph.D. thesis, University of London, 1974.

## *Published material*

'Abd al-Qādir al-Sūfī. *Indications from Signs*. Atlanta, 1979.

——. *The Hundred Steps*. Norwich, 1979.

Abun-Nasr, Jamil M. *The Tijaniyya*. London, 1965.

Alexandre, Pierre. "A West African Islamic Movement: Hamallism in French West Africa," in *Protest and Power in Black Africa*, ed. by R. Rotberg and Ali Mazrui. New York, 1970. pp. 497–512.

'Alī Ḥarāzim. *Jawāhir al-ma'ānī wa bulūgh al-amānī fī faiḍ Sīdī Abī 'l-'Abbās al-Tijānī*. Beirut, no date.

André, P.-J. *L'Islam Noir. Contribution à l'étude des confréries religieuses en Afrique Occidentale*. Paris, 1924.

Arnaud, Robert. "L'Islam et la politique musulmane française en AOF," *Bulletin du Comité de l'Afrique Française et du Comité du Maroc. Renseignements coloniaux et documents*. 1912. pp. 3–20, 115–27, 142–54.

Audoin, Jean and Raymond Deniel. *L'Islam en Haute-Volta à l'époque coloniale*. Paris, 1978.

Bâ, Amadou Hampaté. *L'Étrange Destin de Wangrin*. Paris, 1973.

——. "Jésus et Hasdu; conte initiatique de la mystique peule, enseigné à la Zaouia de Bandiagara," *Bulletin de l'IFAN*, tome 31 (juillet 1969), pp. 754–86.

——. *Jésus vu par un Musulman*. Abidjan-Dakar, 1976.

——. *Vie et Enseignement de Tierno Bokar. Le Sage de Bandiagara*. Paris, 1980.

——. and Marcel Cardaire. *Tierno Bokar, le Sage de Bandiagara*. Paris, 1957.

——. and J. Daget. *L'Empire peul du Macina*. Vol. I (1818–1853). Paris, 1962.

Bonnetain, Mme. *Une Française au Soudan*. Paris, 1894.

Bouche, Denise. "Les Écoles françaises au Soudan à l'époque de la conquête, 1884–1900," *Cahiers d'Études Africaines*, VI, 22 (1966), pp. 228–67.

Brenner, Louis. "Separate Realities: a Review of Literature on Sufism," *International Journal of African Historical Studies*, V, 4 (1972), pp. 637–58.

——. "The Sufi Teaching of Tierno Bokar Salif Tall," *Journal of Religion in Africa*, VIII, facs. 3 (1976), pp. 208–26.

Caron, E. *De Saint-Louis au port du Tombouctou*. Paris, 1894.

Corbin, Henry. *Creative Imagination in the Ṣūfism of Ibn 'Arabī*. Transl. from French by Ralph Manheim. Princeton, 1969.

Cruise-O'Brien, Donal. "Towards an 'Islamic Policy' in French West Africa, 1854–1914,' *Journal of African History*, VIII, 2 (1967), pp. 303–16.

Delafosse, Maurice. "Les États d'âme d'un colonial," *Bulletin du Comité de l'Afrique Française*, 1912, pp. 62, 102, 127, 162, 200, 240, 288, 311, 338, 373, 414.

Dumont, Fernand. *L'Anti-Sultan ou al-Hajj Omar Tal du Fouta, combattant de la foi (1794–1864)*. Abidjan-Dakar, 1974.

Fawtier, Administrateur. "Le Cercle de Bandiagara," *Bulletin du Comité de l'Afrique Française, Renseignements Coloniaux*, 1914, pp. 68–75.

Fisher, Humphrey J. "Hassebu: Islamic Healing in Black Africa," in M. Brett, ed., *Northern Africa: Islam and Modernization*. London, 1973. pp. 23–47.

——. "Dreams and Conversion in Black Africa," in N. Levtzion, ed. *Conversion to Islam*. New York, 1979, pp. 217–35.

Gaden, Henri. *Proverbes et maximes peuls et toucouleurs, traduits, expliqués et annotés*. Paris, 1931.

al-Ghazālī, Abū Ḥāmid Muḥammad. *The Alchemy of Happiness*. Translated from the Turkish by Henry H. Homes. Albany, 1873.

Goody, Jack. "Restricted Literacy in Northern Ghana," in J. Goody, ed., *Literacy in Traditional Societies*. Cambridge, 1968. pp. 198–264.

Gouilly, A. *L'Islam dans l'Afrique Occidentale Française*. Paris, 1952.
Gourdeau, J.-P. "Une Lecture de *L'Étrange Destin de Wangrin* d'Amadou Hampaté Bâ," *Annales de l'Université d'Abidjan*, Série D, 8 (1975), pp. 153–84.
Guy, G. "L'Enseignement colonial en France," *Bulletin du Comité de l'Afrique Française*, 1927, pp. 188–92.
Hama, Boubou. *Contribution à la Connaissance de l'histoire des Peul*. Paris, 1968.
Hardy, G. *Une Conquête Morale. L'Enseignement en Afrique Occidentale Française*. Paris, 1917.
Hiskett, Mervyn. "The 'Community of Grace' and its opponents, the 'Rejecters': a Debate about theology and mysticism in Muslim West Africa with special reference to its Hausa expression," *African Language Studies*, XVII (1980), pp. 99–140.
Houdas, O. *Tedzkiret en-Nisian*. Paris, 1960.
Jah, Omar. "Source materials for the career and the *jihād* of al-Ḥājj 'Umar al-Fūtī, 1794–1864," *Bulletin de l'IFAN*, tome 41, Série B, no. 2 (1979), pp. 371–97.
Kaba, Lansine. *The Wahhabiyya. Islamic Reform and Politics in French West Africa*. Evanston, 1974.
Last, Murray. *The Sokoto Caliphate*. New York, 1967.
Last, D.M. and M.A. al-Hajj, "Attempts at defining a Muslim in nineteenth century Hausaland and Bornu," *Journal of the Historical Society of Nigeria*, III, 2 (Dec. 1965), pp. 231–9.
Le Chatelier, Alfred. *L'Islam dans l'Afrique Occidentale*. Paris, 1899.
Loppinot, A. de. "Souvenirs d'Aguibou," *Bulletin du Comité d'Études Historiques et Scientifiques de l'Afrique Occidentale Française*, 1919, pp. 24–61.
Mage, A.E. *Voyage dans le Soudan occidentale, 1863–66*. Paris, 1868.
Marty, Paul. *Études sur l'Islam au Sénégal*. 2 vols. Paris, 1917.
——. *Études sur l'Islam et les Tribus du Soudan*. 4 vols. Paris, 1920.
——. *L'Islam en Guinée*. Paris, 1921.
——. *L'Islam en Mauretanie et au Sénégal*. *Revue du Monde Musulman*, tome 31 (1915–16).
Monod, Théodore. "Un poème mystique soudanais," *Le Monde non-Chrétien*, no. 2 (1947), pp. 217–28.
——. "Un Homme de Dieu: Tierno Bokar," *Présence Africaine*, 8–9 (1950), pp. 149–57.
Moreau, L. "Les Marabouts de Dori," *Archives de Sociologie des Religions*, no. 17 (1964), pp. 113–34.
Muḥammad Bello. *Infāq al-Maisūr*. London, 1957.
Muḥammad b. Yūsuf al-Sanūsī. *Al-'Aqīda al-ṣughrā*. Accompanied by French translation by J.O. Lucian. Algiers, 1896.
al-Naqar, 'Umar. *The Pilgrimage Tradition in West Africa*. Khartoum, 1972.
Nasr, Seyyed Hossein. *An Introduction to Islamic Cosmological Doctrines*. Revised edition. London, 1978.
Ndiaye, Moustapha. "Rapports entre Qādirites et Tijānites au Fouta Toro au XIXe et XXe siècles à travers *al-Ḥaqq al-Mubīn* de Cheikh Moussa

Kamara," *Bulletin de l'IFAN*, tome 41, série B, no. 1 (1979), pp. 190–207.
Oloruntimehin, B.O. *The Segu Tukolor Empire*. New York, 1972.
Ouane, Ibrahima-Mamadou. *L'Énigme du Macina*. Monte Carlo, 1952.
Paden, John N. *Religion and Political Culture in Kano*. Berkeley, 1973.
Saint-Martin, Yves. *L'Empire Toucouleur et la France*. Dakar, 1967.
——. *L'Empire Toucouleur 1848–1897*. Paris, 1970.
——. "Un fils d'El Hadj Omar: Aguibou, roi du Dinguiray et du Macina (1843–1907)," *Cahiers d'Études Africaines*, VIII, 29 (1968), pp. 144–78.
Schimmel, Annemarie. *Mystical Dimensions of Islam*. Chapel Hill, 1975.
Sow, Alfa Ibrahim. *Le Filon du Bonheur Éternel*. Paris, 1971.
Sukayrij, Aḥmad b. al-Ḥājj al-'Iyāshī. *Kashf al-Ḥijāb 'amman talāqā ma'a 'l-shaykh al-Tijānī min al-aṣḥāb*. Morocco, 1961.
Tomlinson, G.J.F. and G.J. Lethem. *History of Islamic Propaganda in Nigeria*. 2 vols. London, no date.
Triaud, Jean-Louis. "La Lutte entre la Tidjaniya et la Qadiriya dans le Macina au dix-neuvième siècle," *Annales de l'Université d'Abidjan*, Série F, I, no. 1 (1969), 149–71.
Trimingham, J.S. *The Sufi Orders in Islam*. Oxford, 1971.
Tyam, M.A. *La Vie d'el Hadj Omar, qasīda en poular*. Transl. from the Poular by Henri Gaden. Paris, 1935.
'Umar b. Sa'īd al-Fūtī. *Rimāḥ ḥizb al-raḥīm 'alā nuḥūr ḥizb al-rajīm*. Published in the margins of 'Alī Ḥarāzim, *Jawāhir al-Ma'ānī*, Beirut, no date.
Weiskel, T.C. *French Colonial Rule and the Baule Peoples: Resistance and Collaboration, 1889–1911*. Oxford, 1980.
Willis, J.R. "The Writings of al-Ḥājj 'Umar al-Fūtī and Shaykh Mukhtār b. Wadī'at Allāh: Literary Themes, Sources and Influences," in J.R. Willis, ed., *Studies in West African Islamic History*. Vol. I. *The Cultivators of Islam*. London, 1979. pp. 177–210.
Zouber, M.A. *Aḥmad Bābā de Tombouctou (1556–1627). Sa Vie et son Oeuvre*. Paris, 1977.

# GLOSSARY-INDEX OF ARABIC, FULFULDE AND OTHER AFRICAN TERMS


*adhkār*, see *dhikr*

*anndude* (Ful). To know, 144

*anndal* (Ful). Knowledge, 144

*'aqīda* (Ar). Article of faith or tenet of dogma, 79

*'aql* (Ar). Intellect or mind, 88–9, 90, 93, 105–6, 114–6, 154, 161, 164, 166, 168, 181–2, 187, 189

*awliyā'*, see *walī*

*baraka* (Ar). A spiritual quality which is transmitted by holy men or holy places; spiritual grace, 5, 69, 110, 117, 121

*bāṭin* (Ar). In Sufi terminology that which is internal or hidden, such as hidden knowledge; the esoteric, 81, 105–6, 150

*cerno* (Ful). Scholar; equivalent to the Arabic *'ālim*, 66

*dhawq* (Ar). Literally, taste; in Sufi terminology refers to the direct, immediate perception of esoteric truths, 104, n. 61

*dhikr*, pl. *adhkār* (Ar). Remembrance; the recitation of prayers which recall the name of God; "a spiritual exercise designed to render God's presence throughout one's being" (Trimingham, *The Sufi Orders*, 302), 53, 115–17, 120, 130, 153, 193, 195–6

*dīn* (Ar). Religion, 122

*fātiḥa* (Ar). Opening *sūra* of the Qur'an, 87–8, 91–2

*fiqh* (Ar). Islamic jurisprudence, 81

*firugol* (Ful). Translation or commentary; training in Fulfulde literacy, 85–6

*funūn* (Ar). Islamic scholastic disciplines, 85–6

*ghāzī* (Ar). Vaporous, 170–2, 174

*ḥadīth* (Ar). Traditional accounts of the Prophet's words and deeds, 41, 63, 75–6, 81, 83, 113, 120, 149

*ḥaḍra* (Ar). Meeting for Tijani prayers held each Friday afternoon, 193–4

*hailala* (Ar). Praising God by reciting the phrase, "There is no god but God" (*lā ilāha illā Allāh*); a form of *dhikr*, 193–5

*ḥājj* (Ar). Pilgrimage to Mecca; *see* Mecca

*ḥāl* (Ar). In Sufi terminology, those spiritual states of being which man can achieve only with the aid of God, 113

*ḥaqīqa* (Ar). Ultimate reality or truth, 1,77, 96, 105–6, 153

*al-Ḥaqq* (Ar). Truth; one of the names of God, 1, 114

*ḥuḍūr ar-rūḥ* (Ar). Presence of the divine light or spirit, 143–4

*ḥulm* (Ar). Dream, 119

*iḥsān* (Ar). Faultless conduct; the third pillar of Islam in the *mā 'd-dīn*, 96, 188–9

*'ilm al-ḥurūf* (Ar). The esoteric science of letters, related to numerology, 81–2, 148, 159; *see also* Numerology

*imām* (Ar). Individual who leads prayers in the mosque; the leader of the Muslim community, 131

*īmān* (Ar). Faith; the second pillar of Islam in the *mā 'd-dīn*, 96, 188–9

*insān al-kāmil* (Ar). Perfected man, 122

*islām* (Ar). Literally, submission; submission to God and His law, 96, 188–9

*isnād* (Ar). Chain of transmission of a mystical or prophetic tradition, 81

*istikhāra* (Ar). Prayer performed with the intention of seeking resolution to a problem, usually through dreams, 119–20, 129–30

*jawaambe* (Ful). A class of free persons in Pullo society who acted

as clients and associates of the rulers, 200

*jawharat al-kamāl* (Ar). Prayer recited as part of the Tijani *waẓīfa* (Hamallists recited this prayer eleven times, other Tijanis recited it twelve times), 47, 49, 51, 134, 192–3, 195

*jihād* (Ar). Literally, struggle; refers to the Muslim "holy war" to spread Islam; referred to by Sufis as the "lesser *jihād*," 17–23, 33, 42–3, 45, 67–8, 84, 107, 113, 151–2, 199–200

*jihād al-nafs* (Ar). The internal spiritual struggle of the Sufi to master the carnal soul; the "greater *jihād*," 107, 113–118

*ka'ba* (Ar). The holy shrine in Mecca containing the venerated Black Stone which is circumambulated during the rituals of pilgrimage, 196

*kabbe* (Ful). Tenet of faith or dogma; equivalent to the Arabic *'aqīda*; the teaching of *tawḥīd* in the Fulfulde language, 6, 73–4, 90, 96–7, 106, 110, 145, 151; history of, 79–87; sectarian practices related to, 83–4, 86

*kabbenkoobe* (Ful). Adherents of the *kabbe*, 84–5

*karāma* (Ar). Miracle, 5, 120

*karamoko* (Mande). Teacher or scholar; equivalent to the Arabic *'ālim*, 86

*khalīfa* (Ar). Successor or deputy; a specially appointed successor to the *shaykh* of a Sufi order, superior to the *muqaddamūn*, 18, 44, 47–53, 119, 128–9, 195

*khalwa* (Ar). Sufi spiritual exercise of seclusion, 116

*lāzim* (Ar). Sequence of Tijani prayers, 193

*mā 'd-dīn* (Ar). Literally, "What is religion?" The second lesson in Cerno Bokar's catechism, 6, 11–2, 73, 79, 86–97, 106, 111, 148, 152–3, 187–92

*maqām* (Ar). Stages of personal development which a Sufi achieves through his own efforts; not to be confused with *ḥāl*, 113

*marabout* (Fr). Scholar, teacher or cleric; a popular French West African usage derived from the Arabic *murābiṭ*, 38

*muḥāmin* (Ar). Attorney or lawyer, 177–8

*mulk* (Ar). Self-will, 115

*muqaddam*, pl. *muqaddamūn* (Ar). Leader in a Sufi order who authorizes the recitation of its various prayers, 17, 42–55, 64, 70, 101, 118–9, 128–9, 131, 135; appointments of by Cerno Bokar, 123, n. 21; appointments of by al-Hajj Umar, 67–8; Tijani hierarchy of, 97, 106–12

*murshid* (Ar). Sufi spiritual guide, 113, 116, 117

*nafs* (Ar). Carnal or animal soul of man, 113–6, 146, 148, 153–5, 159, 162, 163, 165–6, 172–3, 175–8, 180, 183, 185–6; (*see also jihād al-nafs*)

*naẓar* (Ar). Literally, to see; in Sufi terminology, the profound understanding of principles, 104, n. 61

*qalb* (Ar). Heart; in Sufi terminology, not only the physical organ but also the seat of faith; a source of internal energy, 114–5, 144, 162, 179

*qibla* (Ar). Direction of the *ka'ba* in Mecca, 196

*qutb* (Ar). Pole; the highest level in the Sufi hierarchy of saints or *awliyā'*, 47–50, 52, 128

*qutb al-zamān* (Ar). The pole of the era, 48–9

*rūḥ* (Ar). Human spirit, 114–5, 117, 146, 152–4, 157–9, 161–2, 164, 166, 175, 179, 186

*ru'yā* (Ar). Vision, 119; (*see also* Visions)

# INDEX